Dr. John McGeehan, MD, is a graduate of the University of Pennsylvania, Perelman School of Medicine, PA. He did his residency in internal medicine at the Pennsylvania Hospital. He was a primary care physician for over thirty years and served as the director of medical education and chair of medicine at Mercy Hospital in Scranton, PA. He was an associate dean for student affairs and admissions and is now teaching in the classroom and at the bedside and involved in growing the Center for Humanism at Cooper Medical School of Rowan University. He is currently a professor of clinical medicine and chair of the ethics committee of Cooper University Hospital.

This book is dedicated to my wife, Cathie, whom I met on a Friday and proposed to her less than 48 hours later. We have been together for over 46 years. Her love and the many wise decisions she made for me during my illness allowed me to recover and be able to write these stories. I also thank everyone who shared a part of their life with me as none of these stories would have been possible without them.

Dr. John McGeehan

A DOCTOR'S STORIES

Behind Closed Doors

AUSTIN MACAULEY PUBLISHERS™

LONDON * CAMBRIDGE * NEW YORK * SHARJAH

Ordering Information
Quantity sales: Special discounts are available on quantity purchases by corporations, associations, and others. For details, contact the publisher at the address below.

Publisher's Cataloging-in-Publication data
McGeehan, Dr. John
A Doctor's Stories

ISBN 9781647509880 (Paperback)
ISBN 9781647509903 (ePub e-book)
ISBN 9781647509897 (Audiobook)

Library of Congress Control Number: 2021901497

www.austinmacauley.com/us

First Published (2021)
Austin Macauley Publishers LLC
40 Wall Street, 33rd Floor, Suite 3302
New York, NY 10005
USA

mail-usa@austinmacauley.com
+1 (646) 5125767

Special thanks to Hal Baillie, PhD (a dear friend who opened the door for me to medical ethics), Ed Viner, MD (my model for humanism for over four decades), and David Hunter, (a friend and neighbor whose support and suggestions have helped me create this collection). Thanks also to my son for the picture on the front cover of this book.

Table of Contents

Preface

Why did I write this book? Who was the intended reader? What is the intended message? These are the questions I asked myself before I began this process and they have guided me well. I owe it to the reader to answer these at the start and hope that they will be kind enough to read what follows this introduction as it will provide questions in their own lives. I hope everyone considers taking the time to write down their own experiences. Every life is important and all we experience is worth sharing. I decided early on that even if this collection is never published, it will serve as a way my family and friends can remember who I am and know the path I traveled.

Mortality recently stared me in the face. Even worse, the possibility of going on living and not having my mental capacity became real. I had a surgical procedure and somehow acquired a serious infection afterward that resulted in a long hospitalization. I have no memory of any of it. My brave and brilliant wife served as my spokesperson and protected me in those many weeks. I know that I miraculously recovered because of great care and the sound decisions she made. At one point, they told her to begin looking for a nursing home because if I recovered, it would not be complete and not be soon. To this day, no one can say what caused all that I went through. I got all the records and could not make my own diagnosis either. That only heightened the fear because the enemy was unknown. I was told that I became confused, rigid, tremulous, and not easy to care for. My kidneys were severely affected and I became profoundly anemic. I had many tests and even three lumbar punctures. I was transferred at one point to another hospital. For reasons as unknown as the cause, I began to recover and was able to go home. I still have no memory of the week before the entire long hospital stay and about two weeks afterward. That is a blessing in so many ways from what I was told I was like. I cannot even imagine what my family went through.

All of my passwords were erased from my brain – and since I always relied on a darn good memory, they were not written down. My poor wife had no access to financial and other matters. Over the next few weeks, my brain reprogrammed in some magical way and everything came back except the weeks noted above. My wife insisted that I undergo testing to see if I could function at a high level before allowing me to return to work. I passed these tests and amazed the neurologists who cared for me in the hospital. I went back to work. Every time I would get a pain in my abdomen or forget something, I went into a state of terrible fear. This soon controlled every day of my life. No one knew it but my wife. She guided me to the specialist who saw me in the hospital who diagnosed me with delirium while there and told me I now had PTSD. He is a superb clinician, he was right, and the treatment worked.

Could this happen again? Who knows, since no one ever found out why it happened the first time. I have always loved telling stories and suspect that explains the multiple dinners with friends over the years. I have lived a life that was full of stories. I now needed to write these down, as my memory failed me once. I feel I owed it to those who I have had the honor of meeting in these many years. They have all contributed to who I am. I know my children will enjoy reading this and pass it on to others. Perhaps even some who do not know me might find some insights in the stories told in these pages.

My life has been both ordinary and amazing at the same time. I have enjoyed being a son, a student, a sibling, a child, an adult, a husband, a doctor, a father, a grandfather, a friend, and a teacher. I have enjoyed being alive. I have an interest in medical ethics, and through it, I have served as a chair of the ethics committee at two hospitals over many years and of the medical society bioethics committee of the state where I now live. I have been called to consult on many difficult cases. This collection reflects on all of this. I hope the reader finds that these stories allow them to reflect on their lives, the lives of others, and the meaning of life. I suspect it will often lead to more questions than answers and that is why I love medical ethics.

Every story told is real. I have never used real names and have altered some of the details to protect the identity of anyone whose lives have helped me tell these tales. Many are no longer alive. I thank them all for giving me a life worth living and a story that I hope is worth telling.

Chapter 1

A Box of Chocolates

I love chocolates. My HbA1C does not. I also loved Tom Hanks in Forrest Gump. Those who pick up this book will decide how they would like to tackle the task of reading further. They may sample read and, like assorted chocolates in a box, may like what they picked or might not. To help you in this challenge, I have included in this chapter what I feel are six representatives of what the rest of the book has to offer. I have also included at the end of the book a guide as to topics and content to help you find certain subject matter as well as to display that bit of OCD that is me. My life has been like the box of stories that lie ahead.

The Odor

The smell was awful. It was unmistakable. It worsened as I walked down the hall toward Room 728. I noticed that there were no patients in the rooms close to it – they had all demanded to be moved. As physicians, we are trained to cope with experiences few could imagine, starting with the gross anatomy course in medical school. The accident victims in the emergency room, the babies not surviving the birth process, the abused, and the constant battle with death itself have the effect of numbing us in a way. I continued down the hall and met Charlie in Room 728. He was sitting up in bed, eating lunch. He smiled and said hello and I was stunned by how normal everything seemed in spite of the smell.

Charlie was found lying near the railroad tracks outside of town. He was brought by ambulance to the hospital and admitted. He could not remember when he had seen a doctor last. He was a longtime smoker and drank heavily in the days he could afford to. He was alert and oriented in terms of knowing where he was and who he was. He did not know the date or month, but one would not really expect him to. He was homeless and certainly did not have that instant memory jogger called a cellphone that we all rely on.

His left leg from just below the knee was black, shriveled, and dry with a clear demarcation. There were no pulses and no sensation in that leg. It was dead. The human body is amazing in that it had found its own way to stop the pain and wall off the infection that one would expect of an ischemic limb. The one thing it could not do was to stop the odor or gangrene.

I was chair of the ethics committee for the hospital and called to do an ethics consult because Charlie was refusing surgery. It was clear that he would eventually die of an infection without surgery – and many physicians had made that clear to Charlie. Physicians often consider a patient incompetent when they disagree with them. But competent people can make incompetent decisions – one could say that teens do that every day. A psychiatrist was called and after some time, the odor making every minute seem like ten, Charlie was declared mentally competent. So, somehow this situation became a matter of medical ethics. It was clearly established for decades that no medical intervention can be done on a competent patient who refuses it and the consult note was clear to me until I met Charlie.

I sat down and began to talk to Charlie. I find that honesty is always the best way to a clear solution, so I simply asked Charlie if the smell from his leg bothered him. He said he must have gotten used to it because it did not. He was confused that it bothered others. I asked if he had any pain, and he did not. I then asked why he did not want the surgery and he replied that it was his choice and he simply refused. I asked what he thought would happen if he did not have the surgery and he told me he knew he would die somehow. He was matter-of-fact and content with his answer. There was no fear.

I then asked what he thought would happen if he did have the surgery, expecting a blunt refusal of an amputation and a 'rather-die-than-live-without-my-leg' response. Instead, he calmly told me he could not live by the tracks without a leg. He had not had three meals a day for years. He had not slept in a clean bed with a pillow for decades. He had not had people come to talk to him that were not threatening. He had not been warm on a cold day in forever. What hospital staff and I saw was a man with a malodorous dead leg living terribly when in fact Charlie was having his best days of many years as a patient at the hospital. He saw the surgery as this reprieve coming to an end.

A hospital has many resources. Calls were placed. Social services wove their magic and Charlie was told of how he could be fit for a new leg and taught to walk with it. He would go to a rehab facility with a clean bed, good food, and nice people. They would find him somewhere to live that would be warm and safe. He agreed, and all went well.

Charlie was not incompetent; he was homeless.

Our Dogs

Growing up, I never had a dog. My wife always did. I never wanted one. As with most things in a good marriage, we arrived at a compromise and got our first dog as a puppy a number of years into our marriage – after our three children were old enough. She was a golden retriever. She was smart, happy, playful, and a bit mischievous. Autumn quickly became a part of our family and changed our lives for the better. At age ten, she suddenly fell over without any prior warning. We took her to the vet who told us to take her to a teaching hospital and I was shocked when I faced the reality of what we would do for a dog. Autumn had become more than a dog to us over those ten years. At the hospital, we learned she had a cancer of her heart which had bled suddenly. We were given options and told what might happen. The options were not good and they recommended we take her home and make her comfortable. We decided to create a 'doggy hospice' for her! She was now allowed in the pool. She could eat ice cream and all kinds of 'people food.' She was happy and was not suffering.

After a few weeks, she was acting normally. We knew that did not change the fact that she had a cancer and we took every day as a gift. We got another puppy – Madison – a golden retriever, and with her new friend, she became even more energetic and they played daily. One day, six months later, while in the yard, Autumn fell over again and died. For many weeks, Madison would sit exactly where she died and look around for long periods of time. There is so much we do not know. We all missed Autumn. Doggie hospice was a brilliant idea.

Madison enriched our lives for many years and eventually died as well. We were both working and very busy but agreed that there was a void in our lives worsened by the departure of children to college. My wife came up with the brilliant idea of adopting an adult golden retriever and found one not far from our home who was used as a breeder dog. We went to meet her and out of many happy dogs and puppies at this wonderful home in the country, Sierra came right to us and jumped up on my wife. Love at first sight was in all directions and she was soon in the car heading home. She was amazing –

seventy pounds of pure love. She never barked, never begged, and followed us everywhere even without needing a leash.

At age thirteen, she suddenly became weak and we knew immediately what was wrong. It was a horrible déjà vu. She could not walk and was breathing heavy. The vet took blood from her heart sack and confirmed that she had the same heart tumor. This was apparently not unusual in this breed. She improved dramatically, but days later, it happened again. She did not die as had Autumn but was clearly suffering. She looked at us with such sadness. We knew what the right thing to do was for someone we loved.

The staff at the vet knew her and they greeted us at the door. I carried her in and the seventy pounds proved not an issue with emotions fueling adrenaline. We put her on the floor and got down on the floor next to her. The vet was nothing short of amazing and spent more time comforting us than I ever expected. Sierra kept her eyes focused on us and did not move. We both pet her as an IV was started and she did not flinch. Perhaps we read into what a dog thinks but after years, one gets to know their pet and it was clear she was not anxious and knew we were there for her. The medication was administered and she closed her eyes and, shortly after, stopped breathing. It was so beautiful. It was so comfortable for her. It was so sad for us. It was so right. She was a special dog and is missed every day. She left this world without pain and surrounded by those she loved.

I have been a primary-care physician for decades and have seen many people die. I have lost parents and one in hospice. I know firsthand that we cannot relieve all suffering even with the advances in palliative care. I know that those dying do not want to be alone and they do not want to suffer. In only a few states in this country do we allow the dying to have the option of assisted suicide. The current expressed concerns will eventually give way to the fact that the dying deserve better. When my time comes, I would hope to leave this world as did Sierra – with my dignity, without suffering, and surrounded by those I love.

They Stayed Together

I looked at my schedule for the day and noticed that Mabel was on the list, but not Joe. It was clear that something was wrong and that had me worried until I saw her. I was a primary-care physician and blessed to know people over decades. They welcomed me into their lives and told me things they would not even tell their closest relative or spouse. I came to see this as a great honor and a gift of the profession. My patients taught me about caring, about illness, and about what it means to love and have strength.

I walked into the exam room and Mabel told me she had both good and bad news for me today. Rather than waiting for her to ask what I wanted first, I simply said to start with the bad news. She told me that Joe no longer knew who she was. I was silent and so sad. She then told me that the good news was that he had not yet kicked her out of the house, so he must still like her. I smiled and grabbed her arm. This was classic Mabel. She looked to humor as a coping mechanism. Mabel was here today because she needed time to just talk. She was not looking for answers. Her son was home with Joe and she did not want to burden her family with her reality. She did not want a prescription. She wanted to be safe in her words.

Joe had Alzheimer's. This disease robs the patient of their world, their memories that make them smile when alone, their pride, and their dignity. Its slow relentless course begins with the horrible knowledge of what is happening until it eventually and mercifully takes that reality away. There comes a time when the patient is alive and, by outward appearances, well. That wellness soon leaves as the body, without the unconscious way we move, cough, and eat. The door opens to infections and eventually death. The battle in caring for these patients is relentless and always futile.

What I learned over the years is that the definition of my patient changed. I saw the patient not as an isolated person but a member of a special group. This was usually a family but at times, it was a church group or the group in the nursing home. My job was to reach out to this unit and see how I could ease this terrible journey for them. They provided for the patient the few pleasures experienced daily. They were on this journey and needed support and guidance. They needed to know their feelings were not unique.

The spouse, when present, shoulders enormous burden in this disease. Joe and Mabel had a great life. They had three children and five grandchildren. I watched them grow up through pictures. Many became my patients. Such is not always the case. I have seen couples stay together for decades out of whatever obligation they feel, usually religious-based. They live together often out of financial need and sometimes out of habit. The love is gone and with it the caring. When one becomes ill, the other is forced into being the caregiver. This care is devoid of the critical element of love and often devoid of the nuances that make each day a little better – for both. Is this truly better than being alone?

Joe was not wandering at night, so she was able to sleep, although never securely. The family had met and was of one voice surrounding such things as a living will, the estate, and when the time would be to consider a nursing home. This planning is the key. Joe could dress himself if she laid out the clothes. She described with a smile a description of what he put on when left to his own decisions. There were many moments during each day that brought her satisfaction, even happiness. She was proud: of herself, of her family, and of Joe. She did not yet need home-health help. She was OK, for now.

The next week, I went to see Joe at home. The house call brought with it a true view of what was going on with this expanded patient. There was nothing that fancy tests could do for Joe. Sitting next to him and talking while Mabel listened was my role here today. Tomorrow it may be different. Our current healthcare system is losing out on this invaluable resource. I always leave feeling good for being there, and usually with great cookies provided by Mabel.

Joe and Mabel prepared for this day by the love they gave each other every day for forty-five years. They built something that would not be destroyed by this disease. My role is very small in comparison. They know I will be there and that is more than enough for all.

Burning Up

Scott was the last scheduled patient of the day. I was precepting in an internal medicine office at a teaching hospital. The patients were adults who resided in our city. They were served by our hospital system and had Medicare or Medicaid. The hours were 8:00 AM through 5:00 PM. The patients were seen by a resident training to be a specialist in internal medicine. First-year residents saw a patient hourly, second-year about every thirty minutes, and by the third year, they were scheduled such that they saw more in a day. This allowed for each to learn and to prepare for how it will be upon entering practice. A board-certified internist was present at all times who reviewed each chart, had every patient presented to them, reviewed the care plan and tested proposals, and saw any patient that was problematic or might pose a unique teaching opportunity. I loved this part of my week. I had a regular afternoon such that I got to know a group of trainees well, and I covered for others. The residents were amazing and had an incredible amount of knowledge and I learned from them. What they did not yet have was the wisdom that comes with having done this for decades. I got to teach, impact the care of patients, and learn all at the same time.

Scott, who was scheduled for 4:30 PM, was twenty-one minutes late. The senior resident was tired, since he was seeing many patients that day and almost all showed up. This is often not the case when caring for a challenged population. He pulled himself out of his chair, put on his professional demeanor, and left to see the patient. I then reviewed the chart hoping to be able to provide insights. The room we all shared (me, another attending seeing their own patients, three residents seeing patients, and one serving as the person answering phone requests that day) was a small room with many computers. It is an intense exercise in blocking out ambient noise. He returned and the look on his face was one of frustration mixed with bewilderment. He then told me that the reason the patient was there was because he recently read about spontaneous combustion and he was sure he was going to burst into flames at any moment. He was certain of it. In spite of his fear, he was quite considerate in that he had asked the resident to sit by the door and leave it open so that he would not get hurt by the flames! He said the burning had recently started in his left leg on the outside and the flames would soon follow.

It is for these moments that physicians get up every morning looking forward to work. It is why we sacrifice sleep and personal time. It is not for the money – it is for the stories! Scott was a forty-nine-year-old who had been documented with schizophrenia and bipolar disorder. He was on many meds, some of which I had no knowledge of, and saw a specialist for this. Now it was my time! I reached into my past experiences and a thought came to me. I asked the resident to go back into the room and ask the patient when he first became aware he might burst into flames, where exactly it was burning, and whether he recently got a cellphone. The others in the room turned and looked at me as if I was the one with a mental derangement.

Ten minutes later, he returned shocked. Scott got a new cellphone about two months ago with a large holster to protect it. He always wore it on his left side. The resident pushed on the cellphone and a burning sensation began in Scott's left lateral upper leg and a look of terror came over Scott's face. Scott had neuralgia paresthetica. This is an uncommon disorder caused by something pinching a nerve. When Scott was told this was easily fixed by not wearing the holster all the time, especially while sitting, he was so very grateful. Imagine learning that you are not going to burst into flames! This is great news to give anyone! He walked out smiling. He was to sleep that night.

My father was a policeman. His belt was filled with a gun and various tools. I remember him complaining of a burning sensation just like Scott, that went away when he moved his equipment around. I later had a carpenter as a patient with the same thing. I recently watched a television series where a policeman had neuralgia paresthetica. Now this resident would have this tool in his belt to help others, as would the others in the room for the presentation. Making a diagnosis relies on experience, being taught, reading to reinforce the mechanism, and being willing to consider the possibility. Scott was not 'crazy.' Labeling others is a sure roadblock to helping them. Teaching has made my life rich and rewarding.

The Northern Lights

I knew it was the end of the world. I was about ten years old and returning home just as it was becoming dark. The sky began to be shot full of incredible colors coming from one direction. They became larger and brighter. Having been raised in a strict Catholic household, I had been well prepared for the end of the world – it was here! I raced home at a speed my synaptic junctions did not know they could achieve. I got my mother and pulled her outside and pointed in greater fear than I had ever experienced. She calmly looked up and said that it was really beautiful and was called the aurora borealis – the northern lights.

That same household propelled me to become a physician. I was the child most likely to become a priest and that was the ultimate achievement in a family such as ours. I was sure that would not be my path and soon realized that becoming a doctor would erase that disappointment quickly for my parents. These past forty years have proven I took the right path.

Recently, a first and second-year medical student presented a case to me. I teach in a student-run free clinic in a city challenged by poverty and crime. It is the perfect role for me, as I get to give back, to see patients who really need care, and to teach. The first-year student, having recently learned how to do an organized medical interview, proceeded to tell me of this seventy-one-year-old lady from South America who recently moved here to be cared for by her daughter. She had fallen a few years ago and hurt her back. She was seen by a physician there and was told she had bad arthritis that was worsened by her fall. She slowly worsened and now could not get out of a chair by herself. The pain was now minimal. She did not speak English and the story came from her daughter and an interpreter. She was not on any medications. The story given to me was clear and organized. Nice job!

The role of the second year was to do and report the physical exam. He went through the vital signs, the appearance, and the heart and lung exam, etc. He did not do the neurologic exam, as that had not been taught yet in the curriculum. Normally, there is a third year that presents the assessment and plan but there was none today. The second year did a wonderful job in stating that this lady likely had spinal stenosis from arthritis from the fall, and was now very depressed due to her profound disability and reliance on others. He noted that she was emotionless and appeared sad throughout the evaluation.

We went to see this new patient together. I opened the door and in seconds, I knew what she had. Medicine is seeing the aurora borealis for the second time. Once you see it and learn what it is, you will recognize it quickly. I now had the opportunity of allowing these two students to recognize a disease the next time they see it. This nice lady had advanced Parkinson's. I knew it from the look on her face – it was 'masked' – expressionless. I asked her questions through her daughter who should have made her smile, and her eyes opened and her answers were funny but her face did not move. The students stood in awe. I moved her arms and found the classic cogwheel rigidity and immediately had them do the same. This continued and I was able to teach them why this nice lady could not stand from a chair and why her gait was as it was. I was saddened that this was not picked up earlier but able to hold out some hope to her that treatments will likely help now that we had a diagnosis. The students were amazed. This baton had been passed.

I told the patient what she had and outlined the plan of care. Our hospital did an amazing job of supporting those in our community who do not have insurance. Medicines were begun, a neurology consultation was set up, and physical therapy was begun. All of this was done free, as the costs were absorbed by the charity care of our institution. I told her that she might dance again and that I wanted the first dance! Months went by, and one day, she came in and specifically asked for me to be the attending physician. There were others who worked as I do and we rotated who we saw to allow optimal education by giving students different views and approaches. I walked in the room with a big smile. Her daughter took out her cellphone and began to play music. Her mother rose from the chair without assistance and held out her arms to me. We danced! It was a moment I will always treasure.

Each patient I have seen over these four decades has made me a better doctor. Books do not impact long-term memory the way a real patient can. I once heard the chair of medicine at a teaching hospital say that the worst thing about being on call every other night as an intern is missing half the patients. I now know he was right. Each patient becomes a colored light in our sky.

Please, Call Me 'Doctor'

My parents' smiling faces remain fixed in my mind even though forty-three years have passed since the day I graduated from medical school. The two of them hugged me proudly and called me 'doctor.'

I was raised in a small coal-mining town after the mines dried up, and neither of my parents went to college. When I was young, our family of six lived in a three-room attic of a duplex we shared with several other relatives. My parents sacrificed daily for their children and focused intensely on giving us the education they never had. So, my dream of becoming a physician was somewhat dwarfed by their dream of their son being called 'doctor.' The title used that first day did not simply define my status; it was the word used for a dream come true.

Recently, I've been thinking quite a bit about the title 'doctor,' as several younger colleagues made the case for asking patients and trainees to call them by their first names. But after some reflection, I am standing solid with the 'doctor' I've used for decades.

Words – and names – matter. They set a tone, convey specific types of connections, and establish duties and boundaries. I certainly did not call my father by his first name. He was a tall, stern man named Leo, and I'm amazed that his parents knew he'd grow into the image of a lion. Over the course of many years, my dad and I became friends, and I loved and respected him. But calling him by his first name was unthinkable.

Just as my father was 'Dad' to me, I am 'doctor' to my trainees. My title sets the stage on both sides. When learners call me 'Doctor,' it helps me enter my role of teacher and mentor. It reminds me that I am a physician with knowledge, skills, and experience worth sharing. It challenges me to stay current, grow, and do all I can to prepare those who will care for the next generation of patients. It challenges me to be my best in each interaction.

What's more, calling me 'John' likely could raise questions in trainees' minds. In an interaction, am I a friend or an instructor? Is what I say just interesting, as in a conversation, or is it teaching? Am I an equal or am I a role model?

I gladly accept the responsibility of being a role model. The hidden curriculum – lessons trainees learn by watching how we act – can have powerful positive effects. When trainees see me as 'doctor,' I feel they understand that my behaviors are ones to emulate. Seeing 'John' engage in the same behavior does not convey that it is a professional action and may erode some of its vital impact.

I also see the vital power of being called 'doctor' with my patients. I still remember a woman I'll call Sally who came to our clinic unable to sleep. She was twenty-three and the mother of a two-year-old daughter. The first-year resident assigned to the case had that special quality I knew would make her a fine physician. She reported that Sally would not answer any of her questions and instead just stared ahead.

I entered the room wearing my white coat and introduced myself as Dr. McGeehan. I sat next to Sally and gently touched her shoulder. That's something I often do when it just seems right. I said she looked tired and asked if she was having trouble sleeping. A door opened a crack. She looked at me and said yes. It was the first time she spoke. I asked why, but got no response. Then some instinct in me led to another question. I asked if the voices were keeping her awake, and she said yes. That conversation allowed us to diagnose and treat her for schizophrenia, and she responded well. What made her open up? I believe it was partly because I was not 'John,' but, however briefly, I was her 'doctor.'

I even prefer that friends who see me professionally call me 'doctor.' (If one calls me 'John,' I don't correct them, since I never want to make someone uncomfortable.) Over the past four decades, these patients almost always call me John socially and 'doctor' in clinical encounters. This tells me they want me as their friend at certain times and their physician at others. Knowing these roles allows for the magic that is the doctor-patient relationship. It allows me to assess their health objectively and tell them honestly what they need to know about it. It also allows them to open up. Patients tell their physician things they would never tell a friend, and these details can be critical in diagnosis and treatment.

Over the years, I've even developed a particular message about titles I share with my medical students. Envision this scenario: A first-year student enters the room and nervously washes their hands as they introduce themselves. The patient has a life in process outside the clinic door, perhaps money in a meter or someone at home watching their children. Their time is precious, and they now learn that they are seeing a medical student. So, I tell my students to introduce themselves not by their first name but by who they are in the encounter: their full name, their medical school and year, and the attending for whom they are working. I find that all this can help instill a certain confidence in the patient. Yet, I also urge avoiding the term 'student doctor,' which could spark an expectation that the student will act at quite a different level. To even subtly suggest that a student is a doctor is unfair to all. These learners should be clear about – and proud of – being medical students.

Some of my colleagues say they prefer 'doctor' because they've earned the title. For me, though, the word is not at all about staking a claim on status. My daughter is a brilliant PhD in microbiology and she put in many hard years to earn that degree. She is highly respected, especially by me, but does not want to be called a doctor. She agrees with me the term conveys a role – she doesn't want to be mistaken for a physician – and is not about a rank.

The term also is not about creating distance. I love sharing humor with those I teach, talking about life outside of medicine, and being a person – a 'doctor' is a better doctor if they are more than a doctor. Despite this openness and warmth, I have never had a student or resident call me John or ask permission to do so. I hope that this is because they know how much I want to be their mentor and embrace being a role model for them. Sometimes, a trainee winds up joining the staff where I work, and the relationship becomes one of peers. I then invite the person to call me by my first name.

In time, calling physicians 'doctor' may stop being the norm, but I sincerely hope it does not. I also hope that all physicians will live up to the honor conferred on them by the term. Ours is a profession like few others; we are healers, detectives, scientists, and teachers.

My life has been full because of what my titles have brought me over the years. I have been a son, grandson, brother, husband, father, coach, teacher, friend, and grandfather. And I am a 'doctor.' My patients and my students know who I am and what to come to me for. The title makes that clear.

This article was reprinted with permission from the Association of American Medical Colleges (AAMC).

Chapter 2

The Formative Years

We are all an amazing collage of experiences. Some we remember and most we do not. All play a role in molding the person we become. I do not remember much of my early life and I wish I did. I thank all of those who have shaped me along the way and I know that the task is not yet complete.

Yes, Sister

I went to first grade in an old school that has since been torn down. It was a catholic school in a small town that at one time was economically sustained by coal mining. I walked out of the same door I walked in when I graduated twelve years later. Our graduation class had less than fifty students and many of these began first grade with me. It was run by the Sisters of Mercy and noted for having the only convent in the diocese to have an elevator. To say many of my teachers were past their prime was being kind.

My father was a policeman and he had attended the same school. He never went beyond high school. I recall one day, Sister had Tommy stand up and she asked him if he was going to be a doctor like his father, and of course, Tommy said, "Yes, Sister," and sat down. She next had me stand up and asked if I was going to be a policeman like my father and I recall replying, "No, Sister, I will be a doctor like Tommy's father." So began my path to medicine!

My parents strongly valued education. I will not detail my childhood but only state that we did not have much but I cannot recall anything we did not have. We were safe, supported, and loved. We were taught to work hard and be respectful. My early education was also uneventful. At that time, the atmosphere in the catholic world was one of fear and it was a motivator the nuns were masters at. I was a good student and caused no problems. Having nuns all day and an enormous policeman for a father left no room for mischief.

One nun in high school just did not like me for some reason. She didn't like any of the male students actually. She taught German and Latin, both of which I took. I was told they would supply a strong foundation for a science education. They did not. She was just mean. She had arthritis and I can recall her coming to me and pointing a finger at me as she yelled. I always tried to figure the actual projection of the crooked digit and pretend she was pointing at someone else. On graduation day, she actually pulled me out of the procession line and told me that I would never make anything of myself. To this day, I do not know whether this was meant as motivation or her just being her miserable self.

32

Thirteen years flew by. I went to college and then on to medical school. I loved both, so I never saw either as difficult. I was following a dream. I decided after my residency to leave Philadelphia and go to Scranton, PA. I had married a girl who was born in Scranton and a primary care internal medicine residency was just begun there and they offered me an opportunity to teach. The hospital that became my office location was Mercy Hospital. It was run by the Sisters of Mercy – I had come full circle! One day while walking down a long hallway, I saw my high school language teacher at the end of the hall with two other nuns. They traveled in packs... How old could she be now? She was old then. That terrible feeling came over me like I had not done my homework. That fear I had suppressed came back. I talked to myself. I was no longer a victim of that fear that God would strike me down for my thoughts. I had moved on.

Covered in my clean and pressed white coat, I walked down the hallway proudly. I was about to exorcise a demon. I walked straight up to her and said hello, expecting she would have no idea who I was. She said, "Hello, John," in a way that put her immediately in control. I gathered myself and pointed to the MD after my name embroidered on my white coat while I told her that in high school, she told me I would never make anything of myself. There, I said it, and no thunderbolt had struck! She quickly replied, "Yes, John, but I don't know if you are any good." I walked away beaten once again.

Coming Home Late

Memories make things bigger, more colorful, and more dramatic than reality. In time, the actual memories become blurred and our version becomes stored on the hard drive of our brain and then becomes the actual event. This is one such story. I think it is all real and accurate. If not, that is not by intent, and as long as the message of the event is unchanged, I feel safe putting this story in motion.

My father was a big man. He was a policeman in a small town, and when in uniform, his size seemed to double. His personality was proportional. Everyone knew Leo in town. When he would come home in uniform, take off his gun, put it on top of the china closet, and sit down for a meal, there was seldom a mood for open and honest conversation. He tended to speak in short sentences and had a look that conveyed anything he wanted to say. I admire his parents' insight into the future in naming their little baby after a lion. Every year, he would carry the keg of beer on his shoulder into the Policeman's Picnic and set it down, marking the beginning of the festivities. He was a legend.

Dad was tough but showed his four children he loved them through his actions every day. I saw this and it made his occasional gruffness acceptable. I always tried to please him, partly out of fear but mostly out of respect. He made very little money and always worked many odd jobs over the years. He could not afford to get an education beyond high school and was driven to make sure his four children had that opportunity. We did. I now look back and realize that seeing his work ethic and his dedication to family gave me the essential tools that have led me to a happy and successful life.

I recall going with him when I was a young boy in a black station wagon to pick up dead bodies many miles away for a funeral home in our little town that was one of his many side jobs. We would stop at a Howard Johnson and have to park way in the back so no one would look in the back of the car. I loved the coconut cake at Ho Jo. I remember having to pray the rosary with him on the trip. That cake made all of it worthwhile.

I did well in school and never got in trouble. I tend to be a pleaser and it made for a life with few bumps in the road. Dad let us know he was happy with how we were doing by silence. He was not home much but he was always there in many ways. He idealized Mom but I never recall any show of emotions. We did not go on vacations. When I was young, the four children and my parents moved to the other side of a double house. I now had my own bedroom in the top floor. It was Beverly Hills to us. Before that, the six of us lived in the small three rooms in the attic. Eventually, I went on to college and enrolled in a school a short distance from my home. I was given the opportunity to live at school, and that is the true purpose of college – to mature, become independent, and cut the umbilical cord.

The first weekend away, I wanted to come home but that would not be considered 'cool' by my friends. Second weekend met the same judgment. I came home on the third weekend and met up with my friends on Saturday night. There was not much to do in our little town, so we stayed up and talked at one of the friends' houses. I suspect we told exaggerated tales of our life away but do not recall. I know that I did not drink or stay up all night or party – I studied. I quickly discovered by going to college that my high school was terrible and the other students were far better at everything than I was. I got home a little after midnight and opened the front door so that it would not make a noise. It was an old house and no longer had many ninety-degree angles. I lifted it just right when closing so it would not slam. I then walked the stairs by placing each foot at the side so they would not creak. I got in bed and admired my stealth return to my room and slept.

I was at the kitchen table eating breakfast the next day when my father came home in uniform. He looked at me and said, "Where the hell were you last night?" It was downhill from there. I told him that I was just out with my friends talking about college. He next told me that this was his house and he did not care that I was now in college. When in his house, I would be home before midnight no matter how old I was. Emotions quickly overpowered common sense and wisdom. I told him that was not going to happen and he would have to accept that I was now independent (still living with my parents and relying on their help in every way though). I was hoping that I was in a cartoon and could see the words travel through the air such that I could catch and destroy them before they entered his ears. I failed.

His face turned red and he came over and picked me up over his head with one hand on my upper arm and one on my upper leg. I was six-foot tall but thin. He was almost forty years older than me. He threw me across the room onto the couch and came at me with those huge hands that had hair growing from the fingers, and I realized I would not have to worry about grades anymore. Dad had never hit me in my life. It was not his style. He could always make any point with his face. Then it happened. He started tickling me. He

35

knew from the past eighteen years the right places. He was skilled. I laughed so hard and then it reached that point when you cannot even breathe. As he was tickling me, he told me how his night was. He told me that he trusted me and knew I was OK but he could not sleep because Mom kept asking him to call City Hall to see if there was an accident reported. Mom was an expert worrier. He ended by telling me he was counting on me to get him a good night's sleep.

I was never late again. My dad gave me all the tools I needed in life and I still miss him a great deal.

Coaching

I have seen some great coaches in my life and I thank them for their skills and dedication. Some of these were in the world of athletics, and most in the field of medicine. I went to a very small school in a small city in the coal regions of Pennsylvania. We only had about ninety boys in the entire high school including freshman. When I was a freshman, we got a new basketball coach, fresh out of college. He went from classroom to classroom and had everyone stand up. If you were tall, you were invited to try out for the team. If you did not have sneakers, he took you to the store and got you a pair. He put his heart and soul into the team and took us to the state final where we won. It was an unusual year in that there was rich talent but it came together because of this young man. I was the scorekeeper and ball-boy for the team that year, so I was able to watch the process play out. Once he was asked what the secret to being a good coach was, and he replied, "Knowing who to slap on the back and who to kick in the ass, and when." His name was Digger.

This philosophy plays out in the world of medicine as well. As a primary care internist, my job was to diagnose and treat. I also focused on prevention. To treat someone effectively means that you need a plan that has been practiced on others, and that you can inspire your patient to carry out that plan. It requires that the patient trusts you and buys into the plan. This becomes especially true when it comes to preventing illness. Getting people to change their lifestyle is so very difficult. The physician must know when to slap on the back and when to… Coaches must also be able to rebound from a loss – and such is all too common when it comes to getting people to diet or exercise. The big wins keep us going and we use those to motivate other patients. The game of life is always a challenge.

I made sure I found time to do the things I love outside of medicine. My family was always first on my priority list, so I found that I could coach my son's teams – much to his dismay I now realize. My girls took to dance and music. I was not built to do ballet and I have a hard time tuning in a radio station, much less playing an instrument. I drove my children to school every day, went to every recital, and made sure to be at the supper table with them daily. It was not easy and often resulted in my going back to the hospital after they went to bed. I could survive without sleep, but not without being the best father I could be. It was all worth it.

My first day as a basketball coach was when my son was about five. The rules were that if you coached a game, you had to stay and referee the next game. It was brilliant, as it made all of us shut up when a referee would blow a whistle. This was at an age where the rims were low, the court small, and the rules were impossible to follow. It was a riot. On one play, one of the boys on my team was dribbling down the court. They could not do so without watching the ball, so he ran right into another player's shoulder. His nose started to bleed and I was in my element! I brought a first-aid kit and ice – the combination of my boy-scout past and my doctor present. I sat the boy down and put the icepack on the bridge of his nose and held his head just right. The next thing I knew was that his father ran across the coach and pulled the ice of his face and told me that you should never put ice on the face that way. I looked and smiled and he turned red and said, "Holy shit, you're the doctor who is coaching, aren't you?" He asked me what to do next and I congratulated him as my new assistant coach. He sat next to me that season.

They were the fun years of coaching. When the boys got older and there were more girlfriends than parents in the stands, coaching became a nightmare. Simple layups turned into buttonhooks and hormones ruled the day. It is often better to be lucky than smart, and one year, I was very lucky in the lottery during which we picked players. All the coaches came and watched everyone go through drills and we took some notes. It was clear that Billy, even in sixth grade, would be a star. He was tall and confident. He was also a really good kid. I got the first pick and I got Billy. If your son was trying out, you automatically got to have him on your team. My son was late to grow but one thing never changed – he has always been a joy to be with. He enjoyed practice more than games, worked hard, and never complained. The team made it to the finals. It was down to a few seconds in the championship game and the score was tied, so I called timeout. I had the play ready to win the game, so we got in the huddle. I told them that I had a play, and immediately they all said that we should just give the ball to Billy and get out of the way. Not what I had planned – much wiser. We gave the ball to Billy and won the game. Humility was the key to winning, as it has been throughout my career as a physician.

The Flood

It was the summer of 1972 and it started to rain. The rain continued daily and was very heavy. I was home between my junior and senior years of college with my usual summer job working at a small chain of general and auto stores in a small city in Northeastern Pennsylvania. We were located at a high altitude relative to other areas and flooding was never an issue. My college was about thirty miles away. The news began to show pictures of severe flooding in Wilkes-Barre where my school was located on River Street! The company I was working for had a store there as well. I was asked to go to that store to help them with the cleanup after the flooding.

My college was small and they had just installed a state-of-the-art new basketball floor earlier that year. Shortly after, the Water Follies came to town and the tanks were put in the gym. They leaked! The floor was ruined and replaced right before the summer of 1972. I loved my college. It was small and was not noted for getting people into medical school. It was a catholic liberal arts school run by the Holy Cross Fathers. They gave me a generous scholarship that allowed me to live on campus rather than commute. The school was small enough that I knew people and they knew me. When the flood hit the college and they asked for volunteers to help, I went. They were good to me, so it was an opportunity to pay back.

I would drive to the city but could not drive to the store or the school – we were bused in. The streets were ruined and covered with mud after the water subsided. There was no electricity. I could walk from the store after work and go to the college to help. The days would be long. The stench of the city was terrible. The force of water is astonishing. When it rose above the riverbed, it tore into the neighborhoods and even tore up cemeteries, strewing bodies. It would go into grocery stores, break windows, rise slowly, and carry the food out into the streets. It would cause the sewer waters to be mixed with the floodwater. Unless you have seen it yourself, there is no way to truly imagine what happens when a city is flooded. Homes and businesses get lost. People are without places to live. Truly devastating!

At the college, I was assigned to work in the library. It was a three-story building and fairly new. I knew it well as I was the typical biology major taking eighteen credits minimum a semester and needing to ace everything. I walked in the front door and the receded waterline was about four feet up the walls. The problem was that there was another full floor below filled with books arranged neatly by number as with all libraries. I was given a large bucket, a flashlight, and an ax! I was told to go downstairs and pick a row of books. Using the flashlight, I was to read the book titles and decide which one to destroy with the ax. The reason was that the submersion of the books had them swell such that they could not be removed unless one large book was destroyed. I was then to peel the books out one at a time, tear off the cover made of cloth (and I was told this would be impossible to clean and sterilize), place the books in the large bucket, and bring it upstairs when full. The covers and the destroyed books would get shoveled up from the floor later with more of the mud.

I still remember the emotional impact of destroying books with an ax. It brought back mental pictures I have seen of books being burned in rebellions. The act seemed vile. It was against so much that I held sacred. My parents did not get the chance to go beyond high school and they worked very hard to allow us to get the education they could not. We were brought up to respect knowledge and honor our teachers.

Upon leaving to go home, when it got too dark or the stench became too much to bear, I would leave for home and see the havoc this storm had left behind. Houses were destroyed and, along with them, so many papers and pictures that linked those who lived there with their past. The ax that fell on their lives made the one I was using seem insignificant.

The area was rebuilt and life went on as it always does. Many would not ever be the same and that is a part of life's impact every day. Oddly, I cannot read a book on a tablet or a computer. I need to feel it in my hands, with its cover intact.

Love

Love defies science. Love is difficult to define and almost impossible to understand. Those who have experienced it know what it is. Those that have not are missing one of life's great gifts. It guides out actions, forms many of our smiles, and makes our journey full. I love and have been loved, and because of this, my life has been incredible.

It was Friday night and I was ready for another night of studying. I was in the first semester of my first year of medical school and needed every minute of every day to learn what I was expected to know. I enjoyed the learning process but that does not make it any less challenging. My roommate asked me to take a break and go to a party he had heard of. Why not? We arrived and it was a large venue with lots of people. There was music and it was dimly lit. I hate crowds and began to wish I had said no. I was then introduced to a young lady who was from the region in Pennsylvania where I was from. I was wearing what would now be considered a pretty good costume for Halloween. It was not Halloween however. I had green plaid bell-bottoms on with a silk shirt with few buttons at the top, and platform shoes. It was the thing at the time – absurd now. It was Saturday-night fever. I was standing with one foot on a chair as that would make me look cool – or so I deluded myself. This young lady, Cathie, looked down and told me I had Osgood-Schlatter disease. That was it – she had my attention for sure. Cathie was a pediatric nurse. I had grown many inches one year when I was young and that can cause a pulling on a ligament insertion below the knee and a bump that is permanent. How did she know this, and how did she see it with those ridiculous pants on in that dim room? I had to know more.

The next night, we were having a party in our apartment and I invited her and asked her to bring some friends. That next night, I learned that Philadelphia was not like where I had lived in the coal mining regions of Northeast Pennsylvania. I had gutted our refrigerator and put a keg of beer in for our party. That, a few bags of pretzels, and a turntable, and the party was on! I soon found out that people here drank wine and ate cheese – bizarre! I had neither. A few hours later, and after a few beers, I realized this Cathie was special and that I was going to ask her out. I have always been anchored in ethics and realized there was another woman in my life at that time with whom I was spending many hours each day. I had to let Cathie know – it was the right thing to do. I asked her if she wanted to walk across campus with me that night to meet my cadaver. She did. This was the pickup line of all time.

Cathie went home with her friends later that evening. I woke the next day to find two pieces of letter-sized stationary on my bedside table – one had three numbers on it and the other four. I could not remember at first and then it came to me that I had asked Cathie to give me her number. She was too much of a lady to do that and made me write it down. I guess those seven digits on two pieces of large paper were the best I could manage at the time… I called and asked her to lunch. She said yes. I got in my green '64 VW Beetle with a rollback sunroof that I bought for $674 and set off. After lunch, we went to a local park and sat on a bench and talked for a very long time. I knew I was in love. I asked her to marry me that day! That was forty-three hours after first meeting her. It was crazy, but it was right. She did not say yes. She has always been wiser than me. She did not say no.

We were married nine months later when I had my first break in classes from medical school. That was forty-six years ago. Why did I go to that party that night? Why did I dress like a clown and think I looked cool? What were the chances I would meet a woman who could diagnose my knee condition at first sight? How did I know she was the one? Why did she agree to marry me? I study and embrace science every day of my life. We are in a perpetual search for answers to life's questions. We still do not know what brings two people together. One day, we may know more, but knowing will not diminish the magic.

Research

I was given the amazing opportunity to spend most of my senior year of college doing research at a famous science lab outside of Chicago. It was government-funded, so I even got a stipend for living expenses. They took about fifty students from all across the country and we lived on the facility site. It was enormous and albino deer roamed the grounds. It was in the seventies, so there were very few female students at the time. We lived in small apartments inside the barbed-wire fencing that surrounded the site, with four students in each. There was no gymnasium or cafeteria. It did not take long to discover that none of the four of us could cook. Being resourceful, we decided that it was time to get to know the eight women chosen for this research experience.

The early seventies ushered in what should have been forever: women recognized as equals in the world of science. These young women agreed to cook for us, but we had to agree to cook for the same meal for them in six weeks. This turned out to be a wonderful plan. My research was relatively unsuccessful, but I became quite a chef! To this day, I enjoy cooking and make a mean cheesecake.

Before going to the facility, I had entertained doing an MD-PhD combined degree. I learned a great deal about myself while there, including that delayed gratification was not a part of who I was. Researchers are not given the respect they deserve. These women and men spend countless hours exploring the root causes of events. They are creative and set forth to prove hypotheses. Without their work, we would not have the medications we now have to treat diseases, the diagnostic capabilities, or the vaccines that save millions of lives. They do their work quietly and often without recognition. What impresses me the most is that they are able to deal with delayed gratification. It can take months or years to see the result of work done. The pay is usually much lesser than others. There is comparatively little in terms of socialization.

I decided not to pursue the PhD path, as I needed more immediate feedback. Seeing an infection heal, watching a blood pressure or a blood sugar return to normal, or having a painful joint resolve, all give a physician that slap on the back that is needed. We get to interface with many patients each day and hear the words 'thank you.' Medicine is a profession more rewarding in all ways than most. We tend to fixate on the occasional time when the outcome is not what was expected or hoped for, rather than the many times we make a positive difference in a person's life.

Funding for research has been steadily declining in both governmental support and the private sector. This threatens our future in no small way. Every day, discoveries are being made that will greatly improve our lives and those of our children. Most researchers will never get the Noble Prize or their picture on the cover of a major publication. They will present their work in obscure journals and present at conferences attended only by colleagues. They need our support. The ethics surrounding research is now well defined. The horrors of Nazi Germany and the abuses in the Tuskegee syphilis experiment in this country resulted in the important rulings that protect human subjects. Groups of people known as IRBs (Institutional Review Boards) now must review all research involving human subjects to assure that it is safe and rights are being protected. Abuses will likely always be seen but the efforts to protect research from bias continue to grow.

One of the young men I met and lived with during this research experience was a character. His car looked like it was from Dukes of Hazzard, he wore alligator boots and a string tie, and he was a rugby player in college. He was also brilliant. We were all given a project and his was to program a computer to read cross sections of nerve fibers. Mine was to develop a cell-free protein synthesizing system. He finished his in no time! This was at a time when programming a computer involved card piles with punched out dots. The language behind computing was in its infancy. When the time was drawing to an end, I had been accepted to medical school and I asked him what his plans were. He told me that computing was not going to be big for a number of years and that he planned on being a park ranger in the Ozarks! He was wise enough to know even then that once a career kicks in, there is little time to do other things.

I returned home and bought a '64 VW Beetle with a rollback roof for $674. I called T and invited myself to Missouri. That car broke down in every state but I had the spiral-bound book 'Any Idiot Can Fix a VW,' and that label fit me perfectly. By the time I got to my destination, I had replaced most of that little motor. We canoed the Ozarks for two weeks, and to this day, I have never seen anything more beautiful. I went on to medical school and entered that fast-moving career path. T eventually became a teacher and then went on to become famous. With his intelligence, personality, and wisdom, I would not have expected anything less.

Chapter 3

Medical School

It is fascinating comparing my journey through medical school with the students of today. The changes are amazing while the stabilizing force of the profession remains. The old and new issue back and forth through these pages with messages, I hope, will preserve the magic of the doctor-patient relationship.

Gross Anatomy

I recall vividly the final exam in the gross anatomy course in medical school. This was a do-or-die moment, as there was no way at that time to retake an exam or remediate a course. The latter is common now and I see the reason why, yet something inside me says that such a high-stakes test best prepares you for the future. Every moment we have with a patient might prove to be that time when we have to get it right or the patient might die. I suspect this is a bit of an exaggeration, but people who go through very difficult experiences must try to justify them.

The test was in the gross anatomy lab. For those naive to this, imagine a large, dark room with a very distinct smell. Today, these labs are much brighter, and newer air exchange units keep the odor to a minimum. This was in the early seventies and we had what we had. This room was filled with thirty neatly aligned tables – with dissected human bodies on each! Surrounding the walls were skeletons and glass cases filled with a variety of human organs. It was eerie. During the test, coming from somewhere in each cadaver was a string attached to a body part on one end of what looked like a price tag on the other on which was a number. Cadavers do not look like those dead we might see in a funeral home. The skin does not look like skin and the appearance is a bit like gray-tan leather that is slightly shrunken. We worked on each in groups of five people for many months during which we played a game of hide and seek with tissues, organs, nerves, and vessels by carefully cutting into this body that was once a vibrant, and hopefully happy, person like us. Our group was arranged not by our personality types or some careful plan but by alphabet.

We used books as our guides – books that soon attained the same smell as the room. So did our clothes. People on campus knew who the first-year medical students were with their eyes closed. There were no computers, smartphones, or PDFs. We used books: Gray's and Pansky, and highlighted them in yellow – most of Pansky was yellow after a few months. Yellow meant to pay attention to it, as it would likely be on a test. It became Pavlovian. Recently, I got together with one of the five for dinner with our wives. I had not seen him since graduation over thirty years earlier. He brought his Pansky with him. We reminisced about that time decades ago and I asked him why he brought the book. He told me that I was good at anatomy and tutored him often and credited me with his passing the exam. I doubt that was true but greatly appreciated his memory of those days.

The first day was when we 'met' our cadaver. It was a time of great anticipation. *Will I get nauseated, pass out, or decide medical school is not my path?* Seeing the body is not too difficult, but seeing the face is so very difficult. You wonder who this person was. How did they die? Did they donate their body for us to learn from, or did they die alone and without the resources? This person will allow me to visualize how the body works and perhaps lay the foundation for a career in surgery. Now, medical schools commonly have ceremonies during which they honor these men and women. I helped create one at our school when I was a dean, during which students read poetry, a personal message, played an instrument, and ended the event by each placing a red rose in a vase on a memorial table. These are silent, moving, and real. Many prefer to write a note to this special unknown person. We did not do any of this and perhaps this story can be my way of saying 'thank you.'

Medicine has its own language and learning these new words is a major challenge. The anatomy course is the major test of this language acquisition. Some things have names that make sense. Most do not. It is a world in which many pneumonics have been created to help students remember. I recall spending countless nights pounding each into my memory. In time, I have learned that these would be needed for me to practice medicine and not just for this one horrific test. As the days draw close to the final exam, the worst of humanity comes to the surface. People freak out. I had never been a crammer for tests but preferred to be an obsessive. I neatly planned what to study on what day and kept to that schedule. I went to the gym, ate well, and made sure to watch my favorite show on television. I made sure I got a good night sleep. I went by the rule that the mind works best when treated well rather than given a stress test. On test day, I was ready. I loved tests and I got nervous but enjoyed that feeling as well. It was a natural rush that I felt was a good thing, as adrenaline can be very useful if channeled properly.

Test day came and our gross anatomy course director was a legend at our venerable school. He had a crew cut, was thin, always stood straight, and knew everything. He was both revered and feared. He stood at the front of the room next to a very large timer. We all held a clipboard with one hundred lines preceded by a number. It was on these lines that we were to write the name of the anatomy part to which the string with the associated number was attached. In what seemed like seconds, but were a few minutes, that damn timer would go off and we all rotated in unison to the next cadaver and the next line on our

47

sheet. It was an orchestrated dance that has changed little over the years. After about twenty dings, it finally happened – a student lost it.

I knew him, as he was one of my anatomy table partners. TM was a little older and had worked before coming to medical school. That was rare at the time. He was brilliant and had the maturity to know what was important, and that is not always a good thing. He left his place in the dance and walked up to the course director and asked loudly for the director to state what this TM's name was. There was no reply. We all stood there struck by the moment. A short time went by and when it was clear that this teacher did not know this student's name, the student stated that he had been up all night for a few days, memorizing thousands of names for him and that the least he could have done in the past few months was to memorize his. He turned and went back to his place and another ding sounded. About ten dings later, we heard from the front of the room his name called out, followed by, "… And trust me, I will not forget it when grading the papers!"

TM passed the course and has gone on to become a highly respected specialist. He gave us a wonderful momentary reprieve from the exam that I suspect helped all of us. I remember him well, and amazingly, I also remember many of the names on that test.

Medical School

I will always remember opening the envelope and learning that I had been accepted to the University of Pennsylvania's School of Medicine in Philadelphia. Like many, it has since changed its name to Perelman School of Medicine at the University of Pennsylvania. I was in the Chicago area doing research as part of my fourth year of college. I was alone when opening the envelope and immediately called home. Neither of my parents had the opportunity to go beyond high school. They valued education and supported us such that all four of their children went on to education beyond high school. We did well due to their encouragement and their genes. I had only applied to three medical schools and this was my top choice. I was going to be a doctor!

Upon returning to my college, King's College in Wilkes-Barre, PA, for the second semester of my senior year, I received a message to call Fred. He was a student at another college in the town where I was going to school and had also been accepted to Penn and wanted to meet me. Fred came to my dorm room and he had outlined what it would cost to live alone in Philadelphia with one other person, or with two others. He had itemized costs for food and even different apartment locations. I had not thought of any of this yet and was amazed. He then asked me if I cooked, as he did not. I told him that I loved to cook and he replied that he enjoyed doing dishes and cleaning up. Next, he arranged a van for our move months later and we set off to medical school together.

The first day of school was in a dark, old lecture hall. Penn was rich in history and just being there evoked a feeling of awe. I recall looking around and feeling like I was an experiment and did not really belong. I was surrounded by people from amazing schools and families. Thirty percent of the class was female, which was very high at that time. Thirty percent were not traditional students with science degrees. We said hello to people who would become our classmates for this journey and watched as a large man walked up to the podium. He had a suit and a bowtie and an amazing presence. He just stared out at us and said nothing. Soon, the room became so silent that you could hear the breathing. His booming voice welcomed us to the class of 1977.

He then told us that fifty percent of the material that we would learn in the next four years was bullshit. We quickly glanced around and awaited a laugh but none came. He next said that it will take about thirty years to discover what is actually correct and until then, we would be tested on everything and expected to know it. It has been over forty-five years since that day and I have come to see that he had exaggerated a tad but was right. Science advances and things change. Medicine is in constant evolution and a physician must be a perpetual student.

Classes were the equivalent of going to a show. The greats in medicine were our teachers and their lectures were riveting. The analogy that learning in medicine is like drinking from a fire hydrant was on target. Our classes were pass/fail in the grading system. They wanted us to learn for the sake of learning rather than competing. It worked. Our classmates became resources and friends rather than foes. The anatomy course was the most demanding and a rite of passage. The first two years breezed by. I loved it.

I married after my first year. She was a pediatric nurse. I made up my schedule so that I could do pediatrics first in my third year and we could work together forever as a perfect couple. The third year is meant to provide a broad clinical experience and allow students to experience the various specialties so that they can decide their path in medicine and design their fourth year. I have since learned that this process was severely flawed. Students at that time never really had any outpatient experiences and my eventual career was ninety percent outpatient medicine. Students saw a specialty through the lens of one or two physicians and that view was often biased by that physician's way of practicing. I had diarrhea for all my weeks in pediatrics and finished with a bad cold. It was called CHOP rot. I would scratch pediatrics off my career list and that likely paved the way to a happy marriage forty-five years later! I hated OB. The hours and standing in surgery dropped that off my list of possibilities. We did not have family medicine as a choice back then. My internal medicine weeks were filled with great role models and challenging cases. I also learned that by going that route, I could later decide on specialization into many fields. A decision was made. This game has not changed much over the years. Today, students have a great deal more experience in outpatient areas and also begin clinical exposure early on. That allows for better choices but these are now limited by greater competition and the perils of exam scores. It was a better time in many ways when I was in school.

The cost of medical education has become outrageous. When I went to medical school, the tuition was less than $3000. That was considered high then, and I was fortunate to have been given scholarships. After I married to a nurse who worked in the ICU at children's hospital, I was told my scholarships were being converted into loans as my status had changed and I was now not the son of a man who made far less money. I am still quite unhappy about that. Every year, tuition was raised, and by the fourth year, it was over $6000. I recall going to my advisor and telling him I had to drop out, since I could not afford medical school. He told me that was the dumbest thing he ever heard and told me to leave his office. That was known as advising back then! In retrospect, he was right, of course. I borrowed for tuition and living and, by the end of medical school, owed over $14,000. If we did not marry and lived together, the loans would be minimal but the risk was that my mother, a lovely, strict catholic, may have suffered a heart attack with the thought of her son living 'in sin.' We paid off the loans many years later and celebrated. My mother was still alive and well. We made the right decision!

Upon entering practice, I had minimal debt and could decide my career based upon what I loved rather than what I owed. I could decide not to bill patients who could not afford it and I could teach while not weighing the impact of hours I could not bill for my services. The good old days... Now students leave medical school with over $170,000 in debt on average from medical school alone. Eighty-six percent carry debt from undergrad and many have also gone to graduate school as well. I had students who owed over $400,000 upon entering practice. They must join a hospital system or corporation in need of a guaranteed salary and they begin their lives on a treadmill of production that becomes hard to get off. They must pay off the debt. They are usually over twenty-eight years of age and the time to start a family and buy a house kicks in. The debt and cost of living soar.

This is not a complaint about our income. Our profession is well rewarded in many ways. What people fail to take into account is the effect of the delay in having income, the hours spent preparing for the career, and costs associated with the path to medicine. The traditional path in America is that of four years of college, four of medical school, and between three and seven of residency/fellowship. While there is a salary associated with the latter, it is not close to what a person with similar skills and education would make at that age. I have come to know well that we do this mostly for the love of helping others. Most of us could have begun a career right after high school and used our drive, abilities, and work ethic to carve out a successful career many years sooner and without the debt. Few know these details.

I still vividly recall my graduation from Penn Med surrounded by my wife, my parents, and others. It was then, and is now, a dream come true. Those years laid the foundation for a lifetime of learning. It made magic real.

Surgical Block

I was assigned to do cardiothoracic surgery for the month. This would not have been my first choice but I was certain it would be a month during which I could learn a great deal and one filled with stories. Typically in medical school, students become immersed in the clinical education with patients in their third year. When I was in school in the mid-seventies, students had very little exposure to patients before the third year. Now they begin to see patients early on and this is a very good thing, as it reminds the student every day why they are spending so much time studying – it is to be able to help their patients now and in the future.

Medical students sometimes show up for the first day of school knowing exactly what they want to be. I recently met a first-year student who said they were going to be a plastic surgeon. This is usually fueled by having someone in the family in that specialty or by some personal experience with that field through an illness. Some change their minds many times during medical school and they are the lucky ones because they are enjoying each experience. Some cannot decide and pick a field with various options that stem from it, such as internal medicine, so as to delay the final decision. That was me. I always try to dissuade the student who is focused on a field early on, as they are depriving themselves of the wonder of medical school. All schools must teach to all facets of medical practice. Those who focus on one tend to minimize the importance of others as they 'will never use that.' Had I taken that mindset over the years, trigonometry and Latin would have proven to be more a torture to me than they were.

In the third year of medical school, students rotate through the major specialties. Everyone must do the same things albeit in different ways. I look at it as a Halloween party. We get to dress up and play surgeon for a period of time. We see the lifestyle, learn the lingo, experience the operating room, see patients before and after surgery, and best of all, get to meet the personalities that inhabit the land of surgery. I had the good fortune of going to medical school at one of the best hospitals in the world and the attending physicians were legends. Would I end up becoming a surgeon, even a CT surgeon? It's time to find out! These rotations set the stage for students to pick what they will do for the rest of their lives. I found it best to immerse myself in every way and enjoy it. Those who do not are depriving themselves of incredible adventures.

I have learned over the years that it is very useful to know a little bit about many things. Patients will ask your opinion. Relatives and friends will get diseases in these other areas of specialization. They expect us to know. The exam taken at the end of medical school includes questions from every field of medicine. All graduates must take it, and passing is required to move forward in residency training.

The weeks I spent learning cardiovascular surgery were incredible. The people were demanding, the hours were ridiculous, the conditions I got to see were unique, and the pace was faster than I could have imagined. There was a surgeon at the time who was 'the best.' I have learned that there are many throughout the world who wear that label. The top CT surgeon in Philadelphia is likely equal to the one in New York and so on. They all get people referred to them from near and far. They walk and act differently. Dr. M knew how good he was and wore it daily. I recall one day in the operating room during a surgery a story he told. He spoke of a lawsuit filed against him the day before. He had operated on a prominent local business tycoon who had severe angina for two years. His chest pain got so bad that he could no longer do anything that involved exertion. That included sex. Dr. M did a four-vessel bypass procedure that restored the blood flow to his heart. He was able to resume his former lifestyle and all seemed well. His wife decided that she was no longer interested in having sex. He ran off with his secretary. His wife filed a suit against Dr. M for the loss of her husband! He spoke of this suit with great pride...

One day, I was in the operating room for another coronary bypass procedure. At the time, this involved exposing the heart and removing veins from the leg to use them to bypass the blockages in the arteries. The senior resident would get everything set and begin the procedure. Dr. M would scrub and then walk in and the ritual was set in motion. A nurse gowned and gloved him in a precise fashion. He would then bend forward and a special light was put on his head, after which he walked to the right side of the chest of the patient, hold his hands forward with elbows flexed, and without speaking, the nurse would put a stepstool behind him and he would say, "Adjust the light to the field." She did so and the surgery was on! He was amazing. My job was to be quiet, hold a retractor now and then, and stay near the leg where the veins had now been removed. This was my seventh time doing this. Suddenly, an announcement came over the speaker that the man who was operated on the day before was crashing in the intensive care unit. The resident working on the leg had to run out. Before he did, he told Dr. M that I was very good and he felt comfortable with me sewing up the leg wounds. Dr. M said OK without emotion.

My adrenaline level soared. This was my moment! I would make that resident proud. Just as I was about to ask for the sewing devices needed, the large circular light over the leg went black. Before I could think, the nurse told Dr. M that they had another head lamp that was not being used and wondered if I could try to use it. My head filled with excitement and my pulse raced! She put the lamp on and adjusted it to my head. I stepped up to the leg and just could not help myself. I said loudly, while mimicking Dr. M's voice and tone, "Nurse, adjust the light to the field." Everyone became silent and froze. In the next second, Dr. M had me thrown out of the operating room. I had my shining moment and it was worth it. My surgical path was officially closed. I am an internist and happy as can be – and with another great story to tell!

The Call

I was in an apartment within the Argonne National Laboratory grounds outside of Chicago. It was 2:00 PM. I was with Tom when the mail came. The return address was the University of Pennsylvania, School of Medicine, Admissions. My heart skipped a few beats as I opened it. The one-page letter within welcomed me into medical school! I remember that moment as if it was yesterday. I felt so lucky, so relieved, and so very grateful. I immediately called my parents. After that, it was a blur. That moment changed my life, and I now know it impacted the lives of many. I was going to be a physician!

Fast forward thirty-five years and I found myself as chair of the admissions committee at a new medical school in Pennsylvania. That was followed soon thereafter by being offered the opportunity to create another admissions process and a new medical school in New Jersey. Doing so would mean moving and leaving my practice that had become another family to me. After weeks of mental anguish, I decided to take on the challenge and we moved to New Jersey. I remembered my acceptance letter on that day in 1973, and what it meant to me. I vowed to work hard to create a unique process to select those that might one day care for me. Who would be the best student for our school? How would we find them? How would we select them?

I knew that one needed intellectual capacity to navigate the amount of knowledge a student consumes in medical school. The entrance test, the MCAT, allows one to compare students from all schools. It is imperfect but useful. However, it can give an advantage to those who have the means to go to the best college, to take prep courses, and to have the extra time to study for it. This disadvantages those from various backgrounds. The GPA allows us to see how students do over a number of years and put course load and science courses into the equation. The personal statements are almost always edited and shaped by many and often do not reflect solely on the applicant. The letters of recommendation are done by faculty and others chosen by each student – and therefore most likely to say the best things. The secondary application allows a school to solicit specific answers, but again, these can and are edited by others before submission. How does one navigate all of this information to select the students to invite for an interview? How do we find the person behind the application? There are thousands of applicants to each medical school every year and only about ten percent can be interviewed by a given school yearly. Then I heard about holistic review!

The American Association of Medical Colleges (AAMC) is an amazing organization that oversees medical education in this country. I went to a national meeting and heard a presentation that changed my thinking entirely. They had come up with an idea that allowed schools to identify the attributes of applicants that would best resonate with the mission of the school and developed a way to screen for these. I invited the speakers to come to our new school and meet with administration and the admissions committee. Everyone bought into the holistic review process. It was a beautiful thing to be part of. We were going to establish a process that identified those who would resonate with what the school was creating. It would be blind to background. It worked! We found that we could identify students who resonated with our mission by resonating with their mission.

The last step was figuring out how to identify students who would be comfortable with interacting with patients from the very start of medical school. Our school was creating a free clinic run by students that would provide care for those uninsured who lived in our challenged city. I also wanted to identify students with strong character and moral values, as I see these as essential. I created a process in which every applicant to our school would interview two standardized patients trained to play a role. These would be graded as to their ability to relate, their professionalism, and the way they managed an ethical dilemma the patient posed. Actors were trained and systems were created to allow for reproducible results. The scores on these encounters were made known to the admissions committee and used in the selection process. The students loved it! It gave us a special insight into their ability while giving them an insight into what medical school would be like.

In addition, each student was interviewed by two faculty members at the same time. One was always a member of the admissions committee and had the full application available to them. One was a faculty member blinded to the application so that bias would not enter into the decision. One interviewer focused on facts related to the application and one focused on questions related to our mission. The process worked! I was asked by the AAMC to be on their holistic review board and was given the opportunity to bring the process to other schools. Our inaugural class of fifty students was all in residency programs and on its way to serve those in need. I thank these students for having the courage to come to a new school with a different mission. I thank them for leading the way.

The best part of my job was calling the students to tell them of their acceptance. I wanted them to remember the moment the way I remembered mine. We would email them, and then I would call. The screams, the 'really' reply, and the calling out to others in the room made all the work worth it for me – and for them. One young lady I will always remember. I made the student promise me that they will celebrate the moment. She said, "I already have a small glass of vodka poured." It was 11:00 AM… She came back for our second-look day – a day when accepted students returned as a group to see and hear more, to meet one another, and to get questions answered. I always greeted them at the door. She walked in and handed me a present in a nice bag. I opened it and it was a bottle of vodka! I opened it sometime later when we heard of our school's full accreditation. The young lady graduated and is now doing her residency in emergency medicine. We will both always remember her acceptance to medical school!

Fork in the Road

I have good handwriting, thanks to the nuns. I have cold hands. I never golfed. I work on Wednesdays. I am not into cars. I cut my own lawn. I fix things around the house and love carpentry. My parents never went beyond high school. No one in my family was a physician. I was shy as a child. I did not go to top schools before medical school. Medicine is a coat that does not seem like one that would fit me, and yet, it fits perfectly. I love to help people. I find people interesting. I love to work hard. I enjoy taking tests. I am not a reader but find all aspects of medicine fascinating and prefer to read medical journals than novels. If happiness is doing what you love for a living, then I am one of the happiest people on Earth.

But how did I manage to find this path? The answer lies in a bit of luck, a few gifts, and the unwavering support of my parents. My mother stayed home to take care of her parents, my father, and my one brother and two sisters. She was very bright and skipped a step in school but her family could not afford to send her to school. Pauline never complained. She was quiet, religious, and supportive. I feel I was driven to do anything possible to make her happy and proud of me. She never asked for anything but deserved everything. Leo was a policeman. He never went beyond high school either but was dedicated to make sure we all did. He worked many jobs and never complained. He would chauffeur physicians in the small town we grew up in. My father did not talk much and I knew my smoothest path would be to never get him upset, and yet, I never actually feared him.

I had an older brother and sister and we were separated in age significantly. My brother went on to become an accountant and he showed me why it was best not to get my father angry or my mother worried. My sister was very bright and went to nursing school. She never talked about it that I recall, so I cannot say this paved the way for me to my medical career. I recall vividly the day she told me there was no Santa Claus – I was devastated! She made it up to me years later by teaching me how to dance for the prom. Nothing in the early years would have predicted I would become a physician.

My first twelve years of school were in the same red-brick building. It was a small catholic school and most of my teachers were Sisters of Mercy. Many were quite old, as we had an elevator in the house where the nuns lived. A few actually dropped dead in class. I do not recall being horrified by this but do recall getting a few days off as a result. Fear was a potent weapon in those years. We feared getting hit by the nun, getting struck dead by God, our parents being told of anything negative, and of being bombed by other countries. There were regular fire drills and even practice hiding under our desks in case a bomb came. In retrospect, this was a bad plan. We went to mass often and had to sit and kneel straight while not understanding a word said until the sermon – and that regularly poured gas on the fear fire. It was not a good education overall, but I did the best I could.

Today's medical school applicants have usually done experiences referred to as shadowing. This means they have been with physicians in the clinical setting observing what that career path is like. Such experiences are variable, of course, and depend on the physician and the activity that day. I had no such experience and had never seen a physician other than when I was taken to one, and that was usually for a shot as a child and therefore not a memorable experience. I went to college and had to declare a major. I wrote down pre-med without a clue of what this really meant. I soon found out it meant 8:00 AM classes, more credits per semester, and late afternoon labs. I also found out I lacked the foundation due to my high school not being strong. I studied hard, did well, and kept my focus on a goal unknown to me.

I liked the labs and thought that perhaps research was a good path. I read about MD-PhD tracks and looked into those. I needed a strong research experience and my college was not known for that. On the bulletin board in the biology department was a paper advertising an experience in research at the Argonne National Laboratory outside of Chicago. It had phone numbers on the bottom on pull-off little strips (the original form of the internet). I called, got accepted, and went there for the first semester of my senior year. It was an incredible experience and I learned that research was not my path. I got accepted to medical school while there and the next step in the path was complete.

Once in medical school, I became happier than I had ever been. I loved everything! It was like being a kid in a candy store. Somehow, I had landed exactly where I was meant to be in life. It is not hard work if you love it. The problem was that I loved everything and decided on a residency in internal medicine mostly because of the role models I had on those experiences. Again, right choice – I had wonderful three years in that residency. I could not decide on a specialty, since I liked everything, so I decided to do general internal medicine. Our first child was born and it was time to earn a living! They had just started a primary-care residency in medicine in the city where my wife was born, so we moved there, as it would allow me to teach and begin a practice. It was the perfect choice and has allowed me to do all that I love, and now reflect on it as well.

Early on in my practice, I was asked to oversee the clinical experience of medical students rotating from Philadelphia to our school and I took on this task. I was required to go to Philadelphia and my mentor decided on a plan of creating a way to enhance primary care as a career for early medical students and asked me to help. That led to creating a course in the first two years and I became the director and primary teacher – and yes, I loved it. Years went by and physicians in my community decided to create a new medical school and I was asked to be part of it. That led to me creating and chairing the admissions' process and recreating my course for first years – and no longer needing to travel to teach! I worked hard and loved teaching and that led to me being asked to move to create a new medical school elsewhere and take on the role of an associate dean of student affairs and admissions. This was a great deal of work and very satisfying but I missed teaching and being with patients. I became critically ill and was out of work for some time, during which things at the school changed. I was offered a job by the affiliated hospital system, teaching in the classroom and at the bedside. I could now use all those years of experience to pay it forward. I can honestly say that this is exactly where any dream I could have had would have placed me.

What would have happened if I did not have supportive parents, if I went to a different college, if I had not done research for a few months, or if I had shadowed a physician on a bad day? What would have happened if I had begun practice in a different city, if my wife had not been supportive in moving after three decades, or if I had not become ill? Yogi Berra once said that when you come to a fork in the road, take it. Who knows what I would have been had I taken a different road along the way? I would not change a thing if given the chance.

Medical Education

My path has allowed me to have a very personal insight into medical education in America. I had many opportunities that have given me a view that might be unique in this area. I went to medical school at the University of Pennsylvania in Philadelphia. It was the first medical school in this country. Walking those hallways gave me a wonderful feeling of being a part of history. That was even truer when I went to the Pennsylvania Hospital to do my residency. It was founded in 1751 by Benjamin Franklin and Dr. Thomas Bond. Jacob Ehrenzeller, the first medical resident, was appointed in 1773. His contract at that time included:

"This Indenture Witnesseth, that Jacob Ehrenzeller, son of Jacob Ehrenzeller of the City of Philadelphia hath put himself, and by these presents, with consent of his said father, doth voluntarily, and of his own free will and accord, put himself apprentice to the managers of the Pennsylvania Hospital to learn the art, trade, and mystery, and after the manner of an apprentice to serve the said managers from the day of the date hereof, for and during, to the full end and term of five years and three months next ensuing. During all of that term, the said apprentice his said master faithfully shall serve, his secrets keep, and his lawful commands everywhere readily obey. He shall do no damage to his said master, nor see it to be done by others, without letting or giving notice thereof to his said master. He shall not waste his said master's goods, nor lend them unlawfully to any. He shall not commit fornication nor contract matrimony within the said term... He shall not play at cards, dice, or any other unlawful game, whereby his said master may have damage... during the said term of five years and three months."

Things certainly changed! During my three years there, I was able to walk through the original hospital, peruse the original library, and even go into the first surgical suite. This gave me perspective and made me grateful for all we then had in treating patients. I would encourage all who read this to take a tour of this amazing building.

Medical schools flourished after that and were begun in many places. The first resident and most that followed in the next decades were trained by attaching themselves to a physician and learning the craft from them. There was little in terms of books or classes. The skill of these early graduates often hinged on who they shadowed. The quality of physicians soon became the subject of study. In 1904, the American Medical Association (AMA) created the Council on Medical Education (CME) whose objective was to restructure American medical education. At its first annual meeting, the CME adopted two standards. One laid down the minimum prior education required for admission to a medical school. The other defined a medical education as consisting of two years' training in human anatomy and physiology followed by two years of clinical work in a teaching hospital. In 1908, the CME asked the Carnegie Foundation for the advancement of teaching to survey American medical education and chose Abraham Flexner to conduct the survey. He toured all one hundred and fifty-five schools that then existed and the report called on American medical schools to enact higher admission and graduation standards and to adhere strictly to the protocols of mainstream science in their teaching and research. Many American medical schools fell short of the standard advocated in the Flexner Report and, subsequent to its publication, nearly half of such schools merged or were closed outright. Homeopathy and natural medicines were derided. Some doctors were jailed.

Over the next hundred years, there was very little change in the system of medical education. Then, things began to change and schools were allowed to experiment with how they taught as long as they met certain standards. These were overseen by the ACGME (Accreditation Council for Graduate Medical Education). The ACGME currently oversees the post-graduate education and training for all MD and the majority of DO physicians in the United States. The ACGME's member organizations are the American Board of Medical Specialties, American Hospital Association, American Medical Association, Association of American Medical Colleges, and the Council of Medical Specialty Societies, each of whom appoints four members to the ACGME's board of directors.

I have had the amazing opportunity to play a significant role in the creation of two new medical schools. The standards that have to be met are many, and they are rigid. Every step along the way is reviewed and the time and work it took to create each school was far greater than I could have imagined. Schools must be designed to create a foundation of knowledge and skill that will prepare the graduate to succeed in many different specialties. It appears to me that we will start seeing some change in the overall goals and likely the requirements in the years ahead. History assures us that this will happen.

When I was in medical school, they had begun this slow evolution. Many in my class were female and this was different at that time. Many were not science majors fresh out of college. They shortened the first two years that were traditionally classroom and gave us early patient exposure. They made testing as pass/fail. These were all radical at the time and are now the norm. Medical education is intense in terms of faculty needs. Unlike universities that can have five hundred in a class, medical schools have been moving toward small group format – often with no more than eight in a classroom with one or two teachers. This is amazing and I am delighted to teach in this setting but it is faculty-intense and I wonder how it can survive with the tuition curve being so steep already.

Classroom lectures are fading away. Now everything is captured and students often do not attend lectures. They are a generation that watches videos – sometimes in fast-forward mode, and they use more than one monitor to link various educational formats. Gone are the days of paying a student to take notes. The teaching is often geared to preparing the student for the licensing exam and that test has taken on extraordinary importance unfortunately. I suspect that in the future, all such teaching will be centralized rather than each medical school giving the same material in separate lectures. Cost alone may dictate this change. It also only makes sense that if one professor is more gifted in making the material come alive to students, then all should have access to this.

There have always been pathways through which people could graduate from medical school in less time. I have seen students enter medical school with debt of over $200,000 in my role overseeing financial aid. The typical debt from medical school alone is now near $200,000 and this is an average with some needing to take on over $300,000. That equates to students entering residency owing up to $500,000 and making often less than $60,000. This cannot continue. I fear we will soon see more of our best and brightest options for different careers for financial reasons, and one cannot blame them.

I came from a family that did not have the resources to pay for my education. Today, I might not have been able to go to medical school. Much of what I have reflected on in this book might never have happened. I find this sad and hope we can find a way to maintain the high standards needed for producing the best physicians possible in the years ahead while taking away the cost barrier. More change is definitely needed.

Moving

Moving is a guaranteed way to shorten your time on this Earth! The path to being a physician is full of moves and each one brings new challenges and intense lessons on how to curse. The first is going off to college and the transition from living in a house and being totally cared for to living in what is the equivalent of a jail cell with someone you do not know, while eating horrible food in a cafeteria and sharing a bathroom with many people at the same time. Then there is the matter of laundry, poverty, and a quantum leap in studying compared to being a senior in high school. The next few years involve moving back home again and again. I had four moves in my first three years with different roommates each time. I then moved to Chicago for a semester to do research after my junior year and back to finish college. Six moves!

Next, I was off to medical school with the fears of how I would perform amongst students coming from the best schools. There were three more moves in medical school followed by the move to begin my residency. That was my longest stay since moving away from home in one place, but after three years, it was time to make that move that was the beginning of my professional life. I had decided what field I loved, had a wife and a newborn daughter, and we had settled on a city in which to begin my life as an internist. We found a small home to rent and were very excited about beginning this next chapter in our lives. We went to see the house again a few weeks before the move, and without the rugs, the wall hangings, and the curtains, it was a mess. Upon trying to contact the landlord, we found that he had recently been put in jail! The next question I asked was how long he was in for and what the reason was. We had no options at this point and I was assured he was not getting out in less than one year and that he was harmless, so we decided to fix it up ourselves and move as planned. Our smooth transition had hit its first bump in the road.

The movers came right on time and I was amazed at the efficiency and strength of these three men. In no time, all of our belongings were out of the apartment in time for us to depart and be in our new dwelling before them and to get to the bank before it closed. There was a time before ATMs and banks closed at 3:00 PM. We had packed our valuables (easy to do, as one does not accumulate wealth as a medical resident paying off loans), our new baby, and walked out the door of the apartment to lock it and move forward with our lives. Once outside the door, we noted that everything we owned was piled down the hallway of the apartment house! Only then were we informed that the moving truck would not start and they were waiting for a new one to arrive. We took a deep breath of faith and began the journey.

Once at the house, we felt excited. My father-in-law had done a great job sprucing it up and we had a small yard, bright windows, and a garage. I went to the bank to get the money to pay the movers and to the store to get a few items. Then we waited. We had no phone hooked up yet, and this was long before cellphones. I drove to a pay phone and called the moving company. There was no answer. I called our former apartment and they told me the truck had left four hours earlier. That was four hours for a two-and-a-half-hour trip. I knew this made no sense and was certain all of our belongings were gone forever. I called the State Police to discover that a moving truck was broken down on the turnpike one hour from us. There was no one in it. After another hour, a small van pulled up outside of our house with two of the movers in it and our living-room rug folded up in the back with two chairs. They told me that the van broke down and they had no way to contact me, so they drove to find me (using good old-fashioned maps). Their van was almost out of gas, so I arranged for a service truck to meet us at the moving van that was broken down and I drove the two movers to the truck. Fifteen minutes into that trip, my car broke down. This tale is sadly all true. I called my brother-in-law who picked the three of us up and off we went down the turnpike. On arrival, a service vehicle was there and all they needed was the key to the truck. The mover then realized he had left the keys in the van at our house!

Finally, at about 2:00 AM, a tow truck pulled the truck will all of our Earthly possessions in front of our house. A tow truck lifted the moving truck up such that our belongings and furniture got pushed together and many were damaged. The noise and the lights likely kept up the neighbors and our initial impression on our new neighbors was less than hoped for. But our things were there and we were ready to move on.

After a few hours' sleep on a mattress lying on a floor, I was awoken by a knock on the door. I opened it to encounter a man who asked if I was the new doctor who just moved into the neighborhood. I had no idea how he knew that, but was happy to be in such a friendly neighborhood. His next words shocked me. He said he thought his brother was dead next door and asked if I would come and check! I did. He was.

Later that day, I drove to the hospital to see my new office. The administrator only then informed me that it was not ready and would take a few weeks. No one knew who I was, and I had a wife, a baby, and bills to pay. This was before new physicians were hired by hospitals and organizations and given a salary and benefits. My income depended on my seeing patients and there were no patients! A neighbor asked my wife how she felt about her husband doing internals all day. She then discovered many did not know what an internist was and they thought I was a gynecologist. After weeks without a call, I took a job working night hours in local emergency rooms just to pay the bills. The new phonebook came out (Yes, there were such things.) and I quickly checked my listing in the yellow pages to learn that they had put me a 'McGeehan John, J.'

Today's new physician faces different issues. They now graduate with an enormous debt. I had little because medical school was not expensive by today's standards. I had loans and it took years to pay them off, but today, it is not uncommon for a person to finish medical school with over $300,000 in debt. To have a car, a family, and get a home on top of that results in the need to generate considerable income. I started my own practice and could make my own hours. Today's new physician is an employee in every sense of the word. I had to buy my own copy machine, pay my phone bill, and hire my secretary, but they were mine and generated enormous pride and responsibility. I went to 'my' office and saw 'my' patients. I loved every day!

Times change and the new are protected by not having experienced the past. Physicians who are now working and are over fifty years old remember the way it was and have to deal with what now is. We remember creating a practice and having the time to go to our children's events, since we were in charge of our daily schedule. We remember really communicating with each patient without the need to enter everything into a computer. We remember seeing our patients in the hospital when they needed us most as well as in our office. Burnout is a hot topic in the life of a physician these days. I remember working much longer hours, having far lesser tools to help patients, the years when malpractice fear ruled our day, and making much less money. I do not recall burnout being an issue. Perhaps it exists because many, like me, feel that we were more a physician then and more an employee now.

Chapter 4

Rough Start

The dream did not go as planned. I was young and able to adjust to the many curveballs thrown my way as I set out to establish my practice. Life humbles everyone. At the time, each event accelerated my hair loss and had me second-guessing my plan. In retrospect, the result was an incredibly strong marriage and a ton of stories!

Being Sued

I was working the night shift in the local emergency room. I was fresh out of residency and decided to move to a smaller city and begin my own practice. At the time, the cost of education was low and my debt was reasonable. I assumed that if I would announce my presence, people would realize where I was trained, and my waiting room would be full in no time. Wrong. No one knew then what an internist was or did. I had a baby girl and it was time to support my family, so I took whatever jobs were available.

It was very slow that night. A family brought their mother, Mrs. S, in to be seen for a headache. I did the usual complete history and learned that she had chronic headaches and had even seen her physician for this earlier in the week. They were not getting worse and were not constant. There were no associated symptoms. I then did a complete physical exam. There were no other patients and I enjoyed doing the physical-exam part of the doctor-patient ritual, especially the neurologic exam. I was good at it. When I approach an exam, I always tell myself I am going to find something, as I feel that heightens the senses. Alas! Her exam was normal. I even did a good exam of the eyes and saw normal venous pulsations and that is indicative of the pressure in the brain being normal.

I sat with the family and the patient and explained my exam and encouraged her to call her doctor after 8:00 AM. They agreed. These days, such a patient would likely have gotten a CT scan of her head even before being examined. This reliance on testing is understandable. Yet, I feel it has diminished the role of the physical exam in patient care. At this time in my career, the hospital had just gotten a CT scanner and it was not available on nights or weekends. Times change.

Two weeks later, I was back working the late shift on a weekend in the ER. The same nurses were there and one asked me what I thought when I heard the lady with the headache died suddenly the next day. I did not know. I was shaken by the news. What did I miss? Should I have admitted her? Was this my fault? People do not realize how deeply such an event impacts a physician. I was sure I did everything right, and yet... I was a mess. I slept poorly. I questioned my decision to become a physician and to leave the big city. I also waited every day for the notice that I was being sued. I had built this up to be the end of my career, as I was sure the news would spread quickly and no one would ever come to see me as a patient.

The day did come and the fact that I was another physician facing a lawsuit became real. I was only a few months out of residency and it was all over. I had every possible scenario go through my mind repeatedly. It was not something one could speak to others about. My wonderful wife was supportive and understanding, but also scared. The hospital was being sued as well, since I was working for them in the emergency-room shift. I met with the lawyers assigned to me by my malpractice insurance carrier and the firm representing the hospital. Every detail of that night was dissected over and over. That was when I learned the reason I was being sued. The plaintiff's attorney was asserting that I had written my note after learning the patient had died.

This was the time before electronic medical records. Notes were written. There was only one other patient that night and I recall writing a very long note on Mrs. S, documenting every single detail. I recall the nurses making fun of me, saying that ER notes are supposed to be brief, not a few pages long. I was taught that notes should be detailed and complete – the rule was that if it is not in the note, it was not done. Everything was in this note – thank God.

The court date was scheduled and I was told to take two weeks off work. Expert witnesses were lined up. The nurses with me that night wanted to testify to my long note done right at the time Mrs. S was seen. I was ready. I had to read the 'expert' witness's reports for the plaintiff. These were people from distant states who clearly would say anything for money. They were immoral liars who give our profession a bad name. I was horrified and angry. My attorneys were amazing and became my psychologists. They assured me this would all be OK. They said this was a tactic to get me to settle and they advised me not to.

Two weeks before the trial date, the plaintiff's lawyers moved to change the date. It was moved to ten months later. I was beyond upset. This happened four more times. It took them eight years to take this to trial! The system is so broken. This was hanging over my head all this time and it truly aged me. I cared about what people thought. Finally, it went to trial and for two weeks, I had to sit there and listen to statements so far from reality that I wanted to scream. I constantly watched the jurors and imagined every outcome.

The jurors were charged by the judge and went to deliberate. I cannot put in words what that waiting felt like. People perhaps think doctors do not care. We care. It is what we do for a living. Being right matters. Saving lives drives us. I was shocked when my lawyer came to get me thirty-two minutes later. The verdict was in! So fast – what did that mean?

The jury delivered a not-guilty verdict and my heart rate slowed for what seemed like the first time in eight years. The plaintiff's attorney rose and demanded the jury be polled and I watched as one by one each rose and said not-guilty and looked at me kindly. I smiled again and I could feel each muscle used in that act.

I slept like a rock that night. The next day, I went to the office to resume my dream. My secretary said that three people had called that morning to be new patients and told her that they were jurors at my trial.

Bad People

I was sitting at the nurse's station admitting a man with diabetes and pneumonia. It was 9:00 PM and I was a second-year resident in medicine at a hospital in Center City. A man in his forties came to the desk, took off his clothes, and stood there naked, staring. He was sweating profusely and did not say a word. The other resident at the desk with me quickly stood up, brought him back to his room, and drew blood. My fellow resident was the smartest person I have ever met. He started school young and finished medical school and college in five years. The blood pressure of the man and pulse were both very high and my fellow resident thought he had a pheochromocytoma. This is a very rare tumor of the adrenal gland that can intermittently put out a surge of adrenaline. The test came back positive. The man had the tumor removed and was cured. It turned out he had been arrested many times for exposing himself. The diagnosis enabled him to have all charges removed from his file! He was not a pervert. He had a tumor. I suspect he was the only sex offender who will ever be diagnosed with this condition. The rest are just bad people – but what does that mean?

It was a normal day in the office. I was now in my second year of practice and my patient base was steadily growing. I was not making much money, but I was happy. My secretary did not come into work that day and had not called. That was very odd. She was a lady in her late forties who was married, had worked as a secretary for years, and was great with all of my patients. She had come with glowing recommendations when I called her references upon hiring her. Other secretaries called her for advice on billing and referrals. Everyone loved her. I called my wife and told her AA did not come to work and she immediately said to check my books! I was shocked. I asked her why and she told me she just had a bad feeling. I did as she suggested and the books were all gone, as were the checks and the cash. I drove to her house to find it empty, with no furniture and no lights as I looked through the window. My heart sank. I remembered that when I met her husband, he told me he worked as a car salesman at a local dealership. I went there to learn that he had not come to work that day either. I called the police.

The police were less than helpful and did not seem to want to look into someone stealing from a doctor. My brother-in-law took over, as he is very clever. After some work, we found that they were never married. He was being investigated in a likely scam in which he stole an expensive car through a number of transfers between dealerships and left town just in time. I called the references upon hiring AA to learn that they had all left their jobs mysteriously and no details were offered. I always did the deposits to the bank myself and balanced the books. Multiple calls found out that she had been fixing the books and had ordered a duplicate set, telling the company they had been damaged in a water leak, and forged my name. She did the same with all of my deposits for estimated taxes. Not only was I now broke, I also owed the IRS! They are not very understanding or sympathetic...

My brother-in-law finally tracked her down in Iowa where she was arrested, left out on bail, and disappeared. She has never been found – if anyone was really looking for her. She was a bad person – a sociopath. There was a network of similar people who supported one another in their scams. These are bright and personable people who choose to commit crimes and prey off others rather than direct these gifts in a positive and meaningful way. What makes people act this way? Why do they not care about others? Is someone born this way or does it come from life experiences? No one really knows. We do not understand brain chemistry. We now treat drug and alcohol dependence as a medical illness. Are other addictions the same? When do we call someone intrinsically bad and not amenable to change? These are questions beyond my ability to offer any explanations.

For a short time, I began to trust no one. My faith in humanity was shaken. I was also embarrassed. I recall telling another physician about what happened and heard that after we spoke, he became so nervous about his books that he got in the garage to go to work to check and backed out without opening his garage door. His books were fine. His door was not.

Time heals most wounds. Life went on. I did some things differently but chose not to live a life suspicious of everyone. Most people are good, in fact wonderful. I see the good in people every day. Illness and crisis bring out the best and worst in people – but usually the best. People rise to the challenges of life. I always loved taking care of my older patients. They shared their view of life and were able to tell me what it was like during the depression in the war before we had medications like today. They knew what life was about and were happy to share it. The real payment for caring for others as their physician is having them share their wisdom. Some people are bad and we cannot let them block out the joy of getting to know all the special people who cross our path in life.

Make the Last First

I decided to hang a shingle and start a private practice. That was not uncommon at that time, though unheard of now. With my training, my love for medicine, and my way with patients, it would not be long before I was busy and looking for a partner. Wrong. The waiting room was empty, the phone silent, and the bills mounting.

I was finally called for a consult. It was a Saturday evening around 11:30 PM as I was starting to watch Saturday Night Live. The answering service called and connected me to the ICU at Mercy Hospital where a nurse told me that a surgeon had placed a consult to me for a medical evaluation on a new admission and it needed to be done now. Deep in my heart, I knew I was called because the surgeon did not want to disturb a friend at that hour on a weekend. Whatever the reason, I was off!

On the way to the hospital, I had time to think. Warren was a senior resident where I trained who made sarcasm a science but always seemed to have the answers. When he heard I had planned to leave the university hospital system in the city to go to a smaller town, he gave me advice that now came back to me. He told me that when I do my first consult and make up that long differential diagnosis that makes an internist get up every morning, be sure to list the last one first. His reasoning was that if I make the most likely diagnosis, the one most would think of, the consulting doctor would think, 'Of course.' If I say the cause was an obscure, put possible, diagnosis and I was right, the word would get out about me. What did I have to lose!?

Her name was Ethyl and she was in Bed Four of an ICU that was old and unlike what I had been accustomed to the past seven years. She was unconscious but breathing on her own. She had no family and no visitors and could not talk to me. As over eighty percent of all diagnoses are made by history, I would be starting at a major disadvantage. The story is that a neighbor had called the police after hearing a noise. She had fallen down the stairs and the ambulance brought her to the ER unconscious since the moment they found her. There was no head trauma noted. There was no CT scanner available at nights at that time. It was the age of relying on the exam and the interpretation of data. The exam showed no major bruising and some response to deep pain. The fundi were normal and there was no focal deficit noted. Strange…

The X-rays showed no fractures amazingly, and the EKG was normal. She had a Foley catheter placed and the urine was clear. Basic labs were done and something caught my eye. Her electrolytes were off. The chloride was elevated, resulting in what is called a negative anion gap. To this day, I do not know if I was lucky to focus on that or perhaps I had so much minutia packed into my brain as a result of studying for the licensing exam that the zebra became the horse. I repeated the labs and they were the same! I asked the nurse to get me her primary physician on the phone but none was listed.

At that moment, I decided to list bromism as her diagnosis and I postulated that somehow she had taken an overdose of bromide, resulting in her sedation, her fall, and her chemical picture. I ordered a bromide level, called the consulting surgeon, and proudly went home!

The next day, the consult was ignored, a CT scan done, a neurologist consulted, and there was no mention of this wondrous diagnosis. I came to the bedside daily and saw this lady slowly wake up. She told me she was very nervous and did not remember what happened. She had been seeing a herbalist for her nerves who made a tonic for her that helped her a great deal. On Day Three, the bromide level finally came back and it was in the toxic range. The word spread like wildfire. Within days, I was being consulted and patients were calling for appointments. My career began. I made the last first. Thank you, Warren.

Dark

Karen was a new patient and I knew that she was a psychologist, as she was referred by a friend of mine. She was fifty-five and had not been to a physician other than her gynecologist for a few years. The problem with the medical interview with someone in her field is that inevitably the bright spotlight gets turned back on the interviewer. She just had this natural way of diverting questions in such a way that I felt I was the patient. At one point, after I asked her what she enjoyed doing outside of working, she used that moment to discover that I enjoyed carpentry. She told me her husband's hobby was carpentry and that he had an amazing workshop that I should come and see. I told her that I would enjoy that and tucked it away into the vast file of things in my mind I should have taken the time to do. Karen was healthy and I ordered some screening tests and told her to call me whenever she needed anything and to consider returning in one year.

I was on call one weekend and covering my practice and that of three other internists. I was in solo practice and the path to sanity is having someone you trust cover your practice so that you can have protected time for family and yourself. The problem is that when it is my turn to cover, I must see all the patients in the hospital for myself and three other busy internists as well as answer every call that comes in for sixty hours. We did not have hospitalists or residents covering our patients, so all calls came to the covering physician. I hated those weekends. The other three doctors called me late Friday afternoon to tell me about the patients they had in the hospital and any potential problems with their outpatients. I would call them back Sunday night to tell them about what happened with their patients, major calls, and any admissions. If anything happened overnight, I would tell them on Monday. This was the routine for thirty years.

Friday came and sign-out began. I had a pen in hand, awaiting the bad news only to find out that everyone was light that week in terms of hospital patients, including me. I had no calls Friday night and felt like I had won the lottery. I went into the hospital in the morning and expected to be done before noon and have the time to catch up on things around the house and do things with my

75

children. It was a great day. I got a call around 10:30 AM from Karen. Her mother, who was seventy-seven, had come to visit from Ohio and had a bad cough and a low-grade fever. She was refusing to go to the emergency room and wondered if I would come to her house to see her. I thought about it and realized I had the time and that I would be able to finally do something on my endless 'to-do' list – see the workshop.

Then she told me where they lived and I did not know it was thirty-five minutes away, out in the country. I had committed, so off I went. There were no GPS tools back then, so my map and notes would have to guide me. I am shocked that we got where we needed to go but we always did. I doubt anyone under twenty-five can read a map now. I walked up the walkway to this really nice two-story house set beautifully in perfect landscaping. I rang the bell and the husband opened the door to greet me. It was immediately obvious to me that he was blind! From that first moment, all I could do was think about a woodworking blind person. I quickly looked at his hands and all digits were intact. He told me he was Jim and led me to his wife and mother-in-law in the family room. He then left the room and I had to work hard to focus on the needs of Mary, Karen's mom.

Doctors have this immediate thing we do: we assess whether the person is sick or not sick. It takes a few seconds. After that, we assess 'real sick' or not. She was between not-sick and not-real-sick. That meant that she was not going to be sent to the hospital and I could treat her at home. She was well dressed and had what we call the 'lipstick sign' that is a very good indicator of not-real-sick in this age group. I went on to do a good history and physical while fighting off the constant thinking about Jim's workshop. I concluded my visit with Mary after which Karen asked me if I wanted to see Jim's workshop while I was there. I did not let on that this was part of why I agreed to the house call and it became top on my list when I learned Jim was blind. She called him and he came and led me downstairs to the basement. He never turned on the lights. After two steps, I stopped and asked him to turn on the lights, to which he replied with a sincere apology followed by telling me he did that all the time.

His basement was filled with the best tools. He had a radial arm saw, a table saw, a lathe, a band saw, and walls covered with perfectly arranged tools of all types. The table was large and marked off with rulers in which all the lines were raised and all the numbers in braille. I asked him to show me how he would cut a board and it was amazing. We sat and talked for an hour. I asked him what projects he spent time on and he lifted his arms and said to look around me. In astonishment, I asked him if he built the house! He said he did not do the core construction but did every room and all the wood-working. The house was magnificent. At one point, Karen joined us and he joked that she would not let him do the wiring himself because he could not get that red to red and white to white thing done correctly.

He then became my patient and each visit was uplifting. He was a large man with a much larger persona. On one visit, he told me that he and Karen had recently traveled to Alaska and he told me all about the smells and sounds with a huge grin on his face. My patients have taught me much more than all the journals I have read. I reflect on my carpentry and cannot imagine doing it without sight. Jim was never disabled. He was challenged and rose to meet that challenge every day.

On Call

The experience of being on call is certainly not unique to the medical profession. Every parent is essentially on call whenever their children go out. The 'what ifs' control our thoughts and fears in so many situations. I am a worrier by nature. It is not a switch easily turned off. That made being a doctor a daily challenge.

It began as an intern in 1977. I was lucky enough to get a spot at the nation's first hospital in Philadelphia. You must go and see it. It is steeped in history and the founders wrote in the charter that its doors would never close to the sick and needy. When other ERs would close to ambulances, they would come to Pennsylvania Hospital. It was not unusual to get six admissions every night. We seldom slept when on call. I loved every minute of it and it shaped the doctor I would be for decades. At that time, there were no attending physicians in the hospital after hours. The residents along with their students ran everything – even the ER. In retrospect, it was not ideal medicine but it was a great way to learn.

We would do thirty-six-hour shifts every three to four days. That was being 'on call.' We had a pager that just beeped. The beep could mean a heart attack or a patient request for an aspirin. We would have to call the operator to find out. The beepers went off constantly. It was maddening. I recall being on call for Christmas one year with Marty as my senior resident. We were short-staffed and therefore the beepers never stopped. Finally, Marty lost it. (It was just a matter of when, not whether he would.) He took the beeper and threw it in the toilet. I still can hear the sound as it went under water and finally died. The magic of Christmas!

I then moved to establish a practice. I bought a pager and had to get an answering service. Because I was new and anxious to build my practice, I decided to be on call for myself every day and night of the week and most weekends for the first two years. There was another new internist doing the same thing and we decided to work together and share space and occasional call. For many months, the beeper was relatively silent. Starting a practice where one is an unknown is not a wise financial decision. Regardless, I was at risk all the time. There was no way of knowing when you closed your eyes to sleep whether you would get a call. You could not venture far and always needed to be near a phone booth and have dimes in your pocket. (Remember phone booths? Remember when it cost a dime?) I was always tethered emotionally. That takes a toll on a person – and their family.

My children grew and I decided to coach my youngest in baseball and basketball. I like sports. I love kids. It was at the time when they came out with the large phone in a bag that would work without a wire. It was like watching science-fiction come true. I bought one. It was a nightmare. The phrase 'can you hear me now' became a way of life. Reception was terrible. But it allowed me to be on the field and coach my son, so it was wonderful. I was, however, still on call and there was never a game or practice when I could coach without my assistant present in case my pager would go off and I would have to run to the hospital. At the time, I did not know that it was making my life so difficult.

The next great evolution was when the beeper evolved into a pager that went off and gave you a number to call. There was no message, just a number. One did not know what the call was about or whose number it was. You called and hoped. I must admit that after regular hours, people seldom called unless they were really sick years ago. There were no walk-in clinics. The ER at the time was actually used for emergencies unlike today. People waited to call until office hours usually. I think what changed being on call was when the pharmacies began to compete with one another and stayed open longer and more often. They ruined it. Now if someone called, they might be able to get a medication that night. In fact, some waited to call until the evening and weekend because it was more convenient for them. Being on call became unbearable. Someone would call at 2:00 AM to tell me they could not sleep and I had all I could do not to tell them that now I could not either.

The pagers became more sophisticated and began to give brief messages. This was great because one could hold the non-emergent ones and do them all together after tending to the patients in the hospital. During my time in practice, there were no hospitalists. I took calls day and night for my patients wherever they were. No one could do this nightly, so we developed small groups of physicians who shared nights and weekends. This was great when it was not your night off but resulted in three to four times the number of calls when you were on call. I would go into the hospital at all hours for admissions or crises. I took care of my patients in the office, in the hospital, in the ICU, in the nursing home, and sometimes even at home. This is not done anymore. I really knew my patients and I think I did a good job. It was difficult and a strain on me physically and emotionally. It is not done anymore and I can see why. Being on call can suck the life out of you. Cellphones evolved rapidly and pagers became extinct. This new technology is great but made it so that a physician is basically now always at work.

I left my practice after thirty years. I was offered a position of dean and the opportunity to start a new medical school in a city two hours away. I took the job and recall my very first night of not being on call. I laid my head on the pillow, ready for the best night of sleep in my life. The home phone went off! I had not given anyone this number. It was the Pennsylvania State Police! I was in New Jersey. Every parent knows the terror such a call inflicts. He went on to ask in this stern voice whether I owned a silver Subaru wagon. I told him I did and my son drove it and asked if he was alright. He told me it was caught on camera outside a nuclear power plant earlier that day and wanted to know why. My son is an amazing photographer and I happened to know he was there that day and told him he was just there to take pictures for art. He told me to have him destroy the pictures and stay away from the plant. After a pause, I asked him how he got my number, since it was new and not listed. He replied, "That is what we do, sir." Discussion over! My dream of not being on call had burst.

Suicide

I had only met Nancy once. Her husband and his family were my patients for a few years. Charlie was a very nice man who had cholesterol issues and a strong family history of heart disease. Nancy came because she had a cold that was getting worse. They had three children, all under six. We talked and she opened up about feeling very down over the past year. It began sometime after the last child was born. She thought it was normal, as all her children were so young and she was always tired and busy. Charlie was a great husband and father and he did all he could. She was clearly depressed. I did as I was taught and asked if she had any thoughts of harming herself and she denied those thoughts. I felt she needed to see a psychiatrist and she was willing to do so. We made the appointment before she left the office.

Two years passed and it was 8:00 AM on a Tuesday. I got a call that Nancy was in the ER, unresponsive. She was found that way when her husband woke and he called the ambulance. She was not breathing well and she was intubated. She had a pulse and a good blood pressure. An empty bottle of pills filled two days before was at her bedside. There was no note. I immediately went to the ER. The neurological testing showed no sign of brain functioning. Nancy was never going home to her family. The scene was devastating. Children were crying in the arms of grandparents. Charlie was in a daze, wondering how he could have prevented this. Nancy's parents were just staring and holding each other's hands. Physicians are not trained for this. There is no right thing to say, or proper way to act. What matters, I have found, is to be there and say little. It matters most to care.

Nancy had gone to the specialist two years ago and had been seeing him regularly. She got worse slowly despite also seeing a counselor and taking medications which were changed and adjusted without success. She never talked about suicide. She did not get out much but was always good with the children and told Charlie how much she appreciated him. Suicide was not on anyone's radar. I have come to know that the act is often impulsive, but never without prior deliberation in some form. I have also come to know that we cannot relieve all suffering. At the time of Nancy's death, we did not have the myriad of medications we now employ for depression. I have been very fortunate, as I do not know what it might be like to wake every day without hope, to have no experience of joy, and to see the future as bleak. We cannot treat all pain but we can give those patients hope. Hope is our anchor in life.

Suicide is an act that is carried out by those who are mentally ill – or so I was taught. A sane person would not take their own life. Religions label the act as a sin and teach that by doing so, one would never enter heaven. The law makes suicide illegal. A life insurance company won't pay death benefits if the policyholder commits suicide within a specific period of time after their policy takes effect. In most states, that period is two years. These are all deterrents and serve the purpose of having a person considering suicide try all avenues when possible. They hinge, however, on the belief that there is always a sound alternative to suicide. What if there is not?

Physician Assisted Suicide (PAS) challenges the above assumption. Some states have made it legal for someone who is in the dying process, passed an evaluation for competency, is suffering beyond the effects of medications provided by experts, and has repeated requested PAS to self-administer a dose of medication known to cause a peaceful and certain death. The law was recently passed in New Jersey where I work. This means that suicide can be an alternative chosen by an individual who is competent and sane. Those who have passed this legislation also have allowed for the person to receive such benefits as their life insurance. Many oppose PAS. Many opposed the removal of life support in those properly diagnosed with brain death. Medical ethics is constantly evolving and the lines being redrawn. This is a good thing when done with open dialog and encouraging the input of many.

Nancy was declared dead a few days later when the medication she took was out of her system and her status unchanged. I called the organ donor network on the first day. These amazing people know exactly what to say and when to say it. I was there for support. Charlie agreed to the donation, as did Nancy's parents. The process went smoothly and the way the family was treated was amazing. Nancy's death resulted in a sorrow I hopefully will never know. It also resulted in restored vision for two people, the end of dialysis for two people, restoration of life and hope for a young woman who got Nancy's heart, and a new set of lungs to someone bedbound and oxygen-dependent. I hope that in whatever comes after death, Nancy knows and sees all this.

Charlie was my patient for over twenty-five years. His children grew and also became my patients. Their lives were never the same, but they were good lives. They knew they were loved and, with counseling, they knew her death was not their fault. The children married and had children. Charlie eventually found someone, many years later, and loved again. Nancy's suffering ended and life went on – as it does. We do not know why she developed depression and why it was resistant to treatment. We can say the same about cancer, diabetes, and even the common cold. Yet, we speak differently about those who commit suicide. We should treat those who die by taking their own life as we do the other diseases – as something we do not yet understand but know as real. Nancy had a disease we could not treat at the time. New medications, new insights, and new understanding of brain chemistry and function will hopefully allow those like Nancy to have hope in the future.

Midnight Mass

It had become a holiday tradition. Our church was close to our home and it was a more modern structure in a round design. It had trees and bushes inside year-round behind the altar area. At Christmas, the choir would begin about thirty minutes before mass and the church was very dark. The many candles flickered and created a calming mood. It was solemn and beautiful. The organ and the voices made for a perfect way to celebrate the day. Everyone was dressed up and many of us knew each other well. We joined in the singing.

I looked down the aisle I was in and noticed an elderly lady who just did not 'look good' to me. This is a skill physicians develop that defies objectivity. We come to 'feel' that someone is sick before any words are exchanged or tests done. We soon learn to trust this feeling. Sure enough, a few minutes later, she collapsed where she was standing. The darkness did not alert many and the singing went on.

Then the training kicks in. It is not a matter of thinking and reasoning but reacting and letting experience and skills carry you. I went down the pew, drugged her to the center aisle which was close, laid her on her back, and did a rapid assessment. She was not responsive. She was not breathing and she had no pulse – full arrest. I did not have time to ask for a history and upon initiation of CPR, I stared at the family who did not tell me to stop. I yelled, "Lights!" and the church suddenly became bright. I yelled, "Help!" and all the physicians came forward. The adrenaline was rushing through my body. The horrific scene and the reality became overshadowed by the 'dance.' Becoming removed from the emotions of the moment and the impact on others is what makes us function at these times.

Next, an altar boy pushed through and handed me a plastic case with a handle on it. I quickly opened it and was shocked when I saw needles, an IV fluid bottle, and medications in the case! Later, I would learn that the priest had a condition and his physician gave him this to have on hand. An ambulance was called immediately. The orthopedic surgeon began chest compressions. That left me to do the mouth-to-mouth. The surgeon was no fool... I instinctively removed my tie and used it to start the IV. I got it in first try – thank you, God. Meds were pushed. The time had come to assess the situation. I was told that the ambulance had arrived but it was not the main unit and had only a stretcher. The fully equipped ambulance was in use elsewhere. This Christmas was not starting out well in our area.

It was clear that this poor lady was not responding and enough time had gone by that the attempts should be stopped. I did not want to totally destroy the solemn event for so many by stopping, so I continued the motions until out of the church and in the ambulance. I then pronounced this patient dead. That was when I was told that they could not transport a dead body in the ambulance. After some attempts to reason, I got them to drive to an area where those leaving church would not see them – to offer hope to all. I then went to the office building of the church and tried to console the grieving family. Their mother was in her eighties and well. They were shocked. Amidst the discussion, a man ran into the room, saying, "It is happening again!"

I ran out thinking I had missed the diagnosis and that I had called a lady dead only for her to wake up. The mind does bizarre things at times. I was quickly told that another lady had collapsed during the mass ceremony and they needed me. What were the odds?

This lady had gotten chest pain as a result of the events and took a few nitroglycerin pills. She was unconscious but did have a thready, rapid pulse and shallow breaths. In came the ambulance crew from the main unit that had finally arrived for the first lady. We quickly treated her and got her on the way to the hospital. She survived.

It was not the relaxing religious experience we planned when we left the house that night. They went on with the mass as scheduled and offered special prayers for the two ladies that night. One family had lost a loved one and would grieve that loss. They would, no doubt, find solace in the fact that she died while at mass on Christmas with her family around her. That is certainly a way to leave this life that most would envy.

I have seen many die over my decades as a physician. Most do not die ideally. Many must face a known end of their life and do so while suffering and even alone. Few have the option of arranging their death so that they would not suffer and time it such that those they loved could be there and control their destiny so as not to put loved ones in the position of making difficult decisions. Those who have access to physician-assisted suicide can end their difficult path to a death that is certain and weeks away. Few do.

Chapter 5

Early Experiences

Medical school and residency lay only a small foundation to build upon for the rest of your career. I found that they actually do little to prepare you for the day-to-day complexities of patient care. The key is to admit what you do not know, fix that gap, and vow to be a lifelong learner. Each patient encounter taught me; I owe most of what I now know to incredible patients who had faith in me, worked with me, taught me, and stuck with me through the years.

Old Photos

Susan was the next patient on my schedule for the day. She was sixty-eight and I had never seen her before. Checking the schedule for the day is a ritual entered in with a mixture of hope, excitement, and rarely disappointment. The hope is that of knowing a patient and wishing they were feeling better since last seen and also the hope that they will show for their appointment. Years ago, there were no text and email reminders. Patients could not sign into a site and see their appointments and results. They somehow wrote the appointment down somewhere – often on a large monthly one-year calendar hanging on a wall – and showed up on time even when the appointment was for six months later. I was fortunate to have an extremely low rate of 'no shows.'

The rare times when I was disappointed were always my fault. It usually was for a difficult patient or one that never seemed pleased with what I did but always returned. Physicians must realize they cannot help everyone, but that is a tough pill to swallow. The excitement arose whenever I would see a new patient on the schedule. I loved to see new patients. They brought a challenge, an opportunity, and usually a new long-term relationship. Today, this would be Susan. I saw that she was referred by a nurse, her niece, who worked at the hospital I sent my patients to. I would see all of my patients when they went to the hospital and managed their care. She must have seen something she liked in that care and I felt grateful for the compliment of referring her relative to me.

Susan was striking in appearance, and physicians commonly make diagnoses in the first seconds of an encounter. I had seen someone who looked like her before but not in person – in a picture somewhere at some point in my training. It would come to me as it always did, but for now, I moved forward with the ritual of the interview process. Susan came because of pain in her knees that was getting worse over a few years. Her doctor had recently retired and she was treated for hypertension and various aches and pains over the years. She saw this physician regularly and was on medications for arthritis and hypertension. My routine is to knock before I enter an exam room as a sign of respect and shake every patient's hand after washing mine. Her hand was thick and her grip strong. I got all the details of the history and twenty minutes had passed and I still could not place the face.

I moved on to the physical exam and started with her vital signs. She was sixty-eight inches tall and weighed one hundred and seventy-four pounds. Her blood pressure was slightly elevated. Her joints had classic changes of degenerative arthritis. It was present in all her joints and it was significant. None were red or warm. Then it struck me – the picture. I stopped in my tracks. She had acromegaly! I was sure of it. We are trained to not show emotions when we should not. I did not let her know what was going through my mind. This is a very rare disease caused by a benign tumor of the pituitary gland at the base of the brain. This small organ is like mission control for our endocrine system. It regulates many glands in the body and it produces growth hormone and thereby controls how our bones and ligaments grow among many other effects. If this begins in childhood, it can lead to people becoming 'giants' as one sees in the Guinness Book of World Records. When it occurs in adults, it results in growth that affects joints and cartilage and produces thick hands, arthritis, changes in the jaw, and a facial appearance very much like Susan.

The brain is amazing. The lecture given by the chief of endocrinology at the VA Hospital in Philadelphia that I had heard thirteen years earlier came back to me – that is where those pictures were from. I recall him teaching us that the changes are so slow and gradual that they are often not noticed by family, friends, and even a doctor who sees the patients often. He said the best diagnostic test was a photo album as that would show what the patient looked like over many years. I actually asked her to go home and bring me photo albums over the past thirty years if she had them. She thought I was nuts – a safe bet most days! She came back a few hours later with photo albums in a bag and we sat and went over them. Over the past thirty years, her appearance had markedly changed but very slowly. She did not even appreciate it at first. I ordered the labs needed and an imaging study of her pituitary gland. The diagnosis was confirmed and she was successfully treated. Her arthritic changes would not resolve but they would likely not progress.

With her permission, I presented her at Grand Rounds at my hospital. I have always felt that information not shared is information lost. She allowed me to borrow her album. The presentation went very well. In the weeks that followed, there was a steady stream of referrals of patients who had arthritis and sort of looked a bit like Susan. I guess those who attended my lecture saw a resemblance in some of their patients. After each exam, I would request to see old photos, and every time they showed, they always looked that way. I never saw another case of acromegaly.

What Finger?

A pediatrician I encountered during medical school told us that when we see a child with a bloody nose, we should ask what finger they used to pick their nose, not whether they pick their nose. This has proven useful on many occasions as a way to get to the truth of what you think is going on. I was consulted on a young lady who had been transferred to our hospital for a presumed bowel disorder. She had developed a connection called a fistula between the skin on her abdominal wall and part of the bowel. Studies done at the smaller hospital showed that the connection was with a part of her small bowel but they could not determine why.

RT was a twenty-five-year-old female who lived with her parents. They had a small farm that provided them with food and a meager income. She had a sister who was also still living at home and two brothers that had moved away and worked in the area. She had no history of illnesses. She did not graduate from high school due to academic challenges. RT was significantly overweight and plain. Her hair appeared to be cut by herself and she wore no makeup. She was pleasant but did not make eye-contact when speaking to me. Her parents were in the room each time I visited and were very concerned.

The records came with her and I reviewed them thoroughly. She did have a colonoscopy and this was normal. She had a barium study of her upper bowel that was read as normal but the fistula was seen. Her laboratory tests were normal. She had no history of weight loss or of a change in bowel function. None of this made sense. I asked the nurses to call me when the parents were not in the room. I did not want to ask them to leave, as that might put the patient in a difficult position.

To this day, I do not know why I did it, but I walked into her room, sat down, and calmly asked her to show me what she was using to create the hole in her belly. To my astonishment, she rolled to her side, opened the drawer of her bedside table, and pulled out a hatpin! I hid my shock and asked her if she did anything to sterilize it. I had decided to just have a calm, non-judgmental conversation and perhaps she was relieved to finally be able to tell someone. I called psychiatry after I learned that throughout her life, she was ignored. She did not have the looks, the intellect, or the courage to create a life for herself. She was jealous of her siblings and this illness had resulted in her parents spending more time with her. They cared about her and made it clear that they loved her. She needed that and did not know how else to get it.

It was clear that the parents would not understand – I barely did. The next few days allowed all of us to construct a safe way to allow for a way to not break this new bond she had formed if at all possible. She would have to tell the family but we could teach her how and when. It all went as well as possible. This is a unique story of what happens every day in this world. People do not feel loved and act out in many ways. I wonder how RT is doing now.

Ask Your Doctor

Fred was on my schedule for 10:30 that day – I would have to wait another two hours to see him. Fred was full of life and always made me laugh. He was one of those people who just saw life through a different lens, much like Seinfeld. He was forty-eight, healthy, and came to see me for minor issues usually. He never called in between. I walked in the door prepared for another experience and was not disappointed. Fred's wife had convinced him he was too sedentary and bought him a treadmill for his birthday. He went on in detail telling why that was the worst gift to give someone his age for a gift. I laughed constantly during the visit. He just had that way of telling a story. He then told me how his phone went off and, while reaching for it, lost his balance and fell off the treadmill. He also told me he thought this was all contrived by his wife as a way to kill him and get the life insurance. He hurt his knee and it swelled and bruised. He could walk on it and did not feel anything could have broken, so he did not call me or go to the ER. So un-American!

It felt better but his wife made him come and see me. I would venture to guess that the majority of times a man at his age goes to a doctor, it is because of the significant other. It also amazes me that when I ask them about their meds, they tell me to ask their wife! He spent the last three days sitting on his recliner with ice on the knee and only needed some Tylenol now and then. He just watched TV and relaxed and considered that time of three days well spent. He then pulled a piece of paper out of pocket and showed it to me. It had thirty-two medication names on it. I looked at him and he said that the TV had told him to ask his doctor about each of these medications over the past three days. We both shared a hearty laugh.

Direct to consumer advertising is no joke however. Pharmaceutical companies pour millions of dollars into these television ads and have done extensive research proving that they are worth the investment. Early in my career, it was commonplace for representatives of these large companies to bring lunches to the office, pay for trips, drop off samples in bulk, and pay large sums for speakers at educational venues for physicians. I seldom met with them or allowed them to bring food to the office, as I felt that when the time came that they knew more about the best way to treat one of my patients than me, it was time to retire. I am still working. Many roadblocks have rightly been put up in the medical profession to this type of sales tactic. The shift then came to go directly to the patient. God forbid, they would use the money to defray the cost of the drug!

I have recently read that there are only two countries that permit such blatant methods of promoting medications: the United States and New Zealand. I also read that these two countries lead the world in the number of medications per patient – no surprise. The companies back up their methods by citing freedom of speech and the good they do by bringing knowledge of these treatments to patients. Isn't that why people have a physician? We know best whether a given treatment is safe and best for our patient. Also, they never advertise generic medications – only those that are expensive and often not even covered by the patient's insurance. I have seen the important time I have to positively impact the life of a patient during an office visit gobbled up by medication questions that are not even relevant.

A colleague told me a few weeks ago that he saw a new patient who came in with a list of fifty-two medications she was on! I told him we should investigate how she was still alive. All medications have side effects. All must be taken a certain way (and few ever do so). All have interactions with other medications. Drugs are dangerous and often not needed. Have we come to the point of expediency where it is quicker to write a script than educate? Do our patients expect a script and criticize us if we do not write one? Our profession should sponsor commercials that educate people about the harms of medications, the safety and importance of immunizations, and the importance of diet and exercise. We do not, and perhaps it is because such ads are expensive and the organized profession of medicine has decided to spend money on other fronts. I hope not.

The television ads have allowed me to develop a new approach to watching television – an activity I must admit I have become quite expert at. I now only record shows I want to watch and can fast-forward so adeptly that I stop right at the start of the next segment! Perhaps they have developed a way to implant subconscious suggestions in the rapidly moving video but I will assume that next step is not yet here.

So, please ask your doctor about what is bothering you and about how to stay well. We cannot help you if we do not get your input. When there is a new test or treatment for a condition you have that is better than what you are now taking, we will offer it to you. Why wouldn't we? Generally, physicians are very bright, keep up with advances in our field, and are over-achievers. Our greatest achievement every day is to help our patients.

I do not want to have my grandsons ask me what a medication is that enhances erections. I do not want to try to figure out the purpose of having two old bathtubs next to each other on the beach, much less guide a confused patient who sees that. I do not want to have to tell a patient who is sore after working in the garden that there is no test for fibromyalgia and they do not need the drug they heard about. I suspect that there is no way to get this horse back in the barn, but I know for a fact that it is was easier to practice medicine before direct-to-consumer-advertising was allowed.

Confidentiality

It was an ordinary day early in my practice. It was my month of doing 'teaching service.' This meant that anyone admitted to the hospital without a physician on staff would be cared for by the students and residents under my direction. Usually, these patients were those who did not have the ability to afford care – those suffering from social burdens. Today would be different – so very different.

I got a call from the emergency room. They had a fifty-year-old male there who had pneumonia and needed admission. It sounded fairly straightforward. He was not toxic and did not need the intensive care unit. I called my resident and told him to begin the process until I could free myself up from my office patients and run over. My office was across the street. The resident asked if the medical student could get started with the medical interview and I agreed that this would be a good opportunity.

When I arrived, everything was in motion. The student excitedly told me that this patient was the father of his medical-school roommate and he knew him. This concerned me and I asked if he had called his friend about the admission and he assured me that he had not. I made it clear that he should not share anything about this patient with his son unless the patient gave him permission. I expected all would work out and the patient would enjoy having someone he knew care for him.

It was now my time to do the evaluation. I did so alone for some reason – I usually have the student and resident with me. The patient was a salesman and lived just outside of Philadelphia. He had a vacation home in the Poconos and that was where he was when his cold got worse and the cough was keeping him up. He came to the closest hospital for evaluation and that happened to be where I worked. He did very well financially. He had been married for twenty-six years, had two children, loved to ski, and drank socially. He did not smoke. He told me that he had no other sexual partners and did not use drugs.

He looked sick. He looked sicker than his chest X-ray would have indicated. His oxygen level was a bit low. He had a mild anemia and his white blood cell count was normal when I would have expected it to be high. I asked

94

the team to call for a pulmonary consult to be safe. He was begun on intravenous antibiotics and oxygen. His wife was with him. Tests were pending.

I made my morning rounds with the team and the patient was unchanged. He had a low-grade fever and was still coughing. To make a long story short, an analysis of the sputum that was collected showed that he had pneumocystis. He had AIDS! This was at a time when this was a death sentence – there was no treatment. The infectivity was not yet defined. I sat down and gave him this terrible news.

Further history was now different. He admitted to having unprotected sex with both male and female partners over the past few years. He told me that he and his wife had not been intimate for five years. He denied intravenous drugs. He did not know of a partner who was infected or ill. He was shocked. The art of getting a medical history is a mixture of what is asked, how it is asked, what is answered, and how it is answered. A physician develops a sense of how truthful the information is without being able to objectify how. I did not believe him.

I told him he must tell his wife and any partners of the diagnosis. There was no mandatory reporting of this disease at this time in terms of public-health policy. He again told me that he and his wife had not had sex in some time. He quickly added that if I told her or if his son heard about this, he would sue me and the hospital.

What is the right thing to do? It is an action that is much easier to talk about than to enact. The answer varies with perspective at times. If his wife were not told, she could have the disease and be denied proper testing and hopefully, one day, treatment. I had no way of knowing if she was sexually active outside of the marriage and therefore spreading the disease. Telling her would be the right thing to do. Confidentiality dictated that I not tell her. This was before HIPAA laws spelled this out. I called those I knew, including the hospital attorney. Opinions varied widely.

If I played a role in keeping this from his wife, I knew I would have a hard time with it forever. We override confidentiality when the life of someone else is at stake. Reporting a patient with a new seizure to the motor vehicle agency to remove the driver's license is such an instance. To me, this was no different. Doctors fear being sued. I had to decide.

I walked into the room and told him he had two hours to tell his wife of the diagnosis or I would. He became very angry and made it clear he would sue me and win. I told him that I honestly could not see how a judge or jury would side with someone who deliberately put someone in harm's way and that I expected he did not want his lifestyle coming out publicly. I walked out of the room.

Later that day, I got a call from the wife. He told her. He demanded that I be removed from the case including the student and resident. Arrangements were made. He improved and was discharged a few days later. I never heard from him again. I was never sued. I never knew if the wife was infected. To my knowledge, the student never told the patient's son to his great credit. The calculated risk of being sued paled in my mind to the risk of his wife becoming ill. I still feel it was the right thing to do.

I'm Not Nuts

My secretary walked into my office to tell me that a young lady had just walked in asking to be seen without an appointment. It was early on in my career and I was in no position to turn down business. I had moved from an academic center in a large city to 'hand a shingle' in a small city. That is another story to tell. It was common at the time to get an office, put a notice in the local paper, and wait for patients to call. There was a lot of waiting and little income for quite some time. We did not join large systems or make large incomes. We worked and worked hard and took pride in building our own medical practice. I loved it.

Sally was alone and sat in the examining room with a large tan envelope in her hands. She was twenty-six and looked tired. I began the interview with the usual question, "What is the reason you came to see me today?" That was all I had to do. The tale began and did not pause for the next twenty minutes. She could talk!

Her first child, a healthy baby girl, was born ten days earlier. It was routine and she went home with her husband, thrilled that this miracle had happened. They had been married for three years and the pregnancy was planned. After a few days, she began to feel differently and became concerned. She had trouble sleeping, but not because of the baby. She felt overly alert and worried about everything. She felt her heart racing. She began to have odd thoughts and did not feel comfortable when alone with the baby. She knew something was wrong, so she was brought to a local emergency room. She was admitted to the psychiatric ward there with a presumed post-partum psychosis. She went readily.

She then told me about the twenty-four hours in the psych ward and did so by saying, "I thought I was nuts, but then I found out what nuts really was, and knew that was not me." She signed out against medical advice. Her husband picked her up and took her home. She had worked at a local diagnostics lab as a technician until two weeks earlier. She went to work the night before her visit with me, drew her own blood, and ran every test she could think of. The results were in the envelope that was then handed to me. The reports showed that she clearly had severe hyperthyroidism! This is rare and is known as postpartum thyroiditis – a phenomenon observed following pregnancy and may involve hyperthyroidism, hypothyroidism, or the two sequentially. It affects about five percent of all women within a year after giving birth.

I congratulated her on diagnosing herself and wondered why she had shown up at my door. In smaller places, word travels fast. I had given a lecture on thyroid disease to the medical residents recently and she heard about that from one who was a neighbor. At the time, there were no specialists in that field, endocrinology, in town, so I became the go-to person after one talk to a small group. I also learned over my time there that local residents did not like going to a big city and preferred having their care in their backyard.

The treatment plan worked and she was soon back to normal. Over the years ahead, I saw her regularly, and slowly her thyroid became underactive, as is often the case, and she needed replacement therapy and we managed all this quite easily.

I marvel at the changes in healthcare every day. What Sally did was quite unusual. Patients seldom participated in their diagnostic decisions, much less do it themselves. There was no internet at the time – that place where anyone can soon develop severe anxiety by looking up the most mundane thing. People seldom questioned the tests ordered or the medications offered. It was a time of paternalism where the doctor made the decisions and the patient followed the directions. It was not a good time in retrospect.

Now, patients have access to their tests and their records almost instantly. They get to correct what is in the chart after they read it. I would have thought this would lead to chaos with people calling all the time, wondering why their result was high when it was actually 5.1 instead of 5.0 with the 'norm' being 5.0. We know this is meaningless and I would have thought this would lead to many calls demanding an answer. It has not. People have become smart consumers of healthcare and take their role very seriously. They want answers and honesty. They should. It is their health and their future. Autonomy now rules our healthcare system and even though this can lead to some decisions that are less than ideal, it is and should be the right of each patient to make that decision.

Patients have repeatedly shown me that they can understand even the most complex issues when given the time and information needed. People are smart. They know what they want and it is a much better system when physicians share the journey with their patient as a partnership. Sally was a trailblazer.

Hernia

Relentless pain overtook my body. I tried my hardest to remain calm and to focus on something else, but the truth is: *it hurt like hell!* I began to lose all sense of rationality and professional demeanor. I don't remember much about the surgery itself. The thing that sticks in my mind is being wheeled back to my room. It seemed like I passed at least one thousand people I knew, all of whom were gaping at me, undoubtedly contriving their own versions of what had taken place. I asked the transporter if he had a plastic nose and glasses I could wear to avoid being recognized. Unfortunately, he didn't.

In those few minutes, I felt as if my privacy had been invaded – the idea of 'confidentiality' was a farce. It made me wonder whether or not I would be the topic of conversation at the water cooler. How I longed for anonymity! The next few hours, at least in my opinion, were a study in agony. Of course, I wouldn't admit that to my wife, or to anyone else for that matter. After all, what was I – a man or mouse? While preparing to go home, the answer to that question became apparent. As much as I wanted to be one big *Y* chromosome, the act of bending over to put on my socks sent such a wave of pain through my body that I was sure I was beginning to grow a little pink tail and crave cheese. And if that wasn't enough, the ride home raised the meaning of pain to new heights. Had I been equipped with an 'ouchometer,' PennDOT, the city could have used me to monitor the depth and width of each pothole between Scranton and Clark's Summit.

Finally, at home, fearing that the dog would pounce on my lap, I questioned whether or not I should have taken the medication my surgeon prescribed for pain. Being a physician, I knew that what he had prescribed was a narcotic, and I wasn't sure whether or not I wanted to be under the influence of such a drug. I began to weigh the pros and cons when a minor stumble sent a bolt of pain through my body, instantaneously ending the debate. I guess I was a mouse, but I decided it was better to be a mouse than a martyr. After a few days of recuperation, boredom began to set in, and I longed to return to work. It seemed to me that I had burdened my colleagues long enough, and that I could deal with the level of pain I was experiencing. After trying to conduct some work at home, I realized that rushing the recuperation process was not in my best interest, or in the best interest of my patients. Like it or not, I had to force myself to rest and regain my strength. Finally, I was getting a dose of my own medicine.

About the same time, I began to wonder about a few other things. When could I take off the dressings? Should I be so black and purple? Would I ever find a comfortable position in which to sit? How long was this pain going last? Being a physician, I was embarrassed that I didn't know the answers to these questions. My need to know overshadowed my pride and I called my doctor to clear things up. Soon afterward, I returned to normal. As I reflect back, it was really was no big deal, but at the time, it was the only thing that mattered.

What did I learn from this minor ordeal? First, it was by asking a young healthy person in the pre-op area if they have a living will is less than optimal for instilling a positive attitude. I created the process for the hospital I was at and never thought about the fact that this conversation might be better off done during the pre-op testing days before. Second, when transporting patients within a hospital, do not use the same elevators that are used by others! I worked the morning before my surgery (God forbid, I would take a day off.) and two of the patients I saw in the office that morning walked on the elevator being used to take me to the surgical suite. I suspect their confidence in my ongoing plan of care for them was shaken. Third, minor surgery is surgery done to someone else. Fourth, when a physician becomes a patient, treat them like a patient and do not assume they know what to expect or what to do. Fifth, warn patients who have their groin shaved that for weeks they will be scratching in public. Sixth, nurses run the world, and the world is better off for it. Seventh, pride is not a part of having surgery.

I love to teach. I wrote about my experience in the local newspaper after the surgery, as I felt people might enjoy hearing about it. Within hours, I realized I had become part of the 'hernia club,' with people contacting me to share stories. I wish I knew what I now know – but that wish spans a great deal more subject matter than a simple hernia.

The Attending

I was out of my residency program for only a few weeks and had moved about two hours away to begin a medical practice. I wanted to go out on my own, build a private practice, not have to battle traffic or a long commute, have a safe community with good schools for my children, and be able to teach. I wanted a place where my wife would be happy, as I had already learned that her happiness was essential to mine. I was offered the opportunity to teach in a new primary-care internal medicine program and have some administrative tasks that would supplement my uncertain income. The future was coming together.

They asked me to be the teaching attending for July. I first thought that this was a very kind gesture in terms of giving me work as soon as I arrived. I later found out that no one wanted to do the summer months. It was my first day in the role and I met with the resident team. Everyone should realize that they should never get sick in July and go to a teaching hospital. On one magical day, people who were medical students were now real doctors and able to sign their own orders. Second-year residents now rejoice in no longer being the low person on the totem pole and having less night call. Second-year residents became senior residents as if the stroke of midnight had mysteriously given them all the knowledge they needed to direct other doctors and solve all problems. Lastly, people like myself, who were a resident days before, were all of a sudden an attending – the term given to the physician who oversees the care delivered by the residents and students under them.

This transition is extremely difficult if one stays at the hospital where they did their residency training. Having moved away, perhaps they would see me as a skilled clinician trained at one of the top medical schools and residencies and I would be embraced. That is actually what happened and I could not be more grateful to that group of residents who made this transition a great one for me. After introductions, including two medical students doing away rotations from their school, we began 'rounds.' This is a time-honored tradition during which patients are discussed with the attending who then offers tips on how to best present a case as well as engages everyone in a discussion of possible diagnoses and treatments. The attending then goes to the bedside with the team and talks to the patient to certify some of the facts presented as well as to demonstrate key physical exam techniques. It is a wonderful way to learn and the ideal way to teach. I have found that patients love being the focus of such attention and it tells them they are getting a thorough evaluation.

Jack was a thirty-two-year-old male admitted for an infected leg ulcer. He had diabetes since the age of seven and the type of diabetes he had was devastating. He was already blind, had evidence of nerve damage in his feet, and his kidneys were impaired. This was at a time when there were no devices to monitor blood sugars at home. There were no insulin pumps and none of our new treatments. We do not understand diabetes and I feel we are calling many distinct diseases diabetes only because they share a defect of glucose metabolism. We do not know why some people can be dependent on insulin for fifty years and never get any complications and some are not dependent on insulin and develop severe issues in ten years. We have come a long way in our treatment and understanding of this disease but we have a very long way to go.

Jack was a science teacher at a local community college until his vision failed. He was married to a fantastic lady and had two sons under the age of six. He was now unable to work and was on disability. His attitude and love of learning allowed him to function very independently and he was very bright. He was alone when our team entered the room. The diagnosis was an infected leg ulcer due to diabetes and the deterioration of his microcirculation resulting in poor oxygen delivery to the tissues. It all made sense. He was admitted for intravenous antibiotics and wound care. Because he was blind, he was unable to describe if the wound had changed, so I got his wife on the phone while we were there with his permission. She helped with the description of how it began and how it had changed. These details are critical. I love getting a history of a disease. A few things struck me. Skin breakdown from diabetic ulcers is usually more distal – the toes or even the ankle. This was in the mid-lower anterior shin area. The appearance was also different in terms of the edges and the base. I had seen this before. I am constantly amazed how our brain works and can do a search of our hard drive so quickly. The picture came up in my head faster than Google images – this was pyoderma gangrenosum!

Now it was time to pull upon the behaviors of my favorite attendings over the years of my education and play my little crowd! I began asking questions and pulling information from each in a positive and polite fashion. There is never any reason to embarrass anyone in this process. People always know much more than they think they know. Students have this absurd fear of being wrong. Thinking or saying something wrong is the path to knowing what is right. Doing something wrong unknowingly is the end product of not speaking up to learn. Once, I got them to realize this did not make sense in terms of it being a diabetic ulcer. They had to now think of other options. His pulses and capillary refill in his feet were good, so a blocked artery was out. He did not have a fever or an elevated white count, so infection made less sense. It was not worsening rapidly. I held back as long as I could and then told them what I thought it was. None had seen or heard of it.

I knew this disease and it offered me the opportunity of playing this game out a bit more. I knew that it is a rare skin manifestation of ulcerative colitis – a process that causes severe inflammation and bleeding in the colon and eventually can lead to cancer. I was told that he had surgery for a blockage in his colon as a teen and had a colostomy ever since. I was not told why. The facts do not stop until they are truly exhausted. I asked Jack if he had ever heard the word 'ulcerative colitis' and he said his parents had mentioned that. I then asked if he had his entire colon removed. Doing so would generally mean that he did not have what I thought, as removal cures the disease and prevents this. He then told me that he almost died during the surgery that was done at a major teaching hospital but he did not know anything else.

We left the room and I went right to the phone and got the medical records department at that hospital on the phone. They faxed me the surgical and pathology report. This was in 1980 and we did not have to go through twenty hoops to get these reports – and there was this new device called a fax machine in our medical records department. The team went there and waited fifteen minutes for three pages to come through the large device. We thought we were at the peak of the new age of communication! It turns out that he had a cardiac arrest during the surgery – at the age of fourteen! They had to move quickly, so they could not remove the entire colon and left a small segment in as a 'blind pouch.' His parents never told him about this. I was on the phone again and had him transferred to the university teaching center I had just left and he was sent down. He went to surgery, had the remaining segment removed without difficulty, and within weeks, his wound that was 7 x 3 inches healed completely.

My first day in my new career was a major homerun. Word got around. I love teaching at the bedside as much now as I did then. Jack was ravaged by his diabetes over the next ten years. I got to see his boys grow up and they loved to come to my office and feed my fish that I had in the waiting room. He died of heart disease in his forties. I made the diagnosis on that first day only because I had seen it before. I saw it before because I had the good fortune of training at a top hospital where many difficult cases were sent daily. We used to say that when you hear hoof beats outside, it is usually a horse, so don't look for a zebra. Where I trained, I saw many zebras. The horses were weeded out before the patient was sent there.

I think about the present state of medicine and cannot comprehend how far we have come. Now, a resident would take a picture on their phone and quickly similar images would pop up. The diagnosis would quickly be Googled. They would share it right then and there with the others on the team. It would link the diagnosis to the bowel issue. We would go to the electronic medical record and pull up the records of the surgery if that hospital had a similar system. If not, they would be sent in seconds as an attachment to our phone at the bedside. Current students take all these wonders for granted. If only our treatment of diabetes had advanced this much…

Chapter 6

Medical Ethics 1

I met Hal as a patient early on in my practice. I knew from that day we would be friends. The past thirty-eight years have proven me correct. He is a gifted teacher and a philosopher. He is thoughtful, contemplative, and needs a push now and then. He told me that he and his friend/mentor were writing a textbook on medical ethics. At the time, this was not a common subject in medical school or college. I never took such a course. I told him that it was absurd that anyone who has not been at the bedside with a patient could even think of writing about it. We fought. We did not speak for many months. The draft was ready and he asked me to read it and comment. I cannot remember many times in my life when I was so humbled. I learned medical ethics from Hal and hopefully, he learned some useful case material and applications from me. Subsequently, we went on to collaborate on later editions – and our friendship has even survived that! Over the years since, I have had incredible experiences in medical ethics and this book allows me to share them. I hope they evoke emotions and spark debate so that you might be able to fuel a friendship as special as I have with Hal.

Billy Smokes

The life of a physician is enriched daily by the opportunity to meet people and to be allowed to touch their lives in some small way. Each appointment brings a chance for growth and understanding. To make this the focus of my time with patients made burnout a non-factor in my career. Each patient teaches me something I could not read in a book or hear about. Being open to this flow of knowledge and understanding is a gift I don't take for granted.

Tim was a new patient on my schedule. His physician had recently retired and no records were sent. I had a clean slate to work with and that is what I prefer when seeing someone for the first time. Records often bring opinions and conclusions and hinder new ideas. The new patient history and physical is a well-orchestrated dance that has stood the test of time in terms of its usefulness. I knocked and entered the room to see this fifty-two-year-old male set to begin the process that I loved. I was stopped in one second when I saw that my new patient had Down syndrome.

He was with his brother and very shy. I was told that he did not like doctors and really did not like being touched. He was relatively high-functioning but could not give me a history that was meaningful. Tim lived with his mother, sister, and brother since birth. He had never been in a facility for care. He was able to feed himself and care for himself in terms of bowel, bladder, and dressing. He had tasks that were his at home, which he did methodically and joyfully. Neighbors and relatives came to visit him often. He was always happy and occasionally would get frustrated and angry, but never violent.

Tim was well. He was not born with any other congenital issues and had an occasional cold. He hated needles, so he did not have any recent flu shot or blood tests. I was told he had his childhood immunizations. His family history was free of any major diseases and he did not drink or smoke. I was able to do a review of systems that would only require nodding of his head and he answered all and, according to his brother, did so accurately. Gradually, he began to look at me and I could sense he was less afraid. I was happy he had become my patient and I would do all I could to see him regularly and get him more comfortable with medical care. At the end of his appointment, he smiled and shook my hand. It was a reward I had not expected.

His brother made an appointment to see me on the way out of the office. Apparently, I had passed some unspoken test. A few weeks later, I saw William as a new patient. He was in his late fifties and when I walked into the room, there was Tim with him. Tim loved to go for rides in the car and when he heard his brother was coming to see me, he asked to come along. I did my evaluation of 'Billy' and he was a smoker and drank. He had some mild claudication and the exam showed decreased pulses in his feet consistent with the pain in his leg when walking. Tests were ordered and smoking cessation was discussed at length. Tim listened quietly. Billy told me he would stop smoking and he did not need any help in doing so. He now had a reason.

I saw him again in six weeks and, sure enough, he came with Tim. I had done some reading on adults with Down syndrome so that I could better serve Tim. One fascinating thing I found is that lying is a complex act that is basically 'speaking against the truth.' Intrinsically, it does not make sense to do so. Tim likely did not have the capacity to knowingly answer a question falsely. Being a scientist, it was time for a test! Billy was in his usual jovial spirits and proudly told me he had stopped smoking and that his leg felt better already. I turned to Tim and asked if Billy still smoked. With a big smile, he replied, "Billy smokes."

Billy finally did stop smoking a few months later. He always brought Tim when he came to see me. His love for his brother outweighed the burden of bringing a human lie detector to the office with him. Tim got his brother to stop smoking by being honest. Over time, Tim let me examine him and he even got a flu shot – as long as I would give it to him. I looked forward to his every visit.

Scientific 'advances' are limiting the number of Tims in this world. We have labeled a group of people undesirable by many. Sadly, our 'advances' limit a group of people who love unconditionally and do not lie.

Delivering Bad News?

We started our medical practices on the same day. Over the next three decades, we would refer patients to each other and treat each other's families. It was a professional friendship that worked. One day, he asked me to see Ruth as a patient, and of course, I said yes. From that day forward, he owed me!

There are patients that are just impossible to please. These are the ones who make you not want to go to work when you see them on your schedule. A fifteen-minute visit seems like an hour. There were none like Ruth. I was blessed with an amazing practice that brought me fulfillment and friendships over the many years. Ruth was that patient all physicians have that we do not like to talk about. We have to sort through the many complaints to figure out which might be new and might be real. They are never satisfied. Yet, they always return for their next appointment. They seem to dislike you but remember your birthday. I came to know this is often referred to as a borderline personality disorder – a diagnosis without an easy treatment.

Ruth was married and had no children. Al would bring her to the appointment and take her home. He never said much and never came in the room. After a few years, he made an appointment to see me. It was for a simple issue and I convinced him to return for a full evaluation, which he did. Al was a big man who seemed small. I came to know that he was a respected businessman who took over his father-in-law's company and grew it nicely. He was active in his religion and on many local boards. He never talked about Ruth, and when I would mention anything, he had this knack of rolling his eyes just so. I came to like Al and looked forward to seeing him. I suppose I admired him because of his devotion to his wife of over forty-five years. I dreaded being with her for even fifteen minutes.

One day, Al called with a cough and some shortness of breath. I had him come right to the office. I had not seen him in about a year, as he had no active medical issues. He had lost weight and looked ill. He had rhonchi on the left on his lung exam, with some decreased breath sounds and dullness at the left base. I sent him across the street for a chest X-ray and asked him to return to my office after. I looked at the film and the diagnosis was obvious. Al had one of those lung cancers that you know in one second is not treatable in any way. Chemo and radiation may add a few weeks or months perhaps.

I walked into the room prepared to deliver this terrible news. I liked Al and felt horrible. He came alone to my office and I somehow knew he preferred that. I was honest and, while holding his upper arm, told him he had cancer and it was not curable. I prepared myself for the onslaught of emotion that I had come to know when delivering such bad news countless times. He stared me in the eyes and calmly asked how long he had to live. I told him he could choose a trial of treatment but I did not think he had more than weeks to live. The next moment changed my life. His face lit up with a big smile and he said, "Thank God." I sat dazed. I knew immediately what he was saying. He went into hospice and died comfortably soon thereafter.

I thank God that I look forward to coming home every day to my best friend.

He Wrote

Arthur was a writer. He was seventy-four and never married. He had no children that we knew of. He had hypertension and smoked when he was younger. He had a stroke five years earlier that affected his left arm such that he could not type well. He continued his life dream of writing stories, many of which were published in various media. He hired a secretary after his stroke. Mary came to the house and typed for him. She was sixty-four and her relationship with him was never clear. Over the past three years, she lived with him and according to her, it was a matter of practicality in that she could not afford to live alone and he benefited from her help. Besides, they were friends.

He was found in the morning by Mary, unresponsive, and she called the ambulance. Initial exam and imaging in the emergency room showed a large stroke affecting the left side of his brain. He was unresponsive but breathing on his own. His right arm and leg fell upon lifting. He could not speak. The time of the stroke was unknown and he was not a candidate for the medications used to dissolve the clot. He was admitted. Mary said he did not have an advance directive or a durable power of attorney that she knew of. He had told her he loved to write, and as long as he could do so, life was worth living. The waiting began.

Two days later, he remained unchanged neurologically. Five days later, there was no change. Seven days after admission, he developed a cough and increased respiratory rate. An exam and a CXR showed a new pneumonia. He had aspirated somehow. Over the next twenty-four hours, he worsened and required intubation – a tube through his mouth to help him breath. There as more waiting.

Days went by without improvement. It was becoming very clear he would not recover – never write again. Mary was there every day and all day. The nursing staff came to know her well and to like her. She clearly had a special relationship with Arthur. Were they in love? Was this more than a professional relationship? No one ever asked. It was time to establish a code status for Arthur and to begin the discussion of a surgery to allow him to continue on the ventilator by having the tube in his neck. Social services could find no relatives. Could Mary be the one making these decisions? Should we get a court-appointed guardian?

A consult was placed to the ethics committee and I met Arthur and Mary. I spoke to all involved – physicians and nurses. I spoke to pastoral care and social services, as they had come to know this case. Such is the routine in doing an ethics consultation. Everyone's input matters. The only person who knew this unfortunate man was Mary who had no legal standing in his life. If he died, would she lose her income and her home and, as a result, would she be more likely to want to continue all measures to keep him alive? Were they close and was she named in his will? If so, might she be more likely to stop everything sooner?

Over the years, I have come to know that nurses know the patient best. They are there for hours while physicians come and go all too quickly. Pastoral care had spent hours with Mary. All who knew Mary found her to be a good person with good intentions. They all liked her. By now, and agreed to by all consultants, it was clear that Arthur would never recover. His would be a short life of complication after complication. If he was aware, it would be a life of suffering. Physicians and especially ethics consultants often use substituted judgment when the patient cannot communicate. It is a flawed process that exposes one's internal prejudice – but often the best recourse. Should we ask Mary or spare her the decisions that needed to be made? Could she decide considering the personal consequences of her decision?

I decided to ask her, as it was clear that everyone felt she was a good person who cared for Arthur. She could always say she did not want to decide. If she agreed with changing our care to one of comfort only for Arthur, all would feel relieved. But what if she said that we must continue to do everything? Would we only respect her wishes if they agreed with ours? She had no legal rights in this case, but was her relationship with Arthur such that it trumped legal right? My crystal ball has never arrived in the mail.

I asked her what Arthur would want. She said he would only want to live if he could tell stories in his special way. She knew he never would again and said he would want only to be kept comfortable. Twenty-four days had passed since his admission. She was at his side every day. She cried.

Arthur died peacefully two days later. Mary called me a few weeks later to thank me for involving her in the decision. She told me that she was shocked to find out that Arthur had given her everything he had, including the house, in his will. In my heart, I knew the will had nothing to do with Mary's feelings for Arthur. They were in love.

Capacity

Competence and capacity are related but not the same thing in medical ethics. The law recognizes that mental capacity is a continuous quality that may be present to a greater or lesser extent. Legal competence, however, cannot be present to a greater or lesser extent. A person is either entitled or not entitled, at law, to have their wishes respected regarding treatment. A person may be competent but lack the capacity to make decisions about their care at a given time. This might be due to injury, medications, or cognitive ability to name a few. It can vary from day to day and situation to situation. Someone deemed incompetent legally is also deemed to not have the capacity to make medical decisions on their own. It is complex.

Issues surrounding capacity are common in the world of medical ethics. Maria was a twenty-two-year-old mother whose one-year-old child was in the hospital on a ventilator for pneumonia. He was born prematurely and had multiple problems. Most of his life had been in the hospital. For many reasons, he was put in the care of foster parents. This child needed total care and had significant cognitive issues on top of the physical ones. He would never lead a normal life and most felt he would die sooner rather than later of his issues. Each time he would have a seizure, an infection, or a need for the breathing machine, the physicians would reach out to this mother for permission. She gave it. Today was different. Joey was on the breathing machine for so long that he needed a surgical procedure to put in a more permanent access to his lungs through his neck. She refused. An ethics consult was called.

I read the chart and talked to the nurses and doctors. This poor mother had lived a very hard short life and was socially disadvantaged. She could not care for Joey. I walked in the room and was met with a scenario I never expected. She was in the rocker holding Joey close and talking to him. She was well groomed and greeted me. I told her why I was there. Her reaction was measured and appropriate. She asked why every time her son needed a medical procedure and treatment, they called her, and every time she agreed. Now that she did not agree, we were challenging her decision. Why was her decision respected when it agreed with the doctors and not so when she did not? She told me she cared as much for her son as she ever had. She knew he suffered daily and will never really be well. She felt she needed to draw the line to prevent his suffering. She was indeed competent, had capacity, and had the best interests of her child as her priority.

Capacity should not mean agreeing with the physician. We frequently use our own lives, beliefs, and knowledge as the yardstick to measure others. It is inevitable. It is also wrong. Autonomy means we respect the well-informed choices of our patients – and of their surrogates when the patient cannot do so. Did this mother's lack of education and financial resources make her any less capable of guiding her son's life right now?

Myron was a seventy-one-year-old lawyer who came to me as a new patient. He was delightful. He loved to golf. He was now retired, lived alone, and his family was the club. He went daily and loved life. I do not golf. I have cold hands and excellent handwriting. It is unclear why I chose medicine as a career... Over the next two years, I came to know how respected Myron was. He had spearheaded a process that created a public golf course close to our city. It was his second home. He had a home in Florida where he went to golf in the winter months.

He came to me with a painful right arm. He thought he strained it golfing. I did too. On exam, however, I felt a hard lump in a muscle in his forearm. It was likely a collection of blood from pulling something, I thought. Imaging showed a mass. A biopsy showed it to be a sarcoma. This was a very bad diagnosis. We talked. I sent him to specialists and all agreed it needed to be resected and the best treatment to assure a cure was an amputation. He was right-handed and this was his right arm. He told me calmly that he would not get an amputation, as that would mean he could no longer golf in the fashion he expected. He said that removing that muscle may allow him to golf but less well for certain and that it may not be curative. Another option was radiation therapy that would likely allow him to continue golfing but was not curative and could have side effects. He went with the radiation and did well with it. He golfed for another two years until he died due to recurrent cancer. He was happy with his decision when he died.

Would I have made the same decisions if I were Myron or Maria? Did I walk in their shoes? It did not matter what I would have done. Was Myron more able to make a decision that differed from the medical opinions because he was a lawyer? No. Assessing capacity requires humility. Humility is occasionally lacking in those who practice medicine but being humble opens the door to insights that are invaluable.

He Loved to Sing

I have always enjoyed most doing the social history when seeing a new patient. This is a part of the medical interview focusing on the lifestyle and habits of the patient. I feel it is an exercise that is akin to beginning a new friendship. The life of that patient opens up and I have found that when they see that I am sincerely interested in who they are, the patient becomes more willing to share other parts of their medical history with me. I begin to see them as a person rather than an illness and that is critical in the doctor-patient relationship. We are fighting in medical education to preserve this for good reason.

Bob came to see me because his wife made him come. This is often the scenario. It is odd in this country that men do not see the need to see a physician unless they are ill. It is also odd how many of my male patients when asked what medications they are on say, "Ask my wife." I have also come to know that when a male younger than fifty-five comes for a 'checkup,' that means something has changed physically and they are inviting me to try to uncover that secret. If I do not find anything, that means it must not be serious in their mind and therefore need not be mentioned. I have come to find that simply asking each patient early on what they are worried about concerning their health opens the door to realizing the actual chief complaint.

Bob was a big red-faced man who had a perpetual smile. I liked him from the first five seconds. He just made you feel good. He was forty-six, married, had a son and a daughter who were in their late teens, worked as a janitor, did not smoke, and drank a few beers on the weekend. He was in a barbershop quartet! Now that was something I did not hear every day and when I asked him to tell me more about it, he opened up like a busted dam. I learned of this activity and came to see how much pleasure the competitions, the related friendships, and the simple joy of singing brought to his life. He was a performer.

His wife wanted him to have a medical evaluation because of his weight and her desire to share another few decades with him. I went on to learn that Bob's family had a history of early vascular events, and on exam, he had significant hypertension. I ordered labs and, not unexpectedly, he had an elevated blood sugar and cholesterol. We met again and went over diet, lifestyle, and medications. He bought into the plan and made it clear he loved life and wanted to be able to care for his family, be independent, and sing for years to come. In time, his labs normalized, his blood pressure was controlled, and he even lost weight. Life was good.

Five years later, I got a call that he had suddenly collapsed at home and was not moving. I called an ambulance and met them in the ER. My office was hospital-based and this allowed me to see my patients easily either in the ER or once admitted. This is seldom the case these days and I cannot imagine not being there for my patients when they needed me most. Bob was in a bed and motionless. He did not respond to commands and his eyes were open. His exam showed no focal abnormalities. His labs and CT scan were normal. A neurologist was called and he was diagnosed with a brainstem stroke.

He was admitted and I went back to my office to see patients. After office hours, I returned to the hospital to see Bob. He looked the same. His eyes were open and he was blinking now. I remembered reading about a type of brainstem stroke where the patient is completely aware but unable to move anything but certain eye muscles. I leaned over close to Bob and asked him to blink twice if he could hear me. He did. I became chilled. I repeated this exercise with various questions using one blink for a no and two for a yes. Every answer was appropriate. This man was fully aware!

I asked neurology to come back and he agreed with my assessment and told me that Bob had what is known as locked-in syndrome. This is a rare stroke of the brainstem and people never recover. He was fully aware and would never again be able to do the things he loved. He would never sing. I told his wife and held her as she cried. She immediately told me that they had spoken and he made it clear he would not want to live if he were ever dependent. He saw this play out in his father. A few days passed as we hoped for a miracle – doctors do that as our way of saying we do not know everything. I met with his family daily and told them that since Bob was competent, it was time to ask him what he would want in terms of CPR and ongoing care. They agreed.

The next day was one that will be with me forever. I made sure I had the time to do this properly and made sure any family who wanted to be there was present. Bob made it clear that he understood his prognosis. He did not want CPR, and he wanted all life support stopped. This took a great deal of time and was painful at times. I could not use my skills at reading people's faces or body language. I could only try to imagine what it might be like to be locked in your body forever this way. He was clearly competent. He was not in physical pain. His wishes were both clear and reasonable.

Orders were written. I met with the nursing staff to make sure all understood and shared the goal of comfort and dignity for Bob. He would be asked regularly if he needed anything for pain or anxiety and medications were made available. He died peacefully that night with family present. I also learned that the three members of his quartet had also come to say goodbye. If there is a life after this, and I hope there is, Bob will be singing again.

Our Paths Do Cross

It was early in my practice when I met Anna and Ed. They came to me together as new patients and asked to come into the exam room together. Such was their relationship. They were both seventy. They had no children. They had no siblings and had no relatives. Ed had just retired from his job working in a hardware store for over thirty years. Anna never worked, as was common at that time. They had each other and the way they looked at each other, the way they completed each other's sentences, and the way they comfortably shared silence was simply beautiful. I felt blessed to meet them and have them as my patients and they became part of a practice I preferred to look at as an extended family.

Anna and Ed had heard about me from a patient who was their neighbor. I came to know that our practices grow and thrive by how we treat each patient. They do not know our board scores; they usually do not know where we went to school, nor do they really care. They do not know how much we know. They want to know that we care. This and the work we do to be the best doctor we can be creates relationships with patients that are amazing. I had many patients in my care for three decades and every visit was like seeing an old friend to me.

I saw them intermittently over years and we shared a journey together. Ed presented with weakness and some gum bleeding one day. He had acute leukemia. I was the one to break the news and give the prognosis and options. His was a terrible disease that defied treatment. Anna never left his side. He died in the hospital with Anna and I present. The wonderful care that is hospice had not yet come to be. At that time, people spent long periods in the hospital. There were no hospitalists and as their primary-care physician, I shared their journey in these final days and came to know them very well.

Years went by and Anna was alone. She came to my office for minor issues and annual evaluations. She never became depressed or angry. She had her religion and, through that, a support group. In her eighties, she became frail and by eighty-five, she was a different person in many ways. She had lost weight, no longer stood straight, and did not have that shine in her eyes. Exams and simple tests did not disclose a reason for her decline. She had the frailty of old age and was dying. This is a diagnosis that doctors often fail to accept. There always has to be a reason, something to treat. We all die, and often the cause is the breakdown of this miraculous machine that is inevitable.

We talked about the process and the prognosis. Anna knew and spoke comfortably about death as people often do who have lived a happy life. I asked her to speak with her lawyer and draft a living will and a power of attorney for health affairs. She said she did not need them, as she had me but agreed to do so. She asked me to promise that she be kept out of the hospital. Ed and a frugal life had left her with resources for home care. She made it clear that she would never agree to a nursing home. The plans were set in place.

Over the following months, she got worse and dementia set in. I ordered home nursing and went to visit her on occasion. The house call is a ritual that yields much more than any office visit. She could not eat and did not know where she was. She was in the dying process and hospice was now an entity. I consulted them and made it clear she was a DNR at her request. The nurse told me she could not go on hospice, as she did not have a terminal diagnosis. I was shocked that dying outside of a known cancer or heart ailment was not embraced as a natural process yet. They said they needed someone to speak for her and asked if she had a power of attorney for health affairs.

I practiced in a relatively small town. I knew her lawyer who was also my patient and gave him a call. She said Anna had made up a DPA and kept in her safe deposit box (a common practice for those who had lived through the Depression) and that he had a key she had given him. He went to the bank, got the document, and gave me a call. Anna had listed me as her power of attorney! I was shocked and now faced with so many realities. I had become her family. The gift of such trust was overwhelming. The role conflicted with my role as her physician. What did Anna need most now: a doctor or family?

I made a call and easily transferred her medical care and records to a physician I trusted – and knew Anna would have as well. I knew that I could do more for her as her trusted spokesperson. She died peacefully at home. Friends came to visit. She was never alone. I still miss her.

Bad Idea

Ideas come and go and they are critical to our evolution. Good ideas pave the way to innovation and pride. Bad ideas, when allowed to come to fruition, can be a disaster. This is a tale of one such outcome.

The local medical society came up with the idea that we needed to allow people to see what doctors really do every day. There was a notion that people were losing respect for physicians, and if they knew the lives we lived, they would be enlightened. The plan was to have professionals in other areas follow a physician for a day and see our experiences firsthand. We would then follow them another day and learn of their work life. Bad idea!

This was long before HIPAA (Health Insurance Portability and Accountability Act of 1996) that provides data privacy and security provisions for safeguarding medical information. It amazes me that there are so many laws enacted to mandate common sense.

Sandra came to me for a routine office visit. She was thirty-five and married. She had no children and worked in sales part-time. She did not smoke and rarely drank. She felt well. People at this age rarely come to the doctor just for a routine visit. There is almost always a hidden agenda – sometimes even hidden from themselves. It was with these patients that I took extra time and did an extensive review of systems. That is the part of the medical interview where the doctor asks everything about everything. It is amazingly useful and I refer to it as our safety net, as it saves us from missing something important. I have also learned that patients sometimes come and hide things from us thinking that if we do not discover it as we ask or examine, it must not be important. Human nature is often bizarre.

As a routine, I ask if the patient is happy. It is a simple ploy but has been the key many times. People can lie in the response but I have found that to be unusual. Sandra told me that she was not. The skill of an interview allows one to open a door that yields to a room with other doors and more exploring. After some time, she opened up and I found that she was in an abusive relationship for a number of years. She felt unsafe. She had made plans to leave him and appeared to be in control. We are trained to support those in this horrible situation and make sure they know it is not their fault. We do not contact authorities or do anything that could escalate the abuse but find ways to allow the victim to get out safely. She knew I was there for her and gave her names of people that I knew could help.

I told her that since she was here, we should do a physical exam but I left that to her. If she refused, I would respect that but feared there might be bruises she did not want seen. I had my nurse present for the exam. There were no bruises and she was very healthy. One part of the exam is the lymph-node exam, and as I was feeling the nodes above her left collar bone, I stopped. There was a lump. A seasoned physician can often make a diagnosis with a one-second feel of a mass. This was bad. I carefully did the entire exam and found nothing else. I had her get dressed and met her in my office. I told her what I found and the possibilities. Tests were ordered. I knew it would lead to a biopsy as the only way to be sure. The tests were normal and the biopsy scheduled. The surgeon I sent her to was good and very kind – I worked with him often.

It all went well and it was a simple outpatient procedure that did not take long. My office was at the hospital, so I went to see her in the recovery room. The initial pathology report was that it was a definite lymphoma. She asked me what it was and I was forced to tell her. I hate this part of my profession. I spent as long as I could to get her where I knew she could manage the situation and scheduled to see her in the office in a few days. I would know more of the biopsy findings by then.

Sandra came as scheduled and she looked tired. I had found out that the final diagnosis was of Hodgkin's disease which is a common type of cancer, and with her limited disease, we could usually treat it very successfully, and cures are common. I told her we had excellent specialists locally and she would not have to leave town unless she preferred. I also told her that she would likely be able to hide this from her husband if she preferred. It was then that the bad idea came to fruition.

One of the physicians being shadowed that day was the surgeon who had removed the lymph node. He was a journalist. He wrote an article in the paper the day after the surgery! He told of a young lady who had a biopsy of a lesion in her left upper chest area that turned out to be a cancer and what the procedure was like. There were no names given. Sandra's husband had noticed the bandage when she came home and she had told him she went to the dermatologist for a minor lesion. He read the article and put the pieces together and forced her to tell the truth.

His reaction was the same as after an argument with her; he became the caring husband she fell in love with many years ago. Her window of opportunity to leave him had closed for now. She was covered under his insurance. This is another example of how a single payer system in this country is desperately needed. She knew she was safe and that he would be that other person for some time. These abusers are very predictable. Sandra now had to deal with two cancers.

I saw her often for support and monitoring of her home situation. Her husband would bring her but never asked to be in the room when I spoke with her. That is usually a good sign, as abusers do not want their victim to be able to tell of their plight. I would never speak with him. She did well with the chemotherapy and went into a complete remission from the lymphoma. In time, he reverted to the abuser and she reached out. She left him and got the support needed to do so. She had beaten one cancer and was going to beat this one as well. She was a very brave lady.

Confidentiality can be breached unintentionally, as it was here. Having a journalist shadow a physician and write about it was a bad idea. Asking someone if they are happy is important in a patient encounter. It is usually not done. People often hide their unhappiness and physicians are often afraid of the possible answer. We now get less and less time with each patient. I teach my residents and students to ask the question. Doing a good physical exam always pays off. Shortcuts do not help the patients who honor us by coming to us for care.

Chapter 7

Personal

Life happens. I spent some time as the student affairs dean at a medical school. It was a very difficult job that often tore my heart out. Bright, ambitious, good, and young people are on the path to achieving their dream when something unexpected happens. Life stops for a while. Perspective becomes difficult. This is true in everyone's life. But the world goes on as if nothing happened while it leaves its mark on all of us.

Stroke

I was home in the afternoon that day for reasons I cannot remember. My wife was talking to her mother on the phone and looked very frustrated. MM had a way of doing that to her. My wife loved her mother very much and was always trying to convince her to get medical help. She handed me the phone and said, "You talk to her." She had a cold for a few days and was coughing quite a bit. She did not know if she had a fever and did not check. She denied being short of breath or having chest pain. She was a smoker and needed to be seen – she refused to see her doctor or even call him. I was on my way back to the office that was located in the hospital complex where I worked. I told her I would pick her up on the way and to be ready in ten minutes. After a few minutes of listening to lame excuses, I hung up and drove off. She was ready outside and got in the car. She told me I was much too busy to do this and then in the middle of a sentence, her speech became garbled and her right arm went limp. She was having a stroke!

The mind kicks into another gear in such situations. I processed many options in seconds and decided the best thing was to bring her to the ER myself. I drove fast but safely. I used my phone, which I always swear not to do when driving – but this was no ordinary ride. I called the ER and told them the story and asked that they have a bed ready and the lab there to do blood work immediately. I also told them to tell radiology I needed a CT scan immediately. Lastly, I told them to call neurology and have them meet me there. I knew that every minute between a stroke and restoration of blood flow was critical. I also knew there was a drug recently released to treat strokes that are new and without active bleeding – thus the need for the scan. I arrived and everything went as planned – just like on TV!

The neurologist would not be able to come for about forty minutes. The scan showed no bleeding. I had to make the decision to give the medication. There was a real risk of severe bleeding with it, including into the brain. Without it, she would almost certainly be unable to speak and partially paralyzed. I gave the medication. Within fifteen minutes, she began to move her arm, and by thirty minutes, she was speaking again. We all celebrated. She did well after that and was home in a few days without complications. I had restored my mother-in-law's speech – some would question the wisdom of such an action...

The 'what ifs' go flying after such an event. What if this happened when she was sleeping? What if I was not home and my wife had not called her? What if she bled and died after I gave the medication?

In general, doctors should not care for family members. The risk of being wrong is too great. The risk of taking shortcuts is real and these are what lead to errors. Doctors do manage family all the time, however, and that does not make it right. We often are put in very difficult situations. MM made it clear she was not going to see any doctor but me. If the alternative is no care, does that make it right? If the relative asks your opinion of what the other doctor said or did and you do not agree, then what? It is shaky ground to walk upon. Knowing what the right thing to do is quite different than doing the right thing. Is it the right thing for the patient or for the profession in general? Like so many things, we must make the best decision possible in dealing with the facts of each encounter.

On this particular day, I did the right thing – but only because the outcome was good. In ethics, we refer to this as utilitarianism. Every year of my life, I have put a crystal ball on my list to Santa – no luck yet.

Pastoral Care

My father had an ischemic cardiomyopathy (weak heart muscle) and would go in and out of congestive heart failure. He did not get chest pain or leg swelling. He would get a 'stuffy nose.' I use him as an example to my students of how to get a proper history. Dad was never much of a talker and tended to be concise to the point of having trouble extrapolating to what he meant. On further questioning, I would find out that he could breathe from his nose fine and had no discharge. He would tell me that every time he would lie down, his nose would get stuffy. This really meant that he was feeling short of breath when supine, and this is called paroxysmal nocturnal dyspnea – a phrase Leo was never going to say! I would get in the car, drive for fifty minutes to his home and bring him to my hospital where his physician was, and bring Mom for another stay with us. He was in and out so often that everyone got to know him. He was a character.

The course of this disease is a slow decline over time with exacerbations and remissions and the patient seldom returns to baseline – they slip a little further down on the slope each time. He would have his meds adjusted and was actually very compliant with his diet (because of Mom). He was in his mid-seventies and was slowly dying. We decided to throw a big forty-fifth wedding anniversary party, not expecting him to reach the fiftieth. He did. It was a good idea, however, because by the fiftieth, he was not able to enjoy life anymore. He really enjoyed the forty-fifth!

There are individuals at most hospitals that go unseen and unappreciated. They are the pastoral care teams. These wonderful people visit patients and meet their non-medical needs. Their role is not about religion or about social service; it is about being a friend for a time to everyone in need of one. There is no situation that is not made better by a friend. I worked at a catholic hospital for thirty years. It was run by the Sisters of Mercy. These were the same nuns who taught me for twelve years. It is not uncommon for these dedicated ladies to take on the role of pastoral care upon leaving their primary roles such as teaching or administration. I got to know them well and many were my patients. It was at first very intimidating to provide medical care for this group but I soon learned they are just like everyone else – once getting over the fear from the early years.

Having spent more time in the hospital as a patient over the past two years than I ever wanted, I came to know what it is like to lie there alone. My wife and family came all the time and I am very blessed with an incredible family. Friends dropped in. But there were many hours alone. Lying on the plastic mattress with various beeping going off, with noises and smells unique to hospitals, with the intermittent nurse visits – asking how I am and what my pain score is, the mind does not drift to positive thoughts. Those times alone get filled with thoughts such as: when will the pain come back? Why did this happen? What are they not telling me? Will I ever be the same? The patient does not spend this time thinking good thoughts. The TV becomes an annoying distraction. Roommates become people sent from hell. It is not a positive scene!

Two pastoral-care people came to visit my father daily. Their visits were the high points of his day and my ego could handle that. Sister MD was someone who made me believe there are saints on this Earth. She just calmed a room upon entering and had a smile that was more effective than morphine. I do not know how she always managed to say just the right thing. I saw MD do this to all the patients she visited. Sister HL was a different story. She was a small lady who was gray, tilted, older, and seldom smiled. She had been part of the hospital administration and every doctor was afraid of her. I recall once when a physician had been kept in the hospital after delivering a child that Sister HL brought charts to her room to complete since 'she was off work and had time on her hands.' Sister HL happened to be from my hometown but I did not know her from there. My father did. Every evening around 7:00 PM, she would go to his room and sit down and talk about people and places from the past that they both knew. My mother would be there and able to join in these magical trips down memory lane. The voyage took Dad to when he was young, healthy, and happy. She transported him out of his bed and made his breathing easy. Her visits were what he looked forward to the most every day. I am indebted to both of these fine people who embodied what pastoral care is, and they are now with God.

I would suggest that anyone who has the opportunity to drop by a patient's room and visit, do so. Do not talk about how they are or ask what the doctor or nurse said. Do not ask how their pain is or what the biopsy showed. Do not ask when they will be able to go home. Strike up a conversation that will transport them out of that damn bed and get their mind thinking good thoughts. When you see the patient nodding off, quietly say goodbye for the day, and if possible, tell them you will return and when. They will look forward to it all day and welcome another distraction from reality.

Post-Op

Am I alive? Coming out of anesthesia is a bizarre experience. The first thing that happens is realizing you have survived. As a physician, I could, and did, develop a long list of things that could go wrong. As a person who is skilled at worrying, this list was extensive and made more real as the surgical date approached. The feeling of knowing I survived was so amazing. It was quickly followed by asking the nearest person if everything went as expected. It did! I closed my eyes and enjoyed the remaining effects of those wonderful medications. Then reality set in.

I had never had a major surgery before. For almost a year, I had battled recurrent diverticulitis. The pain, diet, and antibiotics had made my life miserable. I never missed a day of work or needed hospitalization but it was clear this could not go on. I did my homework and decided to go out of town for the surgery. I was very well known in my local hospital and I did not want a stream of well-meaning people coming to see me post operatively. I also did not want to be treated differently than any other patient, as I know that routines enhance safety and deviations from them can lead to errors. I did not let it known when admitted that I was a physician.

Next, I awoke in terrible pain. I was in a room with my wife next to me. She is a nurse and a brilliant one. I felt secure. The pain was more intense than I expected. She rang for the nurse who explained to me that I had a morphine pump, and every time I needed relief, all I had to do was press the button. I had many patients treated this way and knew it worked. I immediately pressed that button, as I knew it would be my best friend in the hours ahead. After some time and three presses, the pain was even worse. It was sharp and more in my right shoulder. I reasoned that it was due to the gas put into my abdomen to allow visualization during laparoscopic surgery.

There were more presses and still no relief. The pain made it a little hard to breathe. The nurse came and my wife asked her to check the delivery system, as she suspected a problem. She is a genius. The tubing was hooked up incorrectly, and every time I pressed that button, morphine dripped onto my sheets! I wanted to suck those sheets dry immediately. The nurse apologized and immediately gave me a dose of morphine. It did not work well. I knew that it is harder to treat pain once it has escalated. I also knew sometimes the medication does not work for a given patient.

Then, in walked the surgical resident – first year. She did a brief exam and told me she thought I had a pulmonary embolism and she was having me taken down for a CT scan of my chest right away. I quickly realized I had made a mistake planning the surgery. It was early July and this young physician was clearly less than two weeks out of medical school. I knew what was wrong and knew I had nothing to clinically suggest an embolism other than pain. The timing was also off. The pain and the frustration finally took over. I looked at her and told her I was the chief of medicine at another hospital and that I knew I was not having a pulmonary embolism and that I refused the scan. She left the room and I never saw or heard from her again. I feel badly about that interaction.

From the other side of the curtain in the room came a voice from a man who would become a consultant. Amos was my roommate. As I had not mentioned my profession on admission, I was not in a private room. "You a doctor?" My cover was not completely blown. "I hear you are having lots of pain and the morphine ain't helping." I then found out that my roommate was an expert at pain management. He told me he had been repeatedly hospitalized for recurrent alcoholic pancreatitis. I decided to ask what he suggested – why not...? He replied, "Try some of that Dilaudid stuff. It is real good." I rang for the nurse and did just that. Within minutes of the dose, I was free of pain and having an experience I never could have imagined. Amos was my new best friend.

The morning came. My pain became minimal and only in the surgical site area. Tylenol was enough for that. My shoulder was fine. I got out of bed and walked. The surgical team came in and apologies were flying. A hospital administrator came to say he was sorry for what happened with my IV. Mistakes happen. I knew it was not done out of neglect. I knew it did not affect my outcome. One day later, I had the thrill of passing gas – an event I did not realize was a milestone! I was given food and the ability to walk on my own without an IV pole. The next morning, I was sent home. That was only forty-eight hours after having much of my sigmoid colon removed. I felt so good when I got home. I trimmed some bushes outside. The science of medicine is amazing.

I now knew what real pain was and treated my patients differently. I now knew what it was like to be in a hospital with all its complexities. I knew what I already knew – that I had married the perfect woman. I had it dramatically reinforced that every patient is a human being with wisdom and insight and should never be labeled. Thank you, Amos.

Mom

My mother was amazing. I so wish everyone could start a tale this way. I was very lucky. I did not have much growing up but I cannot list a single thing that I did not have that was important. I had two parents who were always there for me and I felt loved, safe, and respected. In my early years, we lived in the top three rooms of my grandparents' duplex. There were six of us including my parents there. We moved into the other half of this house when I was very young and it felt like a mansion. My father was a policeman and he is the deserved topic for another tale. Mom was always there for us. She quit her job when she married – such was the way of life then. She was incredibly bright having skipped a year in school but did not have the opportunity to go beyond high school. She did not drive and I am not sure why she decided to give that up. Perhaps it was because we did not have a car at the time...

I hope she was happy. That was not a subject raised back then. She seemed to be fixated on death and part of that might be religious and ethnic. The Irish seemed to not fear death. I still recall my uncle's death when I was very young. He was waked in the house and there was a two-day party. To this day, I recall being so confused. If you ever came to our house and admired some object, Mom would put a small gummy label with your name on its base after you left. That would mean it would go to you after her death. It was a will by hundreds of labels. I recall one day when some friends picked my wife and me up to take us to the airport for a vacation when I was in residency that they came in to our apartment and put labels on out TV and stereo when they picked us up. "Just in case the plane goes down!"

Our grandparents lived next door and connected to our side by an opening in the basement wall. Mom cared for them as she did for us. I learned so much. My grandfather was an amazing man with a great sense of humor. He taught me carpentry and how to tell a tale. He died when he was ninety and I was with him alone. He taught me death. I still do not know why he died but we were less fixated on causes then and more so on heaven. It was a better time in many ways. My father died in his late seventies – right after his fiftieth wedding anniversary. Mom was alone. We had all moved away for our careers. After many discussions, she finally agreed to leave the home she raised us in and move to the city where we lived. She refused to live with us. She moved into a high-rise apartment for seniors and we tried to make it home for her.

What happened next shocked us all. My wife said she achieved self-actualization in her mid-eighties. Quiet, Mom created a whole new life. She had friends. She sat and talked at all hours with them. She developed a pinochle group. When I would visit, the words, "Hi, Pauline," rang out everywhere we walked. She laughed and it was a laugh that made everyone laugh with her. She was happy.

She began to lose weight. She had bad arthritis but never complained. She used knitting to keep her crooked fingers moving. She loved desserts and looked at a meal's only purpose as that it qualified one for dessert. Her appetite waned. I took her to her doctor. It was someone I trusted and knew that he would keep me informed but not rely on me for direction. I needed to be her son. All physicians should avoid treating those they love. It is too precarious and confusing to do so. Testing revealed that she had ovarian cancer. She was told and given options. I sat with her and we talked. I asked her if she had considered the treatments offered. She said with a smile, "I thought you were smarter than that. I am ninety. Treatments would make me sick. I have always been ready to die." Indeed she was. She never spoke of it again.

She became weaker but refused to live with us. We hired help to allow her to stay with her friends. We convinced her it was covered by insurance, as she would have refused it otherwise. My brother and sisters and I paid. Happiness and independence are priceless. Eventually, she could not be alone and needed more care. Hospice was brought in earlier and told us they wanted to bring her to the unit at the hospital. She had no pain. After a few days, she seemed better. I would spend time with her a few times a day. My office was close. One day, we were having a wonderful chat and she asked me what it was like to die. I guess she thought we learned that in medical school. She expected an answer. I felt that this was not the time or place to tell her that her son, the doctor, did not know something. I told her that she would close her eyes and go to sleep. Only when she would wake, she would be with Dad.

She closed her eyes. She died soon thereafter. I could not believe it. There is so much we do not know... We went to her apartment a few days later. We turned over everything and took home what was designated for us. Thanks, Mom.

Religion

I am certain that religion played a significant role in who I am now. This book has references to experiences that I recall. It is what I do not recall that likely had the greater impact. I was brought up in the Roman Catholic religion in a relatively small town in Northeastern Pennsylvania. My early years were spent in church at a time when the mass was in Latin, the priest faced the altar with his back facing you, we could not eat or drink for many hours before receiving communion, and the fear of God was the law of the land. The priest was revered, and the pastor akin to the president. I was taught mostly by nuns for twelve years. That is the subject of another story.

I was an altar boy for many years. That meant getting up very early, dressing in a gown, wearing nice shoes rather than sneakers, kneeling on marble, remembering a complicated dance that lasted between thirty and sixty minutes, becoming an expert at whispering, and being petrified when it was my turn to ring the bell. If not done perfectly, the metal ball would whirl around the inside of the bell and make no noise. The blessing of the host would be delayed because of me! The fear has not left me to this day. Back in those days, the priest would give out communion and I would have to hold a round gold metal plate on a stick and place it under the chin of the recipient. It was terrifying. Would I hit them in the neck? Would I miss a dropped host? Would I catch it and act proud? What do I do if it lands on the floor? It is all as if it were yesterday in my mind.

One thing I must state clearly at the start. I have never had a priest or a nun approach me in any way that was wrong. I know those who have. I fully support the work done in uncovering this horrific behavior and any punishment that is handed out. I suspect this has been an issue for many years and that there are many who have not been identified. My experience was different and that is a blessing. I also feel that anyone who knew this was going on and did not take a stand, especially those in the priesthood, are to shoulder much of the guilt and blame. Lastly, I believe that there are many in religious orders who truly dedicated their lives to God and lived exemplary lives. They need to be admired. A few of those that touched my life deserve a mention, and other entries in this book have done so.

One priest, Father P, became a significant part of my life. He was a young priest in our parish when I was in grade school and I served as an altar boy for him on many an occasion. He had two brothers who were priests as well. My father used to take up the collections at mass and always went out of his way for the priests in our parish. He loved Father P. He went on a trip to Ireland for parishioners and my parents went with him. It was the only time they ever left the country, and since I am from one hundred percent Irish stock, it was a trip they cherished and spoke of for the rest of their lives.

My high school was noted for having a terrific basketball team and we even won a state title when I was there. The gym was packed whenever we had a game. My dad, because of his size and his ability to stop anyone in their tracks merely with a stare, was the cop hired for the games to prevent problems. It was a tough town and fights were not unusual.

When my father died, Father P asked if he could give the homily and say the mass. He was no longer in our parish, but he was the perfect person for this event. Our church was enormous and beautiful. My father died suddenly on Saint Patrick's Day just after telling my mother how much he liked the green flowers she put on the table. It was as if it were scripted. The next day brought eight inches of snow, making everyone's travel difficult. Father P would later remind everyone that my father was good in life and in death at making things difficult! I had my practice in the city where the Bishop resided. He and many priests, including Father P, were my patients. They all came to the funeral. I can still visualize the scene with so many priests on the altar of our amazing church co-celebrating the mass. My father, who never went beyond high school, who worked many jobs to put us through college, and who seldom said a word was being ushered out of this life religiously as if he were a king! I learned more about my father in that one day than I had in decades.

Then came the homily. Father P walked up the stairs into the magnificent marble-enclosed podium overlooking hundreds of people who showed up for Dad's funeral. The church was packed. All the people that he said hello to every day walking his beat, directed at the major intersection in town, or helped in some small way no one knew about showed up to show Leo off. Father P began by saying that Leo was the most blessed man in the town. A noise went through the church that was obviously the collected moans of complete disagreement by those present. My father was gruff, opinionated, and said what he thought unfiltered. My mother poked me in the side and told me that she did not think what people were doing was very nice. That was Mom – always polite and considerate. Then, Father P reminded everyone that Leo was present for every basketball game and stood next to him in the corner of the gymnasium for many years. The picture became clear to everyone. Father P then said that every time the official would make a call, Leo would curse the official, and he had to bless my father for cursing. Yes, he was the most blessed man in the city. Everyone started to clap. It was fantastic. I am sure Leo loved it.

I cared for Father P for many years and always felt as though I was repaying a favor. He was the perfect man, priest, friend, and uncle until he died. He baptized our first grandchild. I would never charge a priest or a nun and had many in my care. I would take their billing slips and put them in a folder in my desk that I labeled *'the ultimate retirement plan.'* I do believe there is a God, even though I am no longer active in the church for many reasons. My trip back into learning the science of medicine has made it even clearer that it is not possible to explain many things. A newborn baby is still a miracle. I suspect science will continue to explain more, but it is my recent experience that with each answer comes more questions. If there is a heaven and there are pearly gates, and there is a question of my entry, please retrieve that folder from my desk...

People Watching

We all do it. The universal form of entertainment is that of observing people day to day. It helps us pass the time. It provides for interesting games where we challenge a person we are with to compose a story surrounding an individual we both can see. The appearance and the location can provide the blocks upon which we build a theoretical life story of the person. We have all been the subject of such musings by others as well. There is no monthly fee, no need for internet connectivity, and it is harmless and challenging.

I once created an online community for students at a new medical school. Their task was to write a brief story surrounding an experience they had while on a one-week clinical away rotation. Each student was required to enter their own narrative reflection and read those posted by other students in their cohort and enter comments on two of the entries by others. I was able to see all the entries. This was a number of years ago and such reflective narratives have become commonplace in medical education. There is now a growing exercise known as a 'story slam' where students, residents, and physicians tell such stories in public format. There is great attention to patient confidentiality and the goal is to heighten humanism and professionalism.

One student wrote a story of a time when he sat in a waiting room at a doctor's office. He had been assigned to be with a cancer specialist that day and the physician was running a bit late, so the student was asked to sit in the waiting room for a few minutes. JR was a gifted writer and was able to paint a colorful three-dimensional scene with words. Upon reading it, I could feel myself in the room looking at the pictures and the magazines and reflecting on the colors chosen for the walls and woodwork. Was this all planned, knowing the type of patients that would sit here? Next, he told of the faces of the others in the room and theorized the associated prognosis, diagnosis, and current state of therapy for each person. I will never know how close he came to being correct with any of this but accuracy is less the purpose of the exercise.

Another example of expert people watching occurred when I was a student at the VA Hospital. We were in the cafeteria as a team with our attending, a well-known cardiologist and gifted teacher. I thank all such incredible people for passing on so many pearls to me over the years. He looked at a table about twenty feet from where we were sitting and pointed to a man about fifty who was eating his lunch and talking with another man. He was a patient or a visitor, as he was not garbed in the various-length white coats that signal who we are. We were asked to observe him and tell us what we saw. We all missed it until he pointed out that we were to watch the man's head and observe how it was moving. We then noted that there was a slight bobbing motion that seemed to have his head move rhythmically to the left. He said that the man had significant regurgitation of his tricuspid valve and went on to tell us why. Next, he rose and went to the man, who turned out to be visiting a friend, and asked him to please unbutton the top two buttons on his shirt and he began to listen to his heart right there where the man sat. He was right, of course, and later that day, this man was seen in his office as a new patient.

Recently, I became the subject of this game as well as a player. My illness resulted in me spending too much time sitting in the waiting room of various specialists as well as my own wonderful internist. The data used included whether the person was alone or, if not, who the person who was with them might be. Did they use an assistance device? What was their age? Did they look at the floor, the television, read a magazine, or use their phone? Did they know the staff? What was their diagnosis? Would they be leaving happy or distraught?

Were they sizing me up? What would they create based on the way I looked on this day? Could they tell that I was concerned about how my blood pressure was on the new medication? Did it show that I had been worried about my kidney function tests ever since the blood was drawn three days before? Was it apparent that I had lost twenty-four pounds from the illness? Could they see the concern in my wife's eyes who had endured my long and serious illness with me? She bore the real brunt of the past many weeks in the hospital, as I had no memory of any of it. Did they look at her and see the saint that I saw? Would I hear the news that I could return to work? Did it show that I wanted to be independent and drive again? I felt so much older but we see different images in the mirror that others see when they look at us. The waiting-room game involves real people who have real lives and the game is all too real to them, as it was to me.

Reentry

"You have been away from it too long to go back to caring for patients." This is what the department chair at the hospital told me. I heard those words and my reaction went from feeling it was absurd to wondering if he was right and to my usual approach which was to embrace it as a challenge. Could I do what I had done for over thirty years as effectively after a seven-year hiatus? Would I enjoy it as much? Did I still have something valuable to offer? What would I discover about myself and medicine?

Planning has a way of making us humble. I had planned to see patients and teach until I retired. I had tried hospital administration part-time but did not possess the political tools to enjoy that. I loved each moment with my patients, and when I had a student with me, I saw so much more in each encounter. What would have been mundane or routine became exciting with a student there. The patients loved it as well. Teaching is the best way to stave off that demon known as burnout.

One thing led to another and I had the honor of helping start a medical school in our community. That led to me being offered a dean position close to where two of my children then lived. The addition of our first grandchild further sweetened the pot. I left my practice to help start another medical school. My wife supported the decision. It would be only for a few years and we would move back. We kept our home and went back often. We came to carve out a new life and we were happy. She was teaching and we became conflicted about what our future would be. Seven years passed.

Then it all came crashing down. I became very ill and through a series of unpredictable events, I lost my position at the medical school. We went through all the options. What did I love most professionally? Teaching! I was extremely good at it and deprived of meaningful teaching as a dean. When one is a dean of student affairs, the rule is you cannot grade a student and that means you cannot teach in a meaningful capacity in a medical school. It is a logical rule but it took away what I loved. I set out to explore options and the pieces came together.

I would be working for the hospital and part of my salary (dramatically decreased) would be supported by the medical school. It would include supervising the care of patients in a medical clinic and oversight of students in a local free clinic and residents in internal medicine in another clinic. What obstacles would I face? The biggest was the electronic medical record. This 'advance' had been known to result in early retirement and decreased satisfaction by both patient and provider. I set out to tackle this demon and found out a few things. An older physician can learn new things – and rather quickly. The tools in the EMR were ones I quickly realized would have made my prior practice run more smoothly – especially those related to tracking medications and tests. One issue was put behind me.

What I learned next shocked me. Outpatient medicine had advanced very little in the seven years I had been away. It has been well documented over the years that more than eighty percent of diagnoses are made by history alone and over ninety percent when the physical exam is added. I had been trained before CT scans and all the modern technology that young physicians now rely upon. I could do what would give me the vast majority of diagnoses and I could do it better than almost everyone else. In three decades, there was very little I had not seen or heard of – I could do this! Better yet, I could teach the skills that served me well over the years. It was exhilarating!

There were very few new tests and they were easy to learn – even an old guy can Google… There were also surprisingly few new medications and most of those were in a category that really needed a specialist to order. I always learned a great deal from consultants, so I would soon learn these as well. Many of the meds from my past were no longer around, as years unveiled side effects not predicted before marketing. There were now tools to predict atherosclerosis and tools to stage dementia and depression. These were embedded in the EMR and were little more than putting math to common sense and making it immediately available for patient care. I was in Disney!

The residents had more knowledge of the intricacies of acute inpatient care but did not have the experience and wisdom necessary for optimal outpatient care yet. We began to trade knowledge and had a blast. I could teach them bedside skills and they could help me navigate the EMR. Both helped each patient seen. The students are the most fun to teach. They know so little and are so appreciative. It is like showing them magic! My other role is teaching first and second-year students in a small group at the medical school using cases to discuss physiology, biochemistry, molecular biology, and pharmacology. I was back in school again and getting paid to learn!

I wake every morning looking forward to the day. My illness and the events that followed closed one door and opened another. Seven years gave me perspective and have shown me what is most important. The statement of Dr. Francis W. Peabody in a lecture to Harvard students in 1925 is as true today as it was then: "The secret of the care of the patient is in caring for the patient."

Payback

Why medicine? I often think back and try to figure out how I arrived at this career that has brought me so many rewards. There was no singular moment but more a series of circumstances, people, and reflections that led me to my profession. I was raised by amazing parents who valued honesty, work, and education. We never had much in terms of material things, but I look back and cannot think of anything I needed that I did not have. My parents never went beyond high school. My two sisters, my brother, and I were all given that opportunity. I was blessed.

My first paying job was when I was thirteen. My father was a policeman in a small town that was well past its glory days when the coal mines were thriving. He worked many odd jobs to bring in extra income. He never complained. One of those jobs was driving a local doctor to a major city every week to operate and teach at a medical center there. My father loved to drive and this gave the doctor time to read and rest. He took an interest in our family and asked my father if I wanted to work for him around his home doing gardening and tending to his special hens.

I would be driven there and work for most of the days in the summer months. I would do gardening, odd jobs, and feed the hens that he raised. His wife was a wonderful lady but somehow terrified me. To this day, I do not know why. I think it was just the way she carried herself – she was stately, spoke directly, and looked right into my eyes. 'Doc' would come home for lunch at times and sometimes had an early day. He took the time to talk to me and that was amazing. He loved life and made it clear he cared about me. Doc told me how much he enjoyed his work, and his house and family made it clear that his career was more than emotionally rewarding. I started to imagine myself as a doctor.

Years passed and I ended up starting a private practice in internal medicine in a city about fifty minutes from where I grew up. That is a tale for another time. One day, very early in my career, I noticed on my schedule for the day that there was a new patient – it was Doc! I was terrified. How could I be his doctor – I was his gardener. He was an idol of mine. This role reversal was more than I was prepared for. Hopefully, this would be a routine visit and I would not be tested. He said hello and was in the room with his wife. Now I was stressed to the max! He smiled and told me he wanted me to 'check him out' because he had prostate issues and was scheduled for a TURP (a surgical procedure to remove much of the prostate from the inside that is done rarely these days) a week from now by a local urologist he knew.

I do what I always do with a patient; I did a thorough history and physical with the patient in a proper gown. I did not skip over anything, nor did I talk to him in a way different than I would with anyone else. Physicians often get short-changed when seeing another doctor. He seemed impressed and satisfied. This tradition of laying on of hands also put me at ease. I was his doctor and his hens were not part of today's encounter.

In the end, I had him get dressed, brought his wife back in, and gave them my evaluation. He was a smoker and overweight. He did not exercise. He did not care to change his lifestyle and the look on his wife's face told me that was a battle for another day. I them told him I did not think he should have the surgery, as I felt his story was more consistent with a cancer at the base of his bladder that can mimic prostate symptoms. I had recently been at a Grand Rounds at my hospital where a urologist presented a case exactly like his. Life is like that. How often do we encounter a patient right when we have read something related? It seems to defy chance.

I sent him to that urologist who saw him the next week. He had a procedure and a biopsy and indeed he had a cancer right where I told him he could. He was treated and cured. I told him how much that summer job meant to me many years ago and how he had become a role model for me. I thanked him and told him how honored I was that he would come to me as a patient. He told me, "Johnny, I knew you were a good kid." I was given the chance to pay him back for his role in putting me on the path to this life I love.

Footsteps

I love being a physician and honestly feel that there is nothing else I would have wanted to be. I also love being a father and I think I did a reasonable job balancing both. The credit for that goes to my wife. I interface with students considering a career in medicine regularly and never once have I told one of them not be a doctor. It is common now to hear of physicians discouraging their children from entering the career of medicine. Many physicians are tired and beaten down by the business of medicine. This is so very sad. I spent time with my kids when they were growing up. They saw me every day and they saw how much I loved my job. I closed my practice to new patients so that I could be home for supper with them, go to their recitals, drive them to school, and really get to know them. All three are bright, caring, hardworking, and honest. None followed in my footsteps.

My children taught me important lessons every day. They kept me grounded and humble. To come home after a tough day and be hugged by a little ball of energy made all the stress melt away. Their joy surrounding the little things in life allowed me to see every day what is important. They are grown and on their own now. I would go back to those days when they were becoming who they now are in a second if I could.

Every day I looked forward to going to work, and every day I looked forward to going home. There is no better script for a perfect life. My oldest was the perfect student and school was her thing. She was very shy when young but has gotten over that in a big way! She was a gifted dancer and watching her ballet solo made me cry. She played the cello and I recall going to the early recitals that should have been titled 'cats in heat.' Only a parent can be proud of the noises they make early on with those instruments. She joined the diving team in high school and I was totally shocked by that. She went to college on a full scholarship and was a premed major. I encouraged her. In her third year, I thought she should shadow some people so that her decision would not be based only on what she knew of me. She was a top student, great at standardized tests, and it appeared certain that she would follow in my footsteps. One of the people I had her shadow was a PhD who ran the local diagnostics lab. She loved what she saw, dropped her medical school applications, and went on to get her PhD in microbiology. She loves it and has a great job, an amazing husband, and three terrific children who call me 'Doc.' She is what every parent wants for their child – happy.

Our second daughter was an artist from birth. School was easy for her and she would talk to anyone at any time. She glowed. We still have paintings she did in grade school that are amazing. She played the clarinet beautifully throughout her education. She had the voice of an angel. We bought a piano and my favorite moments were listening to her play from another room. You could see how she would use this instrument as a way to manage stress when the loud tones would gradually change to soothing smooth tunes. She spent a year abroad while in college and told us she would find pubs with pianos and seldom had to pay for a drink! I knew medicine would not be her path. She pursued her interests and we have seen her become a talented and successful interior designer. She has more friends than anyone I know. She is what every parent wants for their child – happy.

Last came our son. Perhaps he would one day take over my practice? No. He was smart and did well but never really liked school. He was the opposite of me in so many ways. He was not competitive. He was relaxed and comfortable with himself. He was very artistic and did not enjoy sports. He liked computers and was gifted with a special way of seeing things. He played the drums in a band. When your son is the drummer, it means a bunch of teenage boys are always at your house – and the refrigerator is always empty! He went to college but did not like his major or the school and told us so after his first year. I supported him and told him to take a year off and work and find a better school for him. He immediately told me he wanted to go to another school for the next semester. I told him that would not be possible and he replied saying that he was really good at what he did and will get in. I asked him what he did and he told me, "Computer art." I then asked him to create a CD of his work and that I would find schools with majors in that area that would accept transfers. He did and we sent them to two universities. Upon the department chairs seeing them, he was accepted into both before filing an application. In a few weeks, he was in school doing what he loves. He has been a lesson for me in that he opened the door for me to see that there is happiness outside of my world. He is what every parent wants in their child – happy.

Having children is a major lesson in humility. I credit my wife for the vast majority of reasons why ours have become such wonderful people. She gave them the time, the love for art and music, the courage to take a stand, and so many other things. We raised them as a team and what I could not give in quantity, I tried to make up in quality. Our children are a little bit of both of us

144

genetically and in how they live their lives. I had dreams for each of them when they were born. I had ideas of how I could shape their lives. I learned that children shape their own lives and we are there to support, to give some advice, and to enjoy the journey. Whatever we did was successful, as all are happy, and therefore, so are we.

Chapter 8

Medical Ethics 2

I teach a course in medical ethics every semester at a medical school. I have been doing consultations in the hospital setting for years. Issues surrounding dying, autonomy, allocation, and justice are so much easier to talk about than they are to deal with when the issue is real and patients and their families are involved. Life is complicated. Death is tragic. Solutions to the many issues involving medical ethics are not always clear. Communication and honesty are the basis of discovering the optimal approach. A consultation in medical ethics never involves writing orders – our role is to open a dialog, utilize foundational principles, discuss among a committee that includes representatives of multiple areas, and guide those caring for the patient.

Intent

Mrs. Sweeney lived next door and made great cupcakes. She brought them to our door when we became part of the neighborhood. I had moved to the area with my wife and baby girl to 'hang a shingle' and begin my career. Forty years ago, that was what you did. We were not burdened upon graduation with enormous loans. We did not search for large groups that would allow us free time. We were ready to work whatever hours were needed to build our future and support our family. I wanted to teach and this town had a new residency in my field and it was also the home of my in-laws. It was the perfect choice for this next phase of my life.

My first patients were my neighbors. There was no internet. The yellow pages came out once a year and said nothing more than your address and phone number. Word of mouth built your practice and those referrals from other patients were critical. Each satisfied patient brought in new patients. The process took a few years but this became my practice and no one else's. I was proud. I owed these patients who put their trust in me. Mrs. Sweeney was one of my first patients.

She came to me at the age of seventy-six. She lived across the street in big house that was immaculate. She had two sons who were married and had families – they all lived close. Her husband had died fourteen years earlier after an operation. She did not know the details. She never smoked or drank. She had worked in a dress factory for many years. She loved to bake. She was overweight and dressed simply. Her hair was gray with hints of its former redness. She said that she had been feeling short of breath lately.

The physical exam showed dry, fine noises in all lung fields. A chest X-ray showed diffused scarring – fibrosis. Breathing tests and a measure of her oxygen via a blood gas were done. I felt she had a type of lung disease that is called idiopathic pulmonary fibrosis. That means scarring of the lungs for which we do not know the reason. Doctors made up the term idiopathic rather than simply admitting that they did not know. I sent her to a lung specialist. He agreed and there was no effective treatment. We would watch it together and hope it did not progress.

It progressed. By the age of eighty-two, she needed oxygen at home. She could still manage on her own. I would cross the street and see her at home rather than make her come to the office. I love cupcakes. One day, she said her back was hurting in two spots. She was also more tired than usual. I had them come to her house and get some labs and an X-ray. She had a new anemia and her X-ray was riddled with areas where the bone was being eaten away. Further testing showed that she had multiple myeloma. This is a disease that infiltrates the bone marrow where blood cells are made and spreads to bone among other areas. At the time, there was no good treatment. I had her see a cancer specialist and treatments were tried without success.

The pain worsened. She could not live alone and her son moved in. I saw her frequently. It did not take long before we could not control her pain at home and I admitted her to the hospital and hooked her up to a morphine infusion. The pain improved – for a day. The rule is to double the dose if the pain became refractory. I did. It worked for a day or so. The nurses began to notice that her respiratory rate was slowing down. Morphine can do that, so I cut back only to unleash her pain. Other narcotics were tried with the same respiratory effect and less pain relief. I decided to sit down and have the difficult discussion with my patient whom I liked so much. I told her that the medication for the pain was affecting her breathing and that increasing the dose could result in her death through inhibiting her drive to breathe. I made sure she understood and asked her what she wanted. She replied that she was ready for death and that I should just focus on freeing her from the pain. I doubled the dose. She died two hours later without pain.

My intent was to relieve her pain. I knew the risks, as did she. Did I end her life or was my intent a mere justification for euthanasia? In this case, it was quite clear; the medication was used to relieve pain and done at the consent of someone with capacity. It was needed and wanted. Her death was a side effect of the treatment. The known was relentless pain without the medication. Her death was not certain. Very little really is. In life and in death, things are not always clear.

A Brick Wall

Jack was a salesman. He had that unique personality that draws you in, allows you to trust him, and look forward to his next tale. He was tall and overweight – his size matched his character. He was fifty-six and referred to me by his daughter who was a nurse at the hospital where my office was located. The first visit set the stage. He was alone. I knocked and entered the room at which time he rose, grabbed my hand firmly, and took over the room. You could not dislike him.

He had not been to a doctor in many years. He had been losing a few pounds recently and was more thirsty than usual. His diet was a mess. He drank, but not in excess. He did not smoke. He loved to golf. He did not exercise. His father died at the age of seventy-five of a heart attack and had diabetes. He had no other symptoms and made it known that he did not like medicines, or doctors for that matter. He was there to satisfy his daughter. The diagnosis was obvious.

Jack agreed to some tests and went to the lab as requested. His cholesterol, triglycerides, and blood sugar were all very high. Everything else was normal. I had my nurse call him and get him in that week. It was now my time to control the room, to use my persuasive skills and love of teaching, and to get him on the path to wellness. I loved this part of medicine and was quite good at it having practiced daily for two decades. This would be another victory.

He listened and I told him clearly that he needed to change his lifestyle and begin medications. I discussed a stress test but he refused. I went over a diet as well as any doctor can do – and that is poorly, as this important aspect of medicine is never really addressed in medical school or after. He listened and took the prescription and diet with him as he made an appointment for one month after repeat blood work.

The repeat labs came back with his cholesterol lower, his triglycerides improved, and his blood sugar unchanged at two hundred and sixty-seven. He said he felt well and his weight was unchanged. He claimed to be following the diet. I adjusted his meds and repeated the drill. The next visit again showed no improvement in his blood sugar and he was now on what I considered the maximum dose of oral medication. I told him that he needed to start insulin. The atmosphere in the room changed, as did his voice. He told me in no uncertain terms that he was never going to give himself a needle, and neither was anyone else. I asked him what he was afraid of and he refused to answer. He put up a brick wall and made it clear there was no discussion.

I changed his medications, knowing they would not work, and repeated the drill. As expected, his sugar did not drop. Having given him some time to think about things, I expected that the next visit, he would buy into the plan. Wrong. The wall was still there. I asked him if he did not trust me and he was very frank and polite and said that he liked me and respected my advice but would not follow it. He did not want me to talk to his daughter and I had not to this point. I had made it a point on each visit to document my advice and his refusal.

The time had come, in my mind, to advise him to get another physician. I told myself that perhaps he would listen to someone else. I also felt badly that I was playing some role in allowing his vessels to narrow, his kidneys to fail, and his nerves to malfunction. I told him I would always be there for him until he found the new doctor and suggested he do so soon. I made another appointment to see me just in case.

He never came back. His daughter never asked. I got a records release and sent his chart on to this next physician whom I knew. I never asked how he was doing. I felt like I had failed this patient. Did I abandon him? Should doctors fire a patient who does not comply? Are we passing the buck rather than using the knowledge of the patient to continue to try to break down the wall? Was it my ego that was the issue here? Next time, I would try a little harder, a little longer. There is not always a next time.

Alone

Sam was lying in the bed in the intensive care unit when I went to see him for the first and only time. I had been called by the ICU team to do an ethics consult. While I enjoy doing such evaluations, they never lead to an outcome that makes anyone feel good inside. Ethics consults stem from disagreements, loss, issues of futility, and the attempt to do the right thing in what are often nebulous circumstances. Sam was seventy-two, had resided in a nursing home for the past twelve years, and had a stroke at the age of sixty that resulted in his being placed in the home.

Sam had no relatives, no friends, and no one in his life. Those who cared for him at the nursing home did not have any idea who he really was or is. He could not communicate. It is impossible for me to truly understand being alone, as I have been abundantly gifted with many that I can say are close to me and truly know who I am. My life is full and happy because of this. I do not have a living will or a durable power of attorney for health affairs. I have Cathie. My wife of forty-three years knows who I am and exactly what I would want should I be near the end of my life. I speak openly about my wishes and my children also know that if I should be facing a certain and uncomfortable death or prolonged disability with the inability to enjoy my life, I would want to leave this world in comfort. Sam was alone and suffering.

He was painfully thin and on a ventilator. He had a full arrest two hours earlier – that is a sudden failure of breathing and/or heart function such that the person dies without intervention. The 'code' worked in that the heart rhythm was restored but his blood pressure was low and he needed a machine to breathe. He had been in the hospital for seventy-two days for infections in decubitus ulcers. These are deep, large ulcers from the breakdown of the skin on areas of the body submitted to constant pressure. They are seen in people who do not move and have poor nutrition. They are very hard to treat. Sam had been on multiple courses of antibiotics and had the wounds cared for daily. They were not healing.

The ICU team was certain he was going to arrest again soon and they did not want to subject him to the process of a 'code.' He was already on a breathing machine but if his heart should stop again, they would need to push on his frail chest and shock him. He would almost certainly have broken ribs as a result. We now appropriately question the purpose of submitting such patients to a code and have studied the outcome of those who undergo this medical intervention. Patients such as Sam might respond to the intervention but do not recover and do not leave the hospital. The hospital I work at has a policy that allows for a unilateral entry of a do-not-resuscitate order when two physicians caring for the patient certify in the chart that the CPR (cardiopulmonary resuscitation) would not positively affect the outcome for the patient. The patient must be in the situation Sam was now in – without anyone to decide for him legally. The final mandate is that an ethics committee consult be obtained to assure that all the above is correct. A process to obtain a court appointed guardian is possible but takes a number of days and Sam did not have that time.

These consults impact me in many ways, and that impact has not waned with repeated exposure. In medical ethics, we use the term 'substituted judgment.' This implies that another person acts on behalf of the patient who cannot communicate. They voice decisions that they feel would most likely be what the patient would have wanted. This implies that they know the patient well and that they have discussed situations of this nature with them. It is not uncommon for even a family member to be unclear what their loved one would want and then we expect that decisions be made in the best interests of the patient.

What constituted the best interests of Sam? Was his life in the nursing home these past twelve years where he could not care for himself or communicate a life worth living? Was he suffering? Was he in pain? Was he even aware? We can only speculate to answer these questions and we cannot help but substitute our own answers if we would be in the same situation. Is just being alive enough? How do we define being alive? These are deep and difficult questions that bring religious beliefs, cultural norms, and prior experiences to the discussion. Answers will vary. In many ways, this consult I was to enter then was substituted judgment and must be done diligently.

I spoke with the nurse and the physicians. I reviewed the chart. I went to his room and saw Sam. I was able to pull upon my experiences as a physician for decades as well as my knowledge of medical ethics. I spoke to others on the ethics committee. I reviewed the policy carefully. Sam deserved all this.

The decision was made to enter the order in the chart to not submit Sam to a 'code.' He had a cardiac arrest one hour later and was pronounced dead. I hope Sam would be grateful for preventing further pain and suffering through interventions that we knew were futile. I hope I spoke as he would have wanted.

This is a common situation and so very sad. I encourage those who read this to make their wishes known to those who might be asked to speak for them. Make their difficult job easier. I encourage anyone who feels they do not have someone to speak for them to fill out and submit a living will to your doctor and loved ones. Today, it is very unusual for the primary physician who sees the patient in the office to be the caregiver in the hospital. Things have changed. The completed document should be given to friends and relatives. I always tell my patients to review their living will every year on their birthday and replace the old one if there are changes so that this document can speak for them when they no longer can. Likewise, if a durable power document is used and the person listed as the decision-maker happens to die, a new one must be completed and submitted.

There was a major effort put forth since 1991 when the Patient Self-Determination Act (PSDA) was passed to educate and promote advance directives (living wills and durable power for health affairs). Few have created either document in the past twenty-six years, and this likely stems for the fact that people do not want to talk about death. The end of our lives is one of the very few certainties of living. People like to exercise control of their lives, and they should act to exercise that same control of how they might die. Sam may have suffered needlessly for twelve years.

The Guardian

MK was a sixty-seven-year-old female who had been in the hospital for weeks. She had been in and out of hospitals for most of the past year. She has been a resident of a nursing home for most of her life. She had oxygen deprivation during her birth and was left with severe neurologic impairment. I could find no documentation of the quality of her life when she was younger. She had no relatives and no one came to visit her in the nursing home or at the hospital. She could not speak and she was fed with a tube for at least the past year. She was alive and she was a human being and thus deserved the same level of care I would expect for myself.

I was sent to see MK when a consult was placed to the ethics committee at the hospital. She had severe breakdown of her skin with deep large ulcers on her legs that were not healing. They were infected and the bacteria were now resistant to most antibiotics. We do not give these one-cellular living organisms the credit they deserve. When faced with an adversary, they multiply rapidly and in time, some of the new bacteria possess a mutation that renders them resistant to the antibiotic we put in their surroundings. We put in a new antibiotic and it does its trick again. With the way we now use antibiotics broadly and often without reason – such as when treating the common cold which is viral – we are only fueling the fire that is creating the super bugs that will threaten our lives as we run out of new antibiotics.

The infectious disease specialists on the case suggested we amputate the legs of MK as the best way to control the infections. The surgeons treating the ulcers agreed. MK had a guardian. This is an individual whose job is to follow those he is assigned to, and to act on their behalf in situations such as this where a decision needs to be made medically. There are court-appointed guardians and legal guardians of other types. The name caused me to wonder how it came to be. What exactly was this person guarding for MK? Were they acting in her best interest and thereby trying to imagine what she might want in the same situation? Were they guarding her life and all decisions made would be to keep her alive at all costs? What was their intrinsic view of life and death? What was their religious background? Was the fact that they were paid to do this a factor? I did not know and could not know.

I went to see MK and could not help but be taken aback by what I saw. She was glaring at me with eyes that were fixed in a stare. She was painfully thin. Her legs were folded up under her such that she could not sit and obviously had not been able to sit or stand for years. They were contracted and unable to move at the joints. The ulcers were large but clean and well cared for. She did not appear to be in pain but could not respond to anything I said or did. If anyone thinks that physicians are not deeply affected by seeing such patients, they are very mistaken. I felt so sad for this lady and could not help but wonder if she felt, if she knew any joy, and if she lived or was merely just alive. I did not see the amputation as an operation that would remove legs, as these appendages no longer functioned as legs. I was told the guardian would not consent to the surgery.

I have an ability to carry on a civil conversation with almost anyone and can usually educate the person in such a way as to allow for respectful dialog surrounding medical and ethical issues. I called the guardian and was totally unsuccessful. He said that he would not agree to the surgery due to the risk of death. The fact that she would die without it did not seem to be a fact he would accept. I next decided to at least have MK declared a DNR/DNI. This meant that if her heart stopped or she stopped breathing, we would not intervene. I could not even imagine how CPR could be done with her twisted frame. His answer was that when he came to see her, the heart monitor was not skipping any beats and he did not think she was going to die soon and would not consent to a DNR. It became clear he was going to refuse anything we asked for and without any reason given. I was also given a glimpse of his sense of power by the fact that he would consider a heart rhythm a sound indicator of a patient's medical condition.

MK deserved better than this. I called his supervisor who backed him up. I spoke to a lawyer who told me the courts almost always side with the guardian and trying to remove him was difficult. The antibiotic course was completed and MK was transferred back to the nursing home. These wounds that will never heal will become infected once again and she will return to the hospital for another round of antibiotics, and more suffering – if MK felt pain or was depressed or was aware in any way. If she was, then what was being done was akin to torture. If she was not aware, then was this a life worth living?

The story of MK is not unusual. In every nursing home, there are those like MK. We, as a society, have not come to grips with the reality of caring for those in this condition. We err on the side of life but have not come to terms with what life really is. I do not feel it is a matter of having some brain activity and a heartbeat. That is being alive. Living is a matter of experiencing and being able to interact. It is to feel joy. Shouldn't anyone who acts as the guardian of another be mandated to act in the best interest of that person? Were the best interests of MK being met? If death was a better alternative than her current life and this was why he would not allow the surgery, then why mandate that we do CPR? If merely being alive was the goal, then this guardian was not guarding a person but a multicellular organism. MK deserved better. We all do.

Brain Death

Louis was found on the street unresponsive and 911 was called by a passerby. The ambulance arrived quickly and he was not breathing. CPR was begun and a tube was placed to supply oxygen to his lungs. After two shocks, a heart rhythm and faint pulse was restored. It was unknown how long he was not breathing. In the emergency room, his evaluation showed that this was a heroin overdose – all too common these days. He had been given naloxone twice when first found without response. This is the drug that rapidly reverses opioid overdoses. His initial evaluation showed no evidence of brain function. His scan of the brain showed no reversible cause such as a bleed. The brain of an adult does not tolerate being deprived of oxygen for long. He was sent to the intensive care unit on full support. His wallet gave a number to call and his mother was located. She was soon by his side. "Louis was a good boy who got mixed up with the wrong crowd in eleventh grade," his mother said. He did well in school and wanted to be a teacher. He dropped out of school by twelfth grade and was often gone for days. She was deeply religious and prayed at his bedside out loud.

Repeated evaluations showed no sign of brain function over the next few days. His blood work showed that all narcotics were gone from his system. He met the full criteria for brain death and the mother was told it was time for the machines to be turned off. It was done in a respectful and empathic way but there is no right way to deliver this news to the mother of an eighteen-year-old. Somehow, she had heard of the religious exemption in New Jersey and said that their religion did not accept brain death as the end of life. She wanted everything done. An ethics consult was placed and that was how I got to meet Louis and his mother.

Some of the key controversies in medical ethics surround when life begins and when it ends. What is the difference between biological life and human existence? These are questions far beyond the scope of this story but worth reading about. If human existence begins at conception, the arguments against abortion become significant. If human life begins when the brain can sense and react, the time is different. If it begins when born and the baby takes a breath on its own, then we have another end point. If we consider the number of weeks gestation after which a fetus can survive outside of the womb, we have another point of debate. Recently, death has become the focus of debate as well. This is not new. Years ago, people were mistakenly buried alive. They would tie bells on strings and attach to the arms and legs in the coffin and the ringing of bells would signal that the person was alive and they would dig them up. Amazing! We did not use a standard death certificate in this country until 1910. On August 5, 1968, an ad hoc committee at Harvard Medical School published a landmark report that laid the groundwork for a new definition of death, based on neurological criteria. In 1981, a presidential commission for the study of ethical problems in medicine and biomedical and behavioral research strongly recommended that all of the United States recognize the cessation of brain function as a definition of death. The Harvard brain death criteria have become the standard used.

States have issued documents in support of these criteria. Hospitals have policies surrounding the declaration of brain death with specific testing. New Jersey has allowed for a religious exemption to the brain death criteria when it originally issued the document. This was meant to allow for very specific exemptions in cases where the patient was a known active participant in a religious group that had outlined specific objections. Recently, this has become an option for anyone whose family members say that their personal religion and the beliefs of the patient do not accept the brain death criteria.

I met with Louis' mother and asked that the social worker be present along with the nurse. These conversations are often misinterpreted by the grieving. I tried to have her do the talking and tell me about Louis. I then asked about her faith and whether Louis shared that faith. No matter what I said, she continued to voice that her God would save her son. I asked if I could talk to her pastor and she gave me the name of the church. This man was wonderful and came right to the hospital. With his help, she was able to realize that her God had already made his decision and that her son was gone. Religion continues to play a powerful role in the lives of many and those of us in healthcare should always reach out and include this in our care.

The next day, at a scheduled time, with family and the pastor present, Louis was removed from the ventilator and never drew a single breath on his own. He never moved and was pronounced dead minutes later. There was a great deal of crying, but there was acceptance. I suspect the hole now in this lovely mother's heart will never heal.

This is a common story in this country. Young people are dying needlessly, leaving their family with wounds that will not heal. This situation always makes me question what religion is. To some, it is a formal structure with rules and rituals. To others, it may be the personal belief system that guides their life. I am not to judge. In my years interfacing with these sad situations, I have come to know that all communication requires mutual respect. In time, perhaps all will understand that no adult ever recovers if the brain death is met. The internet and magazines are full of false tales that people who face the loss of a loved one will turn to. Our job is to be there for them, to educate them, and to support them until they can cope with the reality of losing a loved one.

STD

Sexually Transmitted Diseases (STD) continue to be a major medical problem worldwide. The knowledge that it can occur does not seem to alter the actions of human beings. We are a flawed species. Over the past forty years, I have seen many things change in the area of STDs, and many stay the same.

A young woman came to the clinic for a general exam and had no concerns. Sandy was married for ten years, was happy, had a six-year-old boy, and was sexually active with her husband. She had noted a slight vaginal discharge over the past few months but nothing she was worried about. Her physical exam was normal and a gynecologic exam performed. A specimen was examined under the microscope and led to the diagnosis of trichomoniasis. Medicine is a combination of knowledge, ethics, and common sense. In this case, we must ask ourselves what might happen if we do not tell the patient that she has trichomoniasis. We know this is acquired by sexual contact. We know the male, and often the female with this infection can be asymptomatic. If we do not tell her, she could pass this to someone else. We do not know for sure that this was acquired from her husband. Such assumptions can lead to errors in treatment. We also know that when a patient has one STD, they are much more likely to have another. Not telling the patient exactly what this means could lead to missing a diagnosis such as HIV and having this disease passed to others by the patient or her husband. In this case, we also have an obligation to society.

Honesty is a cornerstone of the medical profession. Patients rely on us to be honest with them, especially in the scenario of informed consent. Truth is necessary for the patient to make a decision about their health. When a patient loses trust in their physician, the therapeutic bond is broken. Whatever that physician will communicate with their patient going forward will be heard with suspicion and diminish the value of even truthful and important information.

The need to be honest, however, has to also encompass the issues of confidentiality and how the truth might impact a patient. It had been common for physicians to withhold a diagnosis of cancer from their patient, as they felt the fact would hasten their death or lead to the patient giving up. Time has proven that this is not the case and it is a common practice to tell the patient even if the family asks us not to. Our obligation is to the patient and they deserve the truth, as ultimately all further decisions are theirs to make.

One might consider just treating her for the 'discharge' and not opening the door to the actual diagnosis and its implications surrounding infidelity. It is unethical to treat a patient without giving them the exact diagnosis for which we will order therapy. Telling her a lie in this situation is wrong. We also cannot test her without her permission and that includes knowing exactly what we are testing her for. To say that the tests are now routine and recommended in all patients and to treat her for a diagnosis she does not really have are both lies. They are wrong in and of themselves not to mention the possible repercussions if discovered.

Telling her invites the question of how she got this. Telling her the truth might put her marriage in jeopardy – assuming he was the source. Telling the truth is not always easy. Our primary responsibility is to our patient and not to her husband in this situation even if he also happens to be our patient. Despite being a readily diagnosed and treatable STD, trichomoniasis is not a reportable infection, and control of the infection has received relatively little emphasis from public health STD control programs.

I trained at the time when HIV was just being discovered. It was a terrible time. Mostly young men were presenting with odd infections, tumors, and bizarre blood counts. We had no idea what it was but people were becoming very sick and dying from it. Further studies at that time showed that it was primarily being seen in the male gay population. There was no test for it. Everyone was scared. It brought out the best and the worst in people. Parents sometimes shunned their gay sons with the disease. Many physicians and dentists refused to treat people with the disease. Others talked about it as a plague by God intended to punish this population. It was a horrible time. There were also many who stepped forward and into the center of this disease. Clinics popped up, donations made, and support groups formed. Research soon followed that led to the first drug to treat this disease. It was expensive, had significant side effects, and was not very effective. There was no cure.

Years have passed and we now have very effective medications and we can suppress the viral load in most patients and they can live a normal life. They are not yet cured. I have seen the young people become less alarmed, and in doing so, they let their guard down. Fear is a very effective protective mechanism and they are not afraid anymore. They should be. Likewise, Hepatitis C can now be treated very effectively, and as a result, it is treated like HIV – screened for and treated but not feared as they should be. History has a way of teaching those who are willing to learn. There will be another dangerous virus, and another. Some will be sexually transmitted. Safe sex is the only long-term solution. Either Sandy or her husband thought they were being safe. We have this nasty way of lying to ourselves.

Being honest with our patients is not always easy, but it is always the path to take. A simple way to approach these situations is to ask yourself what you would want if you were this patient.

No Big Deal

Mandy was a healthy twenty-eight-year-old who came to see me for low back pain. It began about two weeks ago when she moved some furniture in her house to clean. It got worse recently after stocking some shelves at work. She had a history of back pain off and on and thought she remembered being told her back was not straight as a child but nothing needed to be done. I considered an X-ray and she told me that she did not have insurance and asked if I could write down the possible relationship with the home lifting, as she wanted to file this as work-related so it could be paid for.

Sally was a forty-five-year-old who was married and I had recently diagnosed her with hypertension. Everyone in her family had it as well. I gave her a medication and had her come back four weeks later to see how it was working. Her pressure was perfect and she felt fine. As I wrote a prescription, she asked if I could write it in her husband's name (who was also my patient), as she did not have insurance yet and he did.

Bob was a fifty-year-old who presented with knee pain. It had hurt off and on for years and he played football in high school and college. X-rays showed some mild degenerative arthritis and his exam was not remarkable. He worked in a local large factory and asked me to fill out a form for a handicap spot at work so he would not have to walk so far in the winter months.

Chuck was a seventeen-year-old who presented with a cold. He was sick the week before and missed school. He is better now but missed an important test last week and needed a note to say he was sick. He did not call last week.

Joe was a sophomore pre-med student and his family members have been my patients for years. He asked me for a prescription for Ritalin. He took his roommate's medication the week before and said he was much clearer for his exam the next day and did well. He felt he must have a form of attention disorder and finals week is coming up.

These are examples of what a physician encounters every day in the office. They all have one thing in common: the obligation of the physician to tell the truth. They also have in common the desire to please your patient. The slippery slope is basically the ethical argument that one action can lead to a series of actions once the first becomes accepted as correct by you. Name-calling could lead to discrimination which could lead to abuse of a segment of the population. This is not theoretical but has been all too real in history and even today. Agreeing to any of the requests above opens the door to accepting that sometimes it is reasonable to be dishonest.

The five examples above are the 'easy visits' in our schedule that are often packed with older patients on many medications. The temptation is to take the easy path to free up time for the complex patients. Such an approach will also please the patients and make it more likely that they will return and refer others. Medicine is a business and customer satisfaction is needed for economic survival.

Mandy hurt her back at home and she told you that. We are obliged to document such and altering a medical record is illegal. What if you did not include the home injury and later get a records release arrives from her employer and a notification that she is filing for workers compensation and disability? If you omitted the facts, you open the door for her claim and know it is fraudulent. The rule is that if it is not in the chart, it did not happen. You must tell her that you will document all she said, including the fact that it got worse at work, but you cannot omit the home injury. If she is upset and never returns, you have lost a patient who did not respect your honesty. No loss.

Sally is a victim of the horrible fact that many people in this country are without health insurance. By writing the prescription in her husband's name, you are saying that he had hypertension and needs the medication. That is a lie and will live on in the medical record. You must tell her that you cannot do that but will find another medication that will work as well and will be cheap. If she is upset with you for your honesty, so be it.

Bob does not deserve a handicap spot based on what you know. Perhaps a specialist may decide he needs one and a referral might be in order. There are people who truly deserve ease of access to buildings every day who find others parked in those spots. The easy way out would be to sign the form. Easy is not often right.

You did not see Chuck when he was sick. You cannot declare that he was too sick to be at school without seeing him. He will not be happy. Life will go on.

Joe was wrong to take another person's medication. He should not get this medication without verification by a specialist that he has the disorder and needs it. This is your time to teach this premed what is essential to being a physician – honesty.

These five encounters only require that we are honest. I created brief scenarios and included all of these in an exercise to screen applicants to medical school. The roles were played out by actors and the responses of the applicants who played the role of the medical student in the sessions done on medical school interview day were recorded. I was surprised by how many took the wrong path. Perhaps it was their way of rebelling against our health insurance system. Perhaps they identified with the patient, or perhaps they wanted to play the role of Robin Hood. Regardless, they took the easy path and were dishonest. Many chose the high road and, I feel, had the foundation upon which could be built a caring and honest physician.

Personalized Medicine

RG came to my office after finding a few bruises on his legs after shoveling snow. They did not hurt and he did not remember bumping anything in his seasonal battle to clear his driveway and sidewalk of snow. RG was a very healthy man in his fifties who I knew socially and had seen as a patient for a well visit at least a year before. He had been feeling well recently except for being a bit more tired than usual and he attributed that to being busier with his work. His exam was normal, but the bruise on his upper leg was large and in an odd location. I ordered some laboratory tests.

That night, I decided to read for a while before going to bed. I took a magazine home from the office now and then to catch up on things. I promised that my office would not be one of those with outdated terrible publications. I had Time, Sports Illustrated, and People. The latter was for the patients who did not have the time to wait and read. This night, I would leaf through Time. On the cover of this issue was one large pill. That was a must read, so I pushed on and found that this article was about a new type of drug that had a very specific action. It had been discovered that in certain types of leukemia, ones that had something called the Philadelphia chromosome, there is a fusion protein of abl with bcr, termed bcr-abl. This new drug targets that enzyme and is used to decrease bcr-abl activity. The drug was known as Imatinib and it was one of the first of this new line of targeted medications. I read on and saw that it was in the last phase of trials before being released.

The next day, the lab work for RG became available and it showed that he had leukemia. I called him personally and told him his blood work was 'off' and asked him to come right down to talk. I do not tell people they have cancer over the phone and I do not have them wait wondering what is so bad that I called and asked them to come down. It was a tough conversation and the fact that he was well, had a young child, and that I knew him made it very difficult. I called one our local cancer specialists and he said to send him over. Where I practiced was rich with excellent physicians, and the city was small enough that I got to know them. Around 1980, the large cities had started to become saturated with physicians and newly trained experts looked for an area that was not far away and one where they could practice at a high level with colleagues. We had an influx of great doctors. I seldom needed to send anyone out of town for anything.

I got a call a few days later from the consultant who had confirmed the diagnosis of leukemia as well as the presence of the Philadelphia chromosome-marker. I mentioned to the oncologist that I had just read the article in Time and asked if he had heard of it. We talked and agreed it might be worth a try to have RG seen – especially since the company was only about two hours away. I got on the phone and was amazingly put right through to the physician doing the trial and he told me to have my patient come up to see him the next day. He was accepted into the trial and given this new targeted medication that was on the cover of Time for free. He took it without side effects and, within a few months, went into a complete remission. Many years later, I left my practice to pursue an academic career elsewhere and he was still in remission and doing well.

In 1976, as a senior in college, I had the opportunity to work at the Argonne National Laboratory with a scientist who was then just starting to look at how to sequence DNA. About ten years ago, I had the good fortune to be at a lunch with James Watson who was at the center of the discovery of the double helix. Now we have completed the human genome project in a rare effort that combined government and private resources. Today, we are using the individual's genes to select therapies on a daily basis. In this short time, I marvel at how rapidly this has come forward. Imagine what the next fifty years will bring?

With all the science that evolves so rapidly, there are associated dilemmas. 'Could-we' versus 'should-we' decisions spark necessary debates in bioethics. The cloning of a sheep that led to Dolly did not usher in human cloning – although I wonder how much of that was the difficulty in doing so rather than the decision not to go in that direction. The breast cancer gene has led to important discussions on what to do with the knowledge of a possibility rather than a certainty. We are now at a stage when in many cases, the DNA of a cancer is more important than the pathology seen with the microscope in determining treatment. We are now exploring genetic information in many other disease treatments. One day, we will all know our complete DNA sequence and it will be used in a computer program to tell us what tests we need as well as what treatments may work best. In the right hands, this may be wonderful. There has always been that fear that this information in the wrong hands might affect promotions at work, health insurance premiums, life insurance, and even knowledge of who one's parents are.

The future of medical ethics is very secure. I hope that we can continue to have honest and meaningful discussions on how to use the knowledge and technology that will certainly be here in the future.

MAID Law

The Medical Aid in Dying Law became effective in New Jersey in August of 2019. I served as chair of the bioethics committee of the medical society of New Jersey in the time leading up to the passage of the law. There were, and are, many wise and caring people on the committee and the discussions were rich and respectful on this topic. The medical society as an organization took a stance opposing the law, as did the American Medical Association and the American College of Physicians.

Upon passage the concern was that floodgates would open with patients wanting to end their lives. There was not. Then came COVID and the conversation was wiped from the headlines for a good reason. I have a medical license in New Jersey but do not have a practice anymore. I teach and consult. For me, to say that I would help a patient within the construct of the law to end their own life would be purely hypothetical. The popular saying is that it is easy to be a hero when there is no war. At present, knowing all I know and having seen over four decades, I feel I would assist my patient if I knew them well and knew all else had been tried. Easy to say…

Death remains mystical. Despite its inevitability, most treat it with fear and physicians often see it as failure. We only began to use death certificates in 1915. It was not considered worthy of recording as to cause prior to that. Death was a part of life. It was only in 1991 that the Patient Self Determination Act was passed, opening the door for patients to make their wishes known at end of life and mandating that providers honor those wishes. Living wills and related documents have been promoted since but are seldom created, as we have a very difficult time getting our arms around what is inevitable.

Assisted suicide has been legalized in other countries since 2002. Oregon first passed the act in 1994 – it took until 2006 to be implemented due to court challenges. In Oregon, over the past decade according to records through 2018, there have been 2,216 scripts issued by providers and used by only 1,459 (65.8%). Many see this as an option and do not take the medications, but feel solace in knowing there is that option. Most who ask for it are over sixty-five years (79.2%), with a median age of seventy-four. Most had cancer (62.5 %)

and were on hospice at the time of death (90.5 %), and most died at home (88.6 %). The new law in our state purposely changed the wording and took suicide out. Most see suicide as the act of someone without capacity and as wrong. Is it? That debate is too long for me to include but I suggest the readers to do so with friends and see what direction the conversation takes.

The New Jersey law is quite rigid and restrictive as well as it should be. Humans are subject to flaws, as history has shown all too well. The very possibility of allowing euthanasia is completely wrong. No human can unilaterally take the life of another. The MAID law clearly states that the person requesting a lethal prescription be documented by two physicians independently, as being in the dying process without the possibility of cure, the person must also be documented as being of sound mind. There is a fifteen-day mandatory wait between the request and physician evaluation and the issuing of the prescription. The patient must request the medications three times in that period and once in writing. There is a forty-eight-hour mandatory period between the pharmacist getting the prescription and filling it. The law assures that this is not an impulsive act and that it is completely controlled by the patient. Finally, the patient must be documented to be able to take the meds without assistance and must do so. This removes many with neuromuscular disorders and others. Again, many argue that such diseases as ALS are such that a patient should be able to avail themselves of MAID but, as of now, legislators have decided to be restrictive to prevent abuse.

Medical organizations state many reasons why they oppose physicians assisting in ending lives. The major one is that they feel such an action is in conflict with the fundamental role of the physician. What is the role of the physician? I have read extensively on this, and the fact that there is no one agreed upon the definition is interesting. What do you want your physician to be for you? Think about that. If our role is to prevent death, then we have clearly failed! If our role is to heal, we often cannot do that. If in the absence of healing, the role is to relieve suffering, then that is a noble goal. But can we always relieve suffering? If so, at what cost? Even the definition of suffering is a large topic within medical ethics. Those dying fear being alone, leaving loved ones behind, and losing control. They fear not only pain but much more than that. There is a way to relieve pain called terminal sedation. This is simply to administer a dose of pain medication that will relieve pain but will render the patient unconscious. It is only done when all else fails and at the request of the patient. They are comforted but left with loved ones who must watch this process not knowing if the end will be in a day or two weeks.

There are many roadblocks to those who want to have the option of MAID. These obstacles include cost of the medications and their availability, finding physicians willing to participate, physically getting back and forth for the necessary evaluation, and letting loved ones know and gaining their support.

I was giving an informational session on MAID to a large group just after it became a law here. An audience member raised their hand and told us all of a relative who recently flew to town to visit her overnight. This man was terminal yet fully functional for these few weeks. He decided to visit those he loved and enjoy those visits. He had sent everyone a notification of his diagnosis and prognosis as well as a date that he had planned to die. He wanted to spare anyone the expense and time of coming but all were invited to a 'goodbye party' the night before if they wanted to come. The party was held and many attended a few weeks later. The chosen loved one was willingly at his side as he took the medications. He died peacefully and happily. He was in control of his death as he was of his life. The audience member allowed all present to know how much she missed him but was grateful to have the wonderful last memories of him that he gave her.

Could this be wrong? Everyone must think about it, talk about it, try to put themselves in the same situation, and make their own decisions. I was told medical ethics is judged in terms of decades of experience and reflection. We shall see…

Chapter 9

My View – Medicine

There are so many wonderful things associates with getting old. The fact that I learn anatomy every day through experiencing a new ache or pain is not one of them. The many experiences over this passage of time cannot help but lend themselves to reflection, comparison, and judgment. This chapter is longer than others, as I have many issues I feel are worthy of comment. I know full well that these are personal opinions and subject to debate. I love debate. To go through life and not have topics that one feels worthy of comment is to go through life without purpose. What follows are some of my views.

A Different Time

My favorite patients were the older physicians who came to me as patients. I was humbled, grateful, and awed by each of them. For some reason, I had quite a few physicians as patients, and caring for this group is interesting. It was not until I got old enough and had issues needing a doctor for myself that I learned how hard it is to walk both sides of that fence.

Dr. T was in his early seventies when I first met him as my patient. I knew of him and the word on the street was that he was good, kind, and respected. He was one of the old school in that he had his office at his home, wore a three-piece suit, never cared what time it was, and treated most ailments with words rather than medications. Patients loved him. His family revered him and it was his son who asked me to take care of him. He did not have a physician and treated himself as most did. Despite knowing how it is impossible to be objective about oneself, most physicians continue to be their own doctor to some extent. He was in the hospital when I met him – in the ICU.

The story is amazing. It was winter and he was out making a house call one evening. He was walking through the snow and developed chest pain. He went into the patient's garage and gave himself a shot of morphine. He then knocked on the door, completed his work with the patient, and asked that they call an ambulance. He was taken to the hospital and treated for an acute myocardial infarction – a diagnosis he had made himself, of course! He did well and I could not help but marvel at this stately man.

A few years went by and I put him on blood pressure medications. He stopped smoking after some battles. At that time, most physicians were smokers – it was considered safe and good for stress! Cholesterol was not yet a modifiable factor. His visits were wonderful and he shared his view of those years of being a doctor before all the tests, medications, and diagnoses. He talked about being paid with a chicken before Medicare! I would not refer to it as the 'good old days' because people died younger, suffered more, and a simple strep throat could kill you. His stories made me appreciate what I now had in my tool chest to help my patients.

173

One day, he called and told me he was having a tear of an aneurysm in his belly. Doctors tend to give diagnoses rather than symptoms and they tend to think they have the worst possible problem. I had him come to the ER by ambulance and I would meet him there. He had diagnosed and treated himself correctly for a heart attack, so why would I doubt him now? With this diagnosis, every second counts! He came and his CT scan showed exactly what he said and we happened to have an excellent surgeon trained by Dr. Debakey in the hospital who came right down and took him to the operating room. He survived (most do not) and went home. I went to see him often there – more for his wealth of tales than for anything I could do for him.

During one visit to his home, his wife, a wonderful lady ten years younger, asked if I could come into another room for a minute. I feared she was ill or Doc was hiding something from me. What she now told me made those options much more preferable. She asked me to give her the meaning of a certain gesture. She had driven to the grocery store, and upon arriving home, their handicap spot in front of her house was occupied. She could not carry the groceries far and had no one to help her. She double-parked and was carrying bags to the porch when a young man in a car drove up behind hers as it was blocking the one-way street. He began to beep at her. She went back to the car and took out another bag of groceries. She then told me that she had given him the finger (as she extended her middle finger up from a closed fist with amazing expertise) but had no idea what she had just told him! I stood there and quickly looked at my options in this uncomfortable moment. Medical school did not cover this topic. I decided it would be best to just be calm and matter-of-fact and explain what this gesture usually implies. She smiled, thanked me, and seemed quite pleased with herself…

I cared for both until their deaths. Decades have passed and I find myself telling my current students what it was like when I began my medical career. They are amazed at the changes in this relatively short period of time as I was with Dr. T's stories. One day, they will do the same for those they teach. That is what life is – a journey that allows us to pass on the past and embrace the future. Thank you, Dr. and Mrs. T.

Alcohol

We walked into the room of Charlie who was a fifty-five-year-old male brought to the emergency room after being found unresponsive. He was known to the hospital and is one often referred to as a 'frequent flyer.' These are the patients who come to the emergency room frequently and become almost our teachers in the way they show us how the human body reacts. Charlie was an alcoholic. We knew he goes into 'DTs' after a few days without alcohol and becomes combative and dangerous to himself or others. This is a withdrawal syndrome, but not all heavy regular drinkers go through this. His was a predictable path and he was given all the usual medications to help him and, at times, he needed to be restrained. I had a new medical student with me this morning and we greeted Charlie together. He was tied down. Charlie went on to tell us that there were spiders all over the wall, his dead mother had come to see him, he was in his home, and last night, a lady with blue hair came in his room and asked him if he wanted any magazine to read – his arms were tied down. We left and my student remarked how sad it was that he was so confused. I reassured her that he was coming out of it because, in fact, an elderly lady visits every room in the evening with a cart and magazines – and her hair had a blue tint!

In the room we visited next was a forty-six-year-old female who was thin, smiling, was nauseated, and had a large, rounded belly and swollen ankles. She went on to tell my student that she had just won the lottery and bought a new home on the mainline. Maggie was homeless and had severe cirrhosis – scarring of the liver. Her story of the lottery is known as confabulation and common in alcoholics. They believe their made-up stories and perhaps it is for the best. Often, their daily reality is one we could not imagine. Her only hope was a liver transplant but she would never stay off alcohol long enough to be a candidate despite all the help we had tried to give her. Soon, her liver would become unable to clear her blood and she would become confused, sedated, and likely bleed to death because her liver could no longer make the proteins to clot her blood.

Bea was an eighty-year-old that had been my patient for nine years. She had osteoporosis and some mild arthritis. She lived alone but had local family. She got her hair done every week and went to church on her own. She was happy with her life, widowed, and she was sharp as a tack. One recent problem was that she had fallen twice. She did not break anything but had bruising. Her daughters wanted her to come and live with her but she refused. They looked for a nice independent living place where she could be more secure. Bea took no medications that would affect her balance and she did not drink, as she would proudly tell me when asked, "Never did." She fell again without losing consciousness and I met her in the emergency room. There were no fractures. Her labs were normal. Her breath smelled like alcohol. She denied drinking. I asked her daughter to go to her home and she found empty and full bottles of vodka in many locations hidden in the house. Bea agreed to go to an inpatient unit for alcoholism and did well. She never came back to see me. Her daughter said it was because she felt badly for lying to me.

I could go on forever with stories about how alcohol has affected the lives of people. This has been true for centuries. Every year, there is a story of an acute, senseless death at a college. We are surrounded by people who are alcoholics and we do not know it. Only those who are seriously socially impacted by the disease become obvious to us. We now know this is an illness and treat it as such in the medical world. The real world still treats those battling alcohol as weak and selfish and shun them. Denial rules the world of the alcoholic. Their children are possibly given the gene that predisposes them to this disease and the daily environment that can foster it. It destroys lives and families. Alcohol is a systemic poison that causes deterioration of almost every organ. It is a common reason for lost jobs. Auto accidents and unfortunately deaths occur daily. Like Bea, many deny using alcohol. All medical providers are taught to ask the question, but patients commonly are too embarrassed to give an honest answer. Many do not see it as a problem.

It seems to me that the issue of alcoholism is no longer front and center in the fight against substance use. The current very real and very deadly issue of narcotic abuse is rightly on center stage. My hope is that we do not lose track of the needs of the alcoholic in their battle with this illness. I honestly do not understand alcoholism, but I accept it as real and as a disease in need of treatment. I do not know what causes hypertension in ninety-five percent of adults. No one does. We still recognize it and treat it. Those who suffer from alcoholism are in our lives daily and cannot be linked to any one element of society. The disease crosses all racial and social lines.

I have been part of interventions for my patients. I have met with other physicians struggling with alcoholism when I was the department chair and gotten them (often mandated them) to treatment. I have had many in recovery and seen the pride in their faces. I have seen some of these slip yet get back up. I do not really know why Alcoholics Anonymous works but know that it does. I have seen affected patients die. I have seen families destroyed. I know there is no easy answer but I also know we all must continue to work to identify and treat those who have this very sad disease.

What Is a Disease?

Learning only happens when we accept the fact that we do not know. Labeling often hinders learning, as it concludes that we know what something is and therefore do not need to further explore it. Human nature is such that we love to label everything. This is especially true in the world of medicine. Oddly, people seem to accept being labeled and even seek it out. They use that label as a search term on the internet and enter worlds less based on facts and more so on similarities and opinions. Their label becomes more real and, at times, it becomes who they are.

Many years ago, people died from a disease called dropsy. This was an accumulation of fluid in the legs such that little drops of clear water would 'leak out' of the skin in the lower legs. Over the years, science was able to explore and discover how and why this happened and often it was due to deterioration in heart muscle function that is now called congestive heart failure. That is yet another term and not a reason to stop exploring. We now can be more specific in terms of exact reasons why the heart muscle is not doing its job. Had we just accepted the term dropsy and stopped there, we would not have the myriad of therapies now available.

Before we discovered insulin, people were dying of a mysterious illness that resulted in thirst, frequent urination, and weight loss. Before we knew of tuberculosis, people would die of consumption. Before we knew of psychiatric illnesses, people were getting holes drilled in their heads to let out the 'evil humors.' The more I study, the more I realize that we now have many more answers to 'how' and few more answers to 'why.'

Over the decades that I have practiced, I have seen the good and bad of labeling. Through categorization of findings, we can study people with similar problems and better determine common ground. We also can explore therapies. Uncertainty and a lack of a confirmatory test often results in mislabeling and submitting a patient to needless and sometime harmful treatments. Beyond that, it deeply affects the person mentally in that they now have a 'disease,' and through the misinformation so abundant online, they now project how their life will be.

Even worse, medicine often labels those whose symptoms we cannot neatly tie together as psychosomatic – a term that is yet another label and lends to that patient being shunned by medical professionals and treated poorly. I have found there are three ways to really learn about a disease: to have it, to know someone well that has it, and to study it. The last is by far the least effective. My illnesses have invariably left me enlightened and more empathic.

I know someone fairly well and have known this person for decades. She became fatigued and developed pain in multiple areas. Her exam showed tenderness but nothing else. Her labs were always normal or showed some slight aberration that resulted in more testing and more dead ends. She went from being highly respected in her field to being unable to work. I sent her everywhere without help. She became depressed, as anyone would who is suffering for so long. We treated the depression without any help in her symptoms. Over time, medicine developed a label for this collection of symptoms that are not diagnosed by testing with another cause: fibromyalgia.

The labeling led to national research on treatments and every time something that might work was published, we tried it. No significant response came. New symptoms lead to more tests and treatment trials lead to false hopes. She battles whatever this is daily and with more courage than I can imagine. She suffers and fights real pain. She cannot predict how the day will be when she wakes and yet moves forward with her life.

One day, we will know what this 'disease' is. Just like the discovery of a test for blood glucose allowed us to define diabetes and the testing for human immunodeficiency virus allowed us to accurately diagnose and now treat HIV disease, one day, we will be able to know what causes fibromyalgia. Our current appropriate concern surrounding narcotics has made the medical profession reticent to treat pain with these drugs. Those with fibromyalgia are caught in the middle – with true pain and no new scar or fracture to ease the discomfort of the physician in using narcotics for this disease.

Once again, we must admit that we do not know. This is hard. We do not know what this disease is. Hopefully, we will soon find out and this will lead to successful treatments. In the meantime, we must continue to care for the patients who suffer and this caring begins with empathy. This disease is real and it can be devastating. Is it not a disease without a defining test or finding? We must be humble and accept that applying a label solves nothing.

CME

Continuing Medical Education (CME) is required by every physician in this country to maintain a license. Few outside of medicine know this. Few other professions mandate that their members keep up with the latest knowledge and advances. The education is tracked in terms of the number of hours (credit hours) spent in learning activities. The mandate is for fifty hours per year or one hundred and fifty every three years. A significant portion of this time must be recorded as Category One. This means that the learning activity has met the standards of the Accreditation Council for Graduate Medical Education. I served on a state board for ACGME and know that the criteria are taken very seriously and institutions that sponsor ACGME activities are reviewed thoroughly. The subject matter required can vary by state and by specialty but the number of hours is consistent. A portion of the required total can be met using Category Two programs such as reading specialty journals or teaching.

One of my favorite roles was as director of medical education – a position I held for over twenty years at a teaching hospital. I oversaw three one-hour sessions each week for physicians – all of which were certified as Category One. One session began as a cardiac conference and developed into a general case conference. Physicians would present their best cases and show the findings. I would moderate and elicit the input of the physicians present as the case progressed. The final diagnosis was revealed followed by a brief overview of that disease. We did two cases in each session. Physicians of all specialties attended and it was very popular. We were able to learn through others rather than just through cases we saw ourselves. Another conference was our Tumor Board and this was held every Thursday at noon. The hospital provided lunch for all sessions and this was no small expense, as there were always sixty or more present. The hospital valued education and perhaps realized that these doctors who came and benefitted from the sessions were more likely to send their patients. Two cases were presented in each Tumor Board session and the surgeons, the oncologists, the radiation therapists, the pathologists, and the support staff all came.

The third weekly session was Grand Rounds. This was a traditional type of educational program that reviewed a disease, a treatment, or another topic physicians needed to be current on, such as epidemiology, patient safety, or a new regulation. It was for one hour and done by an expert. Each program had to be reviewed independently by the CME committee of the hospital and approved as qualified for Category-One credit. It was interesting to see the evolution of this process over time and I am very proud of the focus and effort of the ACGME in this regard.

It was common for pharmaceutical companies to sponsor Category-One programs not that long ago. They would provide the speaker and the topic, pay for the meal, and even do the promotion. The presentations were usually excellent and the speakers entertaining. It became clear that these programs were as much about promotion of a product as they were about education and changes were made to the approval process. The speaker's relationship to the company promoting the program had to be disclosed in advance. The company was unable to provide food and soon was unable to be present for the talk. The availability of such programs waned and I was proud to see that our local experts rose to the occasion and did these on their own without support.

I recall the development and marketing of the first statin drug used to treat cholesterol elevations. It was in the 1980s and the true relationship of high levels of cholesterol to blockages in arteries was only beginning to be understood. The tools we had to treat were limited and not very effective. Bob came to my office all revved up about a new drug his company had developed that was just approved for use. Bob was always revved up. He was born to be a salesman. He knew what he was talking about and was able to convey his message clearly. He was a genuinely nice man who believed in what he was doing. I never saw pharmacy reps in my office but did in the medical education role. I agreed to bring in a speaker through Bob and it was a major name from a respected university hospital who gave the best one-hour presentation I ever heard. The audience was packed that day, since everyone wanted to know more about this new miracle drug. We all left knowing about the biochemistry, the physiology, and pharmacology of the topic.

What if this was done now and it was disclosed that the speaker was sponsored by the company that makes the drug? Would the listeners be skeptical and not believe facts? If it was not disclosed, would they believe 'fake news' and use the product based on misinformation? Both happen and, as a result, it is now very difficult to have a Category-One educational session that is sponsored directly by a pharmaceutical company. I think this is a good thing and I am proud of how this was handled from an ethical standpoint. This difficulty in directly impacting physician behavior has also expanded to hospitals deciding not to have representatives in their buildings, written rules surrounding how physicians can interact with these companies, and full disclosure of any conflict by all physicians, etc. Perhaps this evolution is why the companies have turned to direct marketing to patients.

There was a time when physicians went on cruises and vacations disguised as educational trips. That time has passed for the most part. There are negative impacts of this evolution as well. In the years I spent running the CME process, I saw physicians interact directly before and after the meetings. They spoke about patients and it was wonderful to see. They heard the questions and suggestions of their colleagues during each presentation. They got to know who knew what. It created a community of learners. The medical residents present were able to observe seasoned physicians invested in continued learning. This has all but disappeared, as most CME is now done online. The learning is isolated, dry, and devoid of the immediate reviews that live group presentations offer. Physicians continue to learn and keep up to date, but they have drifted away from what I feel is the ideal way to learn – an interactive session with peers.

Teens

The Lost Boys are characters from J. M. Barrie's play Peter Pan. They are boys who fall out of their prams when the nurse is looking the other way and if they are not claimed in seven days, they are sent far away to the 'Neverland' where Peter Pan is their captain. There are no 'lost girls' because, as Peter explains, girls are far too clever to fall out of their prams.

Teenagers are often those lost in the healthcare system. This became very apparent when my three children were all teens at the same time. It was a time in my life that went well, and ended well, but one that I am happy is now history. My wife and I spoke of having a family literally forty-eight hours after we met. Insane, but true! As time went on and she was a pediatric nurse and I became an internist, I thought we had all bases covered and could deal with our children at a level few could match. I was thrown into the harsh reality that I had never learned anything about the medical problems and the care of adolescents. Pediatric stopped around the age of thirteen when most children have little needs and even less desire to go to the pediatric office. Adult medicine started mostly after the age of twenty with few exceptions. That left the land of the 'lost boys.'

When I went to school, there was almost no exposure to outpatient medicine. Where I went to school, there was no exposure to family medicine. It is this field that had the expertise needed to care for teens. I had no tools to use for this task. It was around this same time when HMOs were on the rise and already a menace to physicians. They required us to take on a 'panel' of patients and the age dipped below where I had any comfort. I attacked this dilemma the way I always do – I scheduled myself to do a Grand Rounds' presentation on Adolescent Medicine at my hospital. I have found that in doing so, I would have to become 'expert' in that area and there are few greater incentives than that of not looking foolish in front of colleagues.

There was a student who went to medical school with me that was very bright. She always seemed calm and was just a really nice person. I remembered that she became interested in adolescent medicine when she did her internal medicine residency and went on to get an advanced degree in anthropology – studying human development. She became one of the early experts in adolescent health. This has now become a recognized specialty. I then learned that she was part of a team giving a course on this subject not far from where I lived. I signed up and it was one of the best educational experiences in my life. I returned, ready to teach and ready to treat.

Teenagers' needs are totally different than other age groups. Our youth's longevity and health is impacted not by their genes, hypertension, and diabetes but by behaviors. They are in the midst of exploring and trying to become independent. They make mistakes, costly mistakes. They learn more by doing than by listening. Peer pressure is enormous. They have major needs in our healthcare system and these needs are not being met. Everything we might be uncomfortable talking about must be front and center when seeing a teen. We must be nonjudgmental and not try to talk in their language. We must be ourselves but open to all that they say. Once we jump in and criticize, the dialog ends. The time to teach and guide must come at the end with a plan that is tailored to them. We must see them alone in the office – when a parent is present, the dialog is screened and therefore less useful. We should assume they are doing what we wish they were not and find out. Alcohol, drugs, sex, thoughts of depression, bullying, and abuse must all be put on the table. I have seen teens deny having unprotected sex but jump at the offer of a screening test for HIV and Hepatitis C. Actions are louder than words. They are addicted to their phone and share way too freely in social media. They have eating disorders and fears that make no sense. We need to open those doors and help them through this dangerous stage of life. They will be the ones caring for us one day.

I learned that the usual interview and physical exam rules do not work in teens. The past history is usually not important. The family history of illness is a bomb that will not explode in them for decades. Their review of systems is empty. Their meds, allergies, and immunizations are either in the electronic record or neatly delivered by the parent. The key is an extensive social history. The physical exam is limited to the vital signs done by the nurses and perhaps a peak at a skin lesion or acne that they are concerned about. Doing a complete exam is much more likely to prevent them from ever coming back than to reveal anything. The driver's exam and sports physical get them in the door and that time should be devoted to their real health risks. The sports exam rightly includes a cardiac evaluation. I soon learned that when I saw a teen, I should not use that as my 'quick visit' to give more time to my octogenarian next on the schedule. What I do for this teen can add seventy years to their life.

I taught the introductory course in clinical medicine at our medical school. I loved that role. I wanted all of my students to learn about adolescent health because they had it close in their rearview mirror. Many would rightly ague that teen behavior has extended in the early twenties as parents become more protective and they stay in school longer rather than those experiencing real life. I frequently used structured scenarios using standardized patients to see how my students utilized their knowledge in patient encounters. These were videotaped and students could critique themselves. I got the idea of creating one for the adolescent health topic. This needed to be real to work.

I called the local high school and asked for the name of the person who ran the theater group at the school. We met and she arranged for me to come back and meet with the officers of the theater club. I taught them how to be standardized patients and they loved every minute of it. The case was one that was full of dangerous behaviors and I wondered if it was too exaggerated and if it made them uncomfortable. They all replied in unison that the case was very real and on target. I was pleased but also dismayed. After some practices, they were ready. I went into the room to talk to them before the sessions began and asked them if they knew the script and were ready to play out the role. One asked me if they could do anything they wanted, and I replied no – this had to be reproducible. Their look made me wonder, so I asked what they had in mind. They said they wanted to start the session by texting on their phone when the student entered and ignoring them! Perfect! The script was changed and the sessions began.

The students loved it and we all learned so much. One medical student went up to the actor and took the phone out of her hand and put it on the other side of the room. The actor then refused to answer a single question until they got their phone back. They ad-libbed and it was perfect. We do not give our adolescents the credit they deserve. They will make it through these years but can do so more safely with our help.

Fear

I was a medical student doing a clinical rotation at the Pennsylvania Hospital in Philadelphia in 1976. We had admitted an otherwise healthy young man with a cough, a fever, and pneumonia. He had no known exposures or risks. Despite antibiotics he worsened and needed to be put on a ventilator. Over the course of the next two days, others were admitted with the same clinical picture. The common thread was that they had all been at the American Legion convention at the Bellevue-Stratford Hotel in Philadelphia. This was a contagious infection and very serious. We did not have the antibiotics now available. It was an unknown infectious agent at the time. From the four thousand who were at the American Legion event in Philadelphia, about two hundred and fifty cases were identified, which resulted in between twenty-nine and thirty-four deaths. What struck me was that in spite of the fear and real risk, caregivers all did what was needed. They marched in to fight the disease rather than avoiding self-risk. This goes beyond pay. This is the spirit of a profession dedicated to caring for others. We were afraid to leave the hospital for fear we would bring this home. Over time, the organism was identified as legionella pneumophila – named after the convention. It was determined that this bacterium came from the ventilation system in the hotel. It is now routinely identified as a cause of upper respiratory infections and easily treated.

I was fortunate enough to do my residency in internal medicine at the Pennsylvania Hospital from 1977 through 1980. It was a special time in my life. I had incredible teaching and worked with amazing residents. It is the latter who really teach you. I recall cases being admitted who had odd infections and odd white blood cell counts. They were young gay men who lived locally. We had no clue what this was. It was not until the 1984 when the causative virus, HIV, was identified by French and American scientists. Companies then could begin to develop a test for antibodies produced in response to the virus. The first test used blood and was known as an enzyme-linked immunosorbent assay or ELISA test. It was approved for use on March 2, 1985. The disease caused by this HIV virus was known as AIDS and impacted medical history.

It showed the best and worst of the medical profession and I was able to see this firsthand.

In the late 1980s, Adam became a new patient in my practice. He was thirty-five and had been well until the past months. He was gay and living with his partner for the past year. He worked and was from the area. He did not use drugs or drink. He was outgoing and easy to like. Having trained at a hospital located in the section of a city well known for being the popular location for the gay community, I had come to know and appreciate this group. It was clear to me that Adam was gay and clear to him that he could talk openly with me about it. He had been feeling tired and the initial exam was normal and the blood test showed a mild anemia. I asked his permission to do a test for HIV and he agreed. He was positive. At the time, there was no treatment and he knew well what his future would be. HIV at the time was a death sentence. The death would be one of more than medical issues. To many, it was one of isolation, being shamed for no reason, and being rejected by family at times. It was horrible.

The disease became more common. We were not allowed to test people without their permission. This fear of being positive led to people not knowing they were infected and further spread of the disease. I saw surgeons who refused to operate on anyone who was HIV positive. I knew of dentists who would not accept these patients. I heard of horrific rhetoric surrounding the infection as only a disease of gay men, and progress in funding for research and treatment might have been slowed because of this. Fear of the unknown has always been difficult for humans. Soon, the disease was recognized as a world health crisis. It became obvious that this was also spread by heterosexual contact. It was shown to be a high-risk disease for intravenous drug users who shared needles. It was recognized to be possibly spread by blood transfusions. All those at that time who suffered from a bleeding disorder known as hemophilia were treated with concentrated pooled blood products to get the clotting factor needed – and all became HIV positive. I had one such patient in my practice. People were dying everywhere.

A drug known as Azidothymidine (AZT), a compound first synthesized in 1964 as an anti-cancer drug, was among the drugs initially tested to treat HIV. AZT was shown to improve the immune function of AIDS patients. In 1987, it became the first drug approved by the U.S. FDA for treatment of the disease. I sent Adam to a local specialist and he began AZT. Infectious disease specialists are in short supply now and were then. It is a specialty poorly reimbursed and sorely needed. The pills were large and Adam had to take them often and they made him very nauseated. They did not work. I watched Adam waste away and die. His partner was with him throughout. His family was not. He was one of over forty thousand AIDS-related deaths in the U.S. in 1995.

Thanks to science, we can now effectively treat HIV. We cannot yet cure it. Prevention remains the key and that involves honesty, education, and some fear. My concern is that AIDS does not result in the level of fear it once did and people are drifting back to unprotected sex. Clean needle exchange is effective and yet opposed by many who think it promotes IV drug use – it does not. Free medications have taken down the barrier to treatment and it is now the rule to recommend HIV testing to all on a regular basis. This disease is still prevalent. We have found how to combat it. History tells us that another infectious agent will evolve and result in our next outbreak. How will we react as a society? How will the profession of medicine respond?

Calories

I went to one of the top medical schools in the country and was taught by many considered 'gods' in their field. Lectures went into detail and allowed us to understand the newest in science and medicine. The clinical years were rich and made us look at all aspects of the body and understand its maladies. I spent countless hours studying and memorizing. I do not remember a single lecture on nutrition, and doubt there was one. Four decades later, we have not made a significant impact in this important subject area.

God bless my primary-care physician. I had a private practice for years and was honored to care for physicians, lawyers, professors, and many well-known people. I always tried to treat everyone the same but that is not always possible. The physician patient is a unique beast and I am sure I am such to my doctor. We tend to self-diagnose (how could we not), minimize, maximize, delay, overreact – and often all at the same time! My doctor is wise beyond his years, lets this all play out, and then calmly tells me what to do and explains it to me. I trust him. I need him.

He recently told me I had pre-diabetes. It was no surprise. My father and grandfather both were diabetic. I eat horribly. (There, I said it.) I hate exercise. If left alone with a box of candy, it would certainly hold me hostage and win. With all my knowledge and my love for life and desire to live long and well, why can't I just eat better and exercise? The fact is that we have no clue what drives each of us. Why are some people skinny and eat all the time? We all know people like that and secretly hate them! There are also those who eat little and exercise and gain weight. I have no clue. We say it is their metabolism – but that is honestly not understood. One day, we will know more, but right now, we need to stop judging and accept our ignorance.

There are a few observations I have made that keep me humble. There is a disease called Prader-Willi syndrome (PWS) that is a genetic disorder due to loss of function of specific genes. Beginning in childhood, the person becomes constantly hungry, which often leads to obesity and type-two diabetes. I have seen one case of this and the patient would sneak into other patients' rooms and steal the food. Parents had to put locks on the refrigerator and cabinets.

Life is a bell-shaped curve. Could some cases of obesity be due to a genetic defect in the satiety center? Even if that is the case, the treatment is still to consume less and that is difficult for some people.

For severe obesity, I have had a number of patients have bariatric surgery and I am a major fan of this approach. It changes lives. There are various procedures and a great deal published on this. My patients have told me that they no longer crave food but are not nauseated. They get filled up easily. They cannot eat large quantities. Most lose over hundred pounds in the first year and some go back to near ideal body weight. The diabetes and hypertension go away. The sleep apnea is cured. I find it curious that they do not continue to lose weight and become underweight. Is it just a matter of the volume of food or is there some other metabolic or endocrine pathway that is altered by the surgery? Not every procedure is a success.

Doctors tell people to diet. I suspect some actually know what that means but likely very few. I have no clue. We say to eat less carbs and it makes us feel like we know something. What is too much? What are the alternatives? I have been around long enough to see so many fad diets come and go. To give a patient a diet is merely to transfer the reason for failure to them. Motivational interviewing is the hot new approach and I believe in it. What motivates us? It varies from person to person and from day to day. If I knew more about the science of nutrition without knowing more about each person's personal life situation, would I really help? I think not. I do know that making a patient feel guilty never works. They already do.

So, we wrap up our patient visit telling the patient they are overweight and need to lose some weight. We tell them their blood sugar is a bit on the high side. We tell them to cut down on carbs and try to walk every day vigorously. We did our job as their physician. Wrong. They will leave our office and go back to their life that may involve the inability to take time to cook healthy meals and much less afford or understand the ingredients. They will go back to living in a neighborhood where exercise is dangerous. Telling someone to diet is no different than telling someone to sleep more, drink less, stop smoking, and be happy. Everyone wants all those things and everyone really tries hard. There is something we just do not understand that is at play. I suggest we never give up and be supportive and focus on small wins.

I will try to cut out the candy. On a good day, I will succeed. On a bad day, I will fail. I will try to exercise. On a day when the weather is nice and I feel good and I have time, I will succeed. On a rainy day or a day I need to work longer, I will fail. I am lucky and have the time, have a safe place to walk, have people to encourage me, and have mostly really good days – and yet, the candy sometimes wins. As physicians, we need to work to make people's lives better and the rest will follow.

911

I was at the nurses' station in the hospital completing a consult on the computer. The elevator door opened and out walked two emergency responders. They had gotten a call from the patient in Room 362 who said she was having trouble breathing. The nurse rightly asked him to repeat exactly why he was there, as it made no sense. He made it clear that they had gotten a 911 call from a lady in that room and their protocol was such that they had to respond. All went into the room to find that this patient was indeed having trouble breathing. She was in a private room, her call button had fallen to the floor, she could not yell due to her breathing, and she tried the phone a few times but kept getting voice prompts that she did not understand. She knew how to dial 911! It obviously worked…

One of my visions of hell is being in a room full of phones and the only way to get out is to get someone to answer the call. Everyone has had their blood pressure go up dealing with this insulting way we are dealt with when we want to communicate. My mother worked on a switchboard – yes, they really existed. A person would call, say who they wanted to talk to, and they were connected to that person. Now we call and get an IQ test. Imagine if you are older, have a poor short-term memory, have trouble with your hearing and most of all, do not speak English. I think we should reward anyone who actually gets through to what destination they need the first try with a free gift.

I recently called the emergency room about a patient. I first learned that I could not call directly. I then counted thirty-three rings until the hospital operator picked up after a voice menu that included, "If you are a physician wishing to talk to one of our physicians, press five." I needed to talk to a nurse but that was not a menu item, so I improvised! I was then connected and began my presentation – only to be cut off for unknown reasons. I actually went through this twice more. I know everyone reading this has had multiple similar experiences. I think there is a room full of geniuses designing ways to make people give up when they place a call and major executives who can tell you exactly how much money is saved by not having one of their employees actually talk to someone. Yes, this is another of my rants. No, I do not feel better now that I have said it!

Getting the nerve to actually call a doctor for an appointment is very difficult for many people. They have had a problem and have had time to contemplate what they might have. They sometimes go on the internet and come away with a vast number of diagnoses that will put them in their grave quickly and cost a fortune. Magically, many think that they if they do not go to the doctor, this problem will not be found and, for some odd reason, will go away on its own. This is often the case actually. But for some, the delay in discovery and treatment could be a matter of life and death. The fifty-three-year-old with heartburn may actually have a heart disease and die. The thirty-three-year-old with a lump may actually have a cancer and the delay could allow it to spread and make its treatment more difficult. If they call and cannot get through, they might say this is some way nature is telling them to forget about it. Human beings lie to themselves all the time.

We can send people into outer space. We have Disney! I just cannot accept that we cannot devise a way for people to connect with who they need to speak to easily – a way around barriers of language, hearing, cognition, and fear. There are patients who do not even have a phone – that message that they will call you back between thirty and sixty minutes does not work when standing in the cold using a pay phone. Many people do not have internet access or computer skills – sending an email or looking up information is not possible for them. The gap between those rich and the poor is getting wider each day. It is not just that people cannot afford healthcare – it is that many cannot even access it. I see people daily who take a cab or a bus just to be able to walk into the office to talk to someone because it is easier than calling. The system is so very broken.

A physician who is one of my mentors (Yes, mentoring is important at any age.) is still working and loves it. He gives his cellphone number to all of his patients. He tells me that patients seldom call because they do not want to bother him. He feels he has a special bond with all of his patients and they respect that relationship. I did the same for many of my patients and never felt that it was abused. That will not work in the current system of care in which most patients are now cared for by a team rather than one physician. I honestly do not see a clear answer to this problem but I hope everyone recognizes that this is a serious problem in this country. Admitting to a problem is the first step to a solution.

Alternative

CF was a thirty-seven-year-old college professor who came into my practice having recently moved to the area to establish care. She was single and healthy. The interview was uncomplicated, as she had no prior surgeries or illnesses. She had no allergies or history of family illnesses. She did yoga daily, did not drink or smoke, and occasionally used marijuana. When I ask about medications, I always make it a point to ask if my patient takes anything for their health, by prescription or over the counter, in liquid or pill form. I have found that many do not include vitamins, etc. as medications. With this question, I hit the jackpot! She took out a list and proudly told me that she took barley, beta-sitosterol, black tea, blond psyllium, calcium, cocoa, cod liver oil, coenzyme Q10, fish oil, folic acid, garlic, green tea, and Vitamin C. Moving on, I went through a review of systems which is a standard set of questions. She told me she had back pain a few years ago cured with acupuncture, a rash she had treated with magnet therapy, and used Qigong when fatigued. This would not be my usual patient.

As I have gotten older, I have become less certain of many things. What I would have once called 'nuts' and made a strong stance in stating that there was no scientific proof that a certain herb works, I now choose not to argue on such points. I teach every day and read about the nuances of biochemistry, pharmacology, genetics, and molecular biology. I love it. There is so much more that is known now about how our body works than we knew when I went to medical school. There is also so much we do not yet know. Many of the chemicals we now use in prescription form were originally herbs used for centuries. These medications have undergone extensive trials to prove that they are more effective than a placebo. They have also been studied to determine their side effects, in whom and at what dose they might be dangerous, and with what other drugs they interact. This is not true in the case of much of what is referred to as alternative or complimentary medicine.

Current estimates in this country are that thirty-eight percent of adults and ten percent of children use some form of alternative medicine. I am always skeptical of such statistics, as they often use a definition of a term that will result in the greatest yield. For example, if the use of one multivitamin daily would result in all those individuals being put in the category of those who use alternative medicine, then that group is inflated. On the other hand, since we currently have no good scientific evidence that a multivitamin is of any use in someone who is well and consumes a healthy diet, then perhaps they should be placed in the category. There are many 'therapies' that are used daily and a great deal of money is expended on them by very bright people. Intelligence is not wisdom.

'Alternative' and 'complimentary' medicines are two terms that often used interchangeably. There are people diagnosed with cancer who refuse or delay proven treatments with chemotherapy and radiation to pursue claimed remedies in this country and beyond. These are not alternatives. They might be complimentary if proven treatment is used along with them, and studies have proven that there will not be an untoward reaction with the combination. I have had patients pursue such paths and I make it clear that I strongly disagree and make this known in their medical record. I also send them a letter stating my position clearly. It is so frustrating to see competent people make incompetent decisions. I let them know that I will be here for them if they change their mind or if they have a problem. The few who have decided against proven treatment have never returned to my practice. I hope they found a way to proven treatment for their malignancy before it was too late.

Meetings

I am at that stage in my life where I find myself reflecting on what I might do if I had the opportunity to do parts of my life over again. I must first state that there is very little that I would change. This is a true attestation to how fortunate I have been over the years. The one thing in retrospect that I would change was the time I have spent in meetings. I currently spend little or no time in meetings and this has given me a healthy perspective. It is probably analogous to the statement that your head does not start hurting until you stop banging it against the wall.

Meetings tend to last the exact number of minutes for which they are scheduled. I have been at many meetings that could have, and should have, lasted much less time. When a meeting is ended early, the participant is given a gift. The first part of that gift is simply not having to be at the meeting anymore. The second part is unexpected time to accomplish things that really need to be done. Those who run meetings should be able to gauge when the intended task is done and end the meeting immediately.

The agendas of meetings should be stuck to, or else never made known. Each should have a time allotted to the items. Those at the meeting then have something to look forward to other than the end of the meeting.

Often, the meeting is used to get consensus on issues or elicit opinions. These are worth the time but only if the input is respected and, when possible, acted on. Throwing out what seems like great suggestions and having them ignored or shot down is extremely effective in silencing that participant for future meetings. What could be worthwhile ideas for the organization going forward are lost.

When a meeting is used to deliver news such as a new hire or initiative, it seems worthwhile, but often, such information could be better delivered in a memo.

Those who run meetings should undergo training. There is a skill and an art to having a meeting be effective. Organizations should add up the total amount of hours in a year employees spend at meetings and then look at their hourly salary. Meetings are a major capital investment and every effort should be made to assure they are worth the investment of time and money by all.

Over decades, I have also been at many retreats. These are very long meetings, often run by outside consultants, meant to reinvigorate 'the team.' They are exhausting and I cannot remember one where everyone went back to doing what they did differently.

This was a rant. Much like the meetings that have taken up countless hours of my life, this rant has left me feeling no better about this topic. I will move on and be thankful that meetings are no longer a part of my life!

What Would You Do?

Physicians now run-in fear when asked this question. Students are taught in medical school to avoid a reply. I wonder what would happen if my electrician or plumber came to my house and told me what they thought was wrong and if asked what they would do if they had the same issue replied that it was up to me and their opinion is not to be sought. The physician is now practicing in a world where autonomy rules and paternalism is an evil from the past. Autonomy means that the patient decides what their wishes are and we are only to give them the information to do so. Paternalism basically means that the physician makes the decision for the patient. What if the patient decides to ask for us to decide for them? Isn't that the ultimate demonstration of their trust in us? This is a difficult topic at this point in the evolution of the doctor-patient relationship.

On numerous occasions, I have cared for patients who asked for my opinion. The scenarios are broad and reasonable when the terminal cancer patient is offered a trial of a new chemotherapy regimen, when a patient is told that their cataracts are ready for surgery, or when a patient is given the option of mastectomy or radiation for a breast cancer. This happened all the time. The fact is that we honestly do not know what we would decide if in that exact situation, but we have a pretty good idea. That opinion is heavily weighted with the experiences we have had in our personal lives and may have little applicability to our patient. The more we know the patient, the more likely we can properly guide them, but the opportunity to know patients well over years is fading unfortunately. If a patient is offered a test or treatment by another physician that we know to be useless, not indicated, or dangerous, we are obliged to inform the patient of our opinion.

Today's physician often uses guidelines in decision-making. There are many of these and they are very useful because medicine is constantly evolving. We are expected to practice what is known as evidence-based medicine – that is to employ the most recent knowledge that has been subjected to research and expert opinion. These guidelines are available electronically and often even as part of the electronic medical record. Your doctor may even be looking at one when you go to the office visit and wonder why she is looking at that computer screen instead of actually looking at you when you are talking! It is impossible to keep all of this information readily available in one's memory.

The reality is that the information these treatment suggestions are based on is also the subject of evolution. I have seen so many things that were once considered a standard of practice be proven to be ineffective or even dangerous. Doctors used to suggest that their patients smoke to calm their nerves! There was a time not long ago when half a ward in a hospital was filled with patients having prostate surgery for a benign disease. Today, this rarely happens. When I began my practice, the normal cholesterol was anything under three hundred! Hormone-replacement therapy for menopausal women will always be debated. The list is endless and it always will be. Scientific knowledge is constantly expanding and will bring us new treatments, new tests, and insights into all we are currently doing. This is wonderful and should be embraced.

The most recent guideline published regarding whether or not to offer a PSA (Prostate Specific Antigen) blood test to a male patient as part of screening for prostate cancer is remarkable in that it turns the clock back. The guideline states that we should encourage the patient to have an open discussion with us about the risks and benefits of the test. That means that we are supposed to fully educate the patient in the time allotted about the test's false positive and false negative rate of detecting cancer, the possible risks of further tests needed if it is elevated, and the various options of treatment vs. non-treatment! If the physician can accomplish this without totally confusing, if not terrifying the patient, it is highly likely that will cause the patient to ask what we would do – back to square one!

One could reply that if you were their age, with their family history, with their fears about cancer, with their insurance, and with their personal feelings about what role sexual performance plays in your life, you probably would _____. The current concerns about liability might even stipulate that the patient sign a release to protect you if the opinion you gave might not work as planned. (I have not seen this done but would not be surprised if it is.) There are physicians who simply say they would get the blood test because of a fear that if they said not to and the patient went to another physician who suggested it and the test came back elevated and led to a diagnosis of prostate cancer, they might get sued for failure to diagnose. The fact that this cancer could stay dormant until the patient died of something else would not be reassuring. The fact that the treatment guidelines would be shown in court and state that the physician was to have a discussion and not give an opinion would not help support the physician's decision.

It is a hard time to be a physician. There is so much information and it is evolving faster than we can keep up with. Patients should be informed and encouraged to make their own healthcare decisions, but this is so difficult in the allotted time of an office visit and so easily made impossible by the misinformation now available on the internet. Physicians really do care deeply about their patients and work hard to heal, prevent, and console. I will always encourage my patients to do what is proven to be worthwhile and be honest when there are options that are now not clear. Knowing what we do not know is what makes a good physician. Seeking out new knowledge and information that will help us care for our patients is what makes a great physician.

The Number

Student G.M. is a 228. When she came to our school, she was a thirty-one. When she went to college, she was a 1270. Now we must make this number a caring, feeling person who has the empathy to impact the lives of patients for decades. Makes sense, right? Wrong!

I played basketball in college – intramural. I was not bad, but I was not good. I liked to go to the gym when stressed and work it out. The medical school entrance test was three days away and I needed a game of basketball. Coming down from a rebound, I twisted my ankle on another student's sneaker. It hurt badly. I knew something was wrong more than a simple sprain. I was taken to the nearby hospital and admitted with a badly torn ankle ligament. It had bled up into my calf which became very swollen. I was on ice, elevation, rest, and pain meds. It was forty-eight hours until the exam and I would be fine. These days, there are many dates to pick from to take the entrance test. In the seventies, there were two, and if you waited until the second, your chances of getting an interview to a medical school went down significantly. I was taking that test as scheduled.

The night before, the doctor came by and I convinced him I was good to go. He knew about the exam and I agreed to not walk. Crutches were ordered and I practiced with them. The morning came and my friends picked me up and carried me to the car and then into the exam. I was given a pain medication before I left the hospital. All good! The test began and the first section was verbal reasoning where I had to match a word with another. I had no idea that the pain med was a narcotic and found myself matching syllables within each word. I was high as a kite! I reached the end of the page as the proctor warned us there was five minutes left for this part. I smiled knowing I was now ahead of schedule, as I had finished all of the words. I figured I would take a glance at the next section, so I turned the page to discover there were two more pages of these damn words! I should have panicked... but I was on drugs. I smiled and quickly circled 'C' for all the remaining words and moved on.

I did horribly on the exam. The University of Pennsylvania School of Medicine gave me an interview anyway. They saw me as more than a number and took my entire application, my road in life, and my interview into account. I was accepted. I went on to prove that they made a great choice in the decades since then. This would not happen today. I served as the associate dean for admissions for over seven years at my current school and have come to know the admissions' process very well. I chaired the admissions' process in my past school. It is now not unusual to get six thousand applications for a school with hundred seats to offer. To do this, we reduce applicants to a number they score on the national entrance exam, the MCAT, and if one does not get that number or above, nothing else matters. I honestly would not have gotten into medical school today.

When I was a dean in admissions, I decided to have every student who came for an interview for our school participate in two standardized patient (SP) interviews. This means they interview an actor playing the role of a patient in a clinical setting and these interviews were graded for the ability to empathize and for professionalism. No medical knowledge was required. The results were interesting. Those that did well in the traditional interview usually did well in the SP sessions. This was no surprise – people who relate well to others do so in many situations. What was a surprise was that those with the highest MCAT scores tended to do the worst in the SP process. It seems that we need people in our profession who are both smart and relate well to patients. People are not a number.

The SAT is the first in these series of limbo sticks to pass through. I honestly do not remember taking that exam and have no idea what my score was. It did not matter. I was good in school and it was a certainty I would get in, and go to, our local college. Today, parents go crazy getting their children in the best kindergarten so they can do well and get in the best grade school, and so on. It becomes a treadmill that speeds up constantly and puts our youth in grave danger. Stress, depression, eating disorders, and even suicide are increasing in the current climate of how to climb the ladder of 'success.' When did success not encompass happiness? Our country has lost its focus on what our youth really needs. The path to the Ivy's now starts at the age of five – insane!

Once in medical school, the next number is the United States Medical Licensing Exam (USMLE). Students take this at the end of their second and third year and after graduation. When I took these, they were pass/fail in nature. The scores were not important. If you studied and did well in medical school, it was a given that you would pass these exams. The USMLE has become a monster that sucks the life out of medical students. The score has become critical. Students focus on preparing for the first exam at least one year in advance and buy more than one product to prepare and these cost hundreds of dollars. By the second year of medical school, many students stop being active in other activities as they immerse themselves in USMLE prep. They can become reclusive. Anxiety levels go off the scales. When schools present topics such as professionalism, humanism, empathy, and others, they receive less than warm acceptance, as they assume these are not on the test. Medical students now often do not go to lectures. They listen to and watch lectures from home, as they can fast-forward and save time. When they are at lecture, they almost always have their laptops open and are doing USMLE prep. It is very discouraging to those who are present.

The score determines their future. Without a certain score, a student who dreams of being a dermatologist or orthopedic surgeon can kiss their chances goodbye. It is devastating. Those with lower scores are forced to apply to less competitive specialties. Those who fail the exam do not move forward. There are many who pass the exam and yet do not get a residency position because their score was lower than others who applied in the same field. Students can finish medical school and graduate, and pile up enormous debt, only to be left without the opportunity to do a residency. Without this, they cannot practice medicine. Imagine being a student facing these obstacles! The incidence of stress-related issues and burnout are rising every year. And why? Why did the test score not matter in the past? The top students got the best residencies. That was defined by the grades, the school they attended, their letters of recommendation, their dean's letter, and other factors such as research done. We still have all of those to work with. Why should one test taken on one day define a person's future?

No one ever asked me for my SAT, MCAT, or USMLE score in the decades of seeing patients. They came back to see me and sent friends and relatives to me because I was a very good doctor. I listened. I cared. I made sure they understood. I did all I could to help them. They felt that. I enjoyed each visit and hope they did as well. I have been very fortunate to have had an amazing career filled with opportunities and filled with many tales. Today, that student who sprained their ankle in one second of their lives would be denied that opportunity.

Chapter 10

An Education

Life is an education and there is no summer off or spring break. Classes are never over and it is truly pass/fail. The faculty is enormous. Besides books, videos, and observations, there is a never-ending stream of three-dimensional instruction. Human interaction has been a source of my most profound discoveries. Everyone is interesting and nothing is without meaning. I thank everyone who has helped me to be me and encourage everyone to continue assisting in my education. I have discovered that age can satisfy but it can also result in a hunger for more.

Communication

The medical student had just presented her case to me perfectly. I was precepting in a student-run free clinic at an academic medical center. The patient was a thirty-six-year-old female who had all of the symptoms of depression. The physical examination that was presented to me was free of abnormalities. This young lady was a mother of two, single, and unemployed. She had no history of alcohol or drug use. She came to the clinic complaining of a lack of energy and difficulty caring for her children.

I had just left a primary-care practice that I had established thirty years earlier. I saw patients every day in the office and in the hospital and truly loved patient care. I enjoyed teaching and had purposely surrounded myself with medical students throughout my career. The opportunity to be involved in medical school administration on a fulltime basis had just come my way. I moved to a different state and I knew that I would have to find some way to utilize my bedside skills in a teaching capacity. The free clinic was an ideal opportunity in that I could both teach and give back to a community in need.

I had come to enjoy the opportunity to care for people with psychiatric issues. My years in practice had allowed me to see how psychiatric illness impacts not only the patient but those around them. The community I worked in did not have many psychiatrists and I came to understand mood disorders well. Over the thirty years, I had been able to see a remarkable improvement in the medications available to treat depression. Having a patient come to see you who is unable to function and unable to enjoy life and watching them return to a happy and productive individual is amazing. A part of the reason I had chosen primary care is that I enjoyed interacting with people and felt comfortable talking to them. The nonverbal clues reflecting a patient's true state of mind had become a very useful tool.

After the presentation by the student, I got up and confidently went to see the patient with the student. I was ready to demonstrate my seasoned history-taking abilities and show the importance of watching for the nonverbal cues while conversing. I knocked on the door, as I did with every patient encounter, as I see this as a sign of respect. What happened at that moment humbled me in a way that I could never have imagined. This patient greeted me in Spanish. She did not speak English and the student had not relayed this key piece of information. The students who work at this clinic on a regular basis know that it is commonplace for the patients not to speak English and had assumed that I knew that.

My many years of experience communicating with the patient suffering from depression suddenly became useless. There was a translator phone in the room and all of my questions and verbal interactions with this patient were through a third party and delayed in such a way that it became difficult to understand the feelings behind the words. I felt both humbled and embarrassed by the reality that my years of experience were significantly less valuable when I could not directly communicate with the patient. The interview took significantly longer and we were able to accomplish what needed to be done but the interaction lacked the level of empathy and humanity that I came to know as critical in the treatment of patients suffering with emotional disorders.

I quickly came to realize that there is an enormous segment of our population which is deprived of the level of healthcare that those without language barriers experience on a daily basis. If I had learned the Spanish language, I could have treated this young lady the way she deserved to be treated. It has been well documented that over eighty percent of medical diagnoses are made by history-taking alone. When this history must be done in the less-than-optimal circumstances, diagnoses will be missed, counseling diminished, and the treatment often is less effective. The other reality is that healthcare in this country is timed. We only have a certain amount of time for each encounter, and if we exceed that time, the result is that another patient's time is cut short. Communicating with the patient using an interpreter takes significantly more time. Providers are appropriately educated to avoid using family members as interpreters whenever possible. The reasons for this are many and include the breakdown of confidentiality that is critical in the doctor-patient relationship.

Over the course of the past few years, I have learned that the ability to communicate in Spanish would only break down the wall in the treatment of one group of patients. People of all backgrounds, speaking many languages, come for healthcare every day in this country. They deserve the same level of care as those who speak English. We must further improve the availability of translators as well as find a way to allow for longer patient encounters when the individual does not speak English.

All my years of experience and the many skills in communicating with patients were of little use to me on that day.

The Interview

I practiced for many years in a city with three hospitals close to one another. The physicians were talented and kept up to date. My patients got excellent care from my colleagues and all the hospitals. The nursing was amazing. The area was deteriorating in terms of the economy. Most physicians were in solo practice or small groups. Few were employed. Reimbursement for the same care was lower than a city one hour away. The cost of practice was increasing faster than the ability to pay for it through the insurance payments. The electronic medical record added another major cost in more than just dollars. It was a tough time and place for physicians.

The doctors were dedicated to this community and came up with a plan to start a medical school. This was quite rare at the time and a formidable task. I had been driving over two hours every other week to teach at a medical school in a major city at the time. I would make rounds early in the morning, answer calls in the car both ways, go back to the hospital upon return, and was exhausted. But I loved it! A medical school where I worked was perfect! I jumped on board and shared the enthusiasm of many. This was a community project and it was contagious. I was given the opportunity to develop and teach the clinical course in the first year. I was also asked if I would chair the admissions committee. I knew nothing about it, so of course I said yes.

The world of medical school admissions is one of trying to sort out great from terrific, trying to find a match for your school, and trying to predict who would be a solid physician years down the line. Sorting through applications became an art. It is humbling. These young women and men manage to have amazing metrics while doing volunteer work, research, and numerous other things. Their stories are engaging. In addition to the metrics, the application is detailed and the work sorting through it is all daunting. They also submit a secondary application created by each school with specific questions to answer.

The number of available interviews is quite limited. Only a small percentage of those who apply are offered an interview. I was able to create the interview process and took great pride in doing so. This would be an experience that would impress the applicant, give them the information needed, and allow us to meet the person behind the application. The actual interview for medical school is a high-stakes dance and honestly can be a matter of luck as much as attributes. Did what the applicant write happen to resonate with the interviewer? Were the personalities compatible? It is very much like speed-dating. I looked forward to every interview.

I read through the entire application of the young man I was about to interview and I was very impressed – top metrics, very active in college activities, leadership, shadowing, and research including a paper. He had strong letters of recommendation. He was the first to go to college in his family. He was born in America but both parents were immigrants. It appeared that he was on track to becoming a physician. He entered the room and shook my hand firmly. He was well dressed and polite.

In interviewing, there are usually a set of stock questions that everyone is asked to allow for fair comparisons. The answers given may lead to additional areas of discussion. There is always time to ask specific questions based on the application or responses given. I like people. I like to talk to people. This would be fun. My first question was met with a simple 'yes' with no expansion of the answer. The interaction was totally one-sided. It was the worst interview I had ever had with an applicant. My next question was direct: "Why are you doing such a poor job with this interview?"

This poor young man was not expecting this question and the answer will always be with me. He told me that his parents' dream was that he would be a doctor in America. They sacrificed everything to pave the way to this day. They always introduced him to others from when he was a child as 'our future doctor.' He learned in his shadowing experiences that medicine was not the path for him. He knew it would break his parents' heart if he told them, so his plan was to apply to schools and hopefully not get an interview. Now that he had, he intended to make sure he would be rejected. They might accept his failure but he knew they would not accept his choice.

My heart sank. I tried to convince him to tell them but knew deep down that he was right. My three children shine in my eyes every day. I support their choices the way my parents supported mine. We are honest with one another even when I might often prefer not to hear something. There have certainly been times when I have been disappointed – that is part of being a parent. There has never been a time I did not love and believe in them. This talented man made me so sad. He will not be a physician but I hope he has found the path that brings him joy and the love of family.

Journals

Keeping up to date in the field of medicine is daunting. General medical journals began at the end of the eighteenth century and specialist medical journals at the beginning of the twentieth century, followed by subspecialty journals later in that century. The growth in scientific and medical journals was exponential until a decade or so ago when it slowed for economic reasons. Now, due to electronic publishing, it is again on the rise. Those who publish do not get paid but there is increasing pressure to publish, as it is often linked to promotion within academic institutions. Most recently, there are journals that require authors to pay to have their work published. Not all publications are rigidly reviewed before being put forward. The end result of all of this is that it is impossible to keep up with all this information and equally difficult to know the value of what one reads.

Arthritis is a common problem. Patients suffer daily from this illness and treatments can be difficult. The common arthritis medications, referred to as non-steroidal anti-inflammatory drugs (NSAID), often cause irritation of the stomach. A new drug hit the market after approval by the FDA in 1999 called Vioxx. It was in a category called prostaglandin inhibitors. It reduced inflammation and therefore joint pain, but unlike NSAIDs, it did not cause significant stomach issues. It was widely promoted and studies published on it were positive. I used it for my patients and found that it was effective and indeed was much easier on the stomach.

In 2004, the drug was withdrawn from the market. In that time, an estimated twenty million people had taken the drug. Studies were showing that it might be causing heart attacks, especially in those who had been on it for many months. I had prescribed it. I had patients who had heart attacks and strokes. Could it be possible that I had done this to them? I looked through the charts of all who had an event and were on the drug. This was not easy before electronic medical records. No one stood out, as those on the medication were not on it for long were in the age group at risk for cardiovascular events and had other reasons. It did not stop me from wondering if this medication could have played a role. It also made us wonder how such a serious side effect was not discovered prior to the approval of the medication.

The initial trials looked at the effect of the medication on pain and compared it to other drugs for arthritis. They looked at gastrointestinal side effects. They did not specifically look at differences in cardiovascular events. If you are driving and decide to see how many red cars are on the road, the mind begins to not register the number of blue cars on the road. They studied five thousand and four hundred patients. In 1999, another study began of over eight thousand patients and began to show a question surrounding cardiac events. By December, there was a question on the safety of the drug – after approval by the FDA. The committee overseeing the studies by the company decided to continue the study and not make the concern known to the public. In 2000, the New England Journal of Medicine (NEJM) published a study based on the data given and did not question the safety of the drug based on a statistical review. The NEJM is considered by all to be highly prestigious and – what we call refereed – carefully looked at and critiqued before publication. I read it routinely.

Another review of the Vioxx data later showed that three patients who had heart attacks were not included in the initial data given. Statistics are such that only three excluded patients changed the outcome and now indicated that the drug could have played a role in causing heart attacks. More studied followed and led to the removal of the drug from the market. What happened?

The chair of the committee that oversaw the studies surrounding Vioxx at the pharmaceutical company has been investigated. The question was whether Vioxx was bad for the heart or whether the comparison drug was actually protective for the heart. It was a reasonable question but should not have prevented a red flag of concern to be raised. This chair had over $72,000 in stock in the company. It was also found that his contract was renewed in early 2000 after the possible concerns were known. The company eventually lost 4.85 billion dollars as a result of this drug. There might have been over eighty thousand heart attacks caused by the drug and thirty-eight thousand deaths.

This is a terrible story and honestly quite unusual. The safeguards surrounding medications are many and the process rigorous. There are times when drugs that are needed are held up in the approval process and rightly so. Those who work for the FDA, and those who make these drugs, are ethical and well intentioned. The process, however, is one that involves human beings and we have proven over centuries that we are a flawed species. Conflicts of interest can sway judgment. There is a major emphasis on this topic now and rightly so. Anyone who presents any medical information must note if they have any potential or real conflicts. All who are employed as physicians must note such conflicts annually. Even the appearance of a conflict is wrong. Bright people can justify almost anything to themselves.

We need new drugs to help our patients. It seems like less are being developed. Most new drugs are either what we call 'me to' drugs – another similar chemical used for the same disease, or very expensive drugs aimed at illnesses that are not common. We need new antibiotics, as the bugs are becoming resistant to all we have right now. We need better ways to treat pain. Issues such as Vioxx might result in companies being unwilling to sink money into new therapies. We cannot let this happen. Our patients need innovation and those who innovate are always best served by adhering to high ethical standards.

Why Learn?

Julie's father called while I was having supper. There is something that happens when you are a physician that defies all explanation. It is that moment when you just feel that something is wrong before there are any facts to support it. I returned the call and he went on to say that he felt Julie was having an anxiety attack or a reaction to her medications. She was feeling pins and needles in her arms and legs and felt dizzy when she tried to sit up. I immediately got in the car and headed to her house.

Those drives to see a patient you are worried about seem to go by in minutes because you are constantly thinking of the possible diagnoses. I remembered when Julie first became my patient at the age of sixteen. I seldom took a new patient at this age but I knew her well for the past seven years through her father who was my patient. When I first saw her, she had already had fourteen surgeries and six joint replacements. She was well until the age of nine when she developed juvenile rheumatoid arthritis.

Her disease was relentless, as her joints swelled and her ligaments tightened while her body and mind fought back after each surgery. The length of her arms and legs became arrested while the disease and surgeries affected her growth plates. She went to specialists throughout the east coast. Her parents dedicated their lives to her while her sister and brother sacrificed time with their parents. The driving force was love disguised as 'you do what you have to do.'

It was a time before biologics and disease-modifying agents. Finding artificial joints the right size was difficult. There were periods of time when Julie was without pain but these were few and far between. In those times, and even in the painful crises, this family managed to have life go on. As physicians, we are gifted to see people show amazing courage every day. We meet people who manage to bring the best out of everyone. Julie was such a person. Her classmates in high school carried her up the stairs. She went to the prom. She went to college. Her courage was contagious. She abhorred sympathy.

Medical school does not create physicians – patients do. They make facts stick in our brains and they push us to know more. Julie taught me about joints, ligaments, and experimental surgery and she taught me about pain. I knew juvenile rheumatoid arthritis – I owed it to Julie. I had read that a synovial joint exists between the top of C2 and the arch of C1. The disease can therefore produce C1-2 instability by eroding the dens or the transverse ligament. This creates an increase of the space between the two bone surfaces on the lateral cervical X-ray. This can result in a slip of one vertebra on the other and the odontoid process pushed on the brainstem and the vertebral arteries. I also knew that this could cause the tingling she was feeling and the postural weakness.

I arrived at her home. My exam showed bilateral decreased sensation and decreased reflexes everywhere. I called an ambulance and called her insurance company to find out what center would be covered for emergency cervical surgery ⌐not something we could do locally. Cervical stabilization, a stat CT which showed what I feared, and a helicopter ride to another state all happened quickly. She was put in halo traction that same night and had surgery two days later. All deficits resolved.

Julie finished graduate school – masters in counseling. In medicine, we all have patients that make all the work we are now doing worthwhile. They make learning not just fun but the key to other people's survival. My time in medical school taught me the anatomy of the spine, the dermatomes, and muscle and joint function. I built on this with each patient I saw. It all became easy when I stopped studying for the test and started learning for my future patients. I encourage my students to do the same.

Tomorrow's Physician

Holistic review is a process used in many medical schools to help focus on the characteristics of medical school applicants to allow for the interview and subsequent selection of candidates. I thought this was a great method and I had representatives from the Association of American Medical Colleges (AAMC) come to our school to educate administration and members of the admissions committee on the process even before our first cycle of selection. The process is mission-driven. I was the associate dean for admissions at that time at our school. Over the following years, I went to other schools to educate them and was honored to serve on the Holistic Review Board of the AAMC. The central message is that each school can and should identify what attributes of an applicant they considered most important for their school. Not all schools are the same. All must teach the same content but how they do so and what is outside of the curriculum varies significantly. The best thing about holistic review is that it is bidirectional – the candidate can better determine what school matches their mission.

Metrics remain extremely important in medical schools. I have yet to see that a score in a standardized test can predict who will be a great physician. Yet, schools continue to raise that bar. The score makes it easier to narrow down the list of applicants as a computer can really do it. There is also the matter of all medical schools needing their students to pass exams to move forward to residency, and these scores even determine what residency programs will even consider a given student. Entrance exams can often predict who will do well in these subsequent exams. I have never heard of a patient telling a friend about their doctor's test score when suggesting they go to see them. Patients do not feel a test score. They recognize intrinsic abilities such as empathy, professionalism, and humanism. They care that the correct diagnosis and treatment is made and that they recovered. Will this change in the years ahead?

Computers will continue to evolve. Artificial intelligence is already the subject of many publications. Science-fiction from decades ago predicted this. There is no doubt that in the future, physicians will rely heavily on tools to search data and integrate this data. Algorithms are now used extensively in treatment decisions. These are already being incorporated into the electronic medical record. The rate of growth of new knowledge in science and medicine is at a pace that the human brain cannot keep up with. Tomorrow's physician will not need to 'know everything' because they cannot and because all that knowledge will be easily available. The physician of tomorrow will need to know how to access information more than recall it. Will the current exams be replaced by a demonstration that a person can access information that is relevant quickly? I hope so. Once this is realized, perhaps we can go back to focusing on the interpersonal skills of those who apply to medical school. Perhaps, we can better identify the doctor who is best at the bedside.

Many doctors also need to have excellent hand-eye coordination, such as surgeons. Many need to be visually gifted, such as radiologists and dermatologists. In this country, students usually come to medical school after college, graduate schools, or a time working. They usually do not know what type of physician they want to be. Finding ways to select for attributes for the above in the medical school selection process would not be useful. In residency selection, I feel these will become more important than the scores in standardized tests in the years ahead.

When I was asked to create an admissions process for our school, I carefully looked at our mission and asked for the input of many. I had a dean who lived by our mission and was very supportive of the holistic approach. I wanted to find strong students who felt comfortable working with patients in a socially challenged city. Looking at the experiences of these applicants enabled us to identify those who had worked with the underserved. I wanted to find students who embraced diversity. I needed to identify students who would pass the exams but found through studies done by the AAMC that even students with lower metrics finished medical school and went into residency training at a very high percentage. We were going to have our students begin seeing patients in their first year, and therefore, I wanted to find a way to identify who would be best able to do so.

I had worked with standardized patients (SPs) over the years and loved it. When I went to medical school, we learned on real patients. That means we made mistakes with real patients – that is just wrong. Today, students practice and learn how to do the interview and how to do the physical exam on actors trained to play the role of the patient in a reproducible way. They are also trained to assess and give feedback. It is an ideal way to learn. We also now have sophisticated devices that allow students to learn procedures that are very realistic. Medical schools have dedicated the space and money needed for this type of education. Our new school had a beautiful space in which they had created twelve fully equipped exam rooms that were identical to a typical physician's office. These were also outfitted to allow for all interactions in these rooms to be captured audio-visually. This allowed for assessment and feedback.

The idea came to me that we could use this space in our admissions' process. The MCAT (medical college assessment test) would assess cognitive skills. The traditional interview would assess interpersonal skills and allow for specific questions surrounding application content. Perhaps an SP encounter could identify students who were capable at the bedside and able to manage an ethical dilemma in real time. Schools at the time were beginning to use an MMI (multiple mini-interviews) process in their admission process. These schools did not do the traditional interviews but evaluated students based upon a series of gradable performances. A few were using something similar to an SP encounter. I developed a number of scenarios and trained the actors. Each encounter would have a real-life dilemma. Each interview would be brief and graded on the ability to begin a conversation, be professional, and react appropriately to a dilemma. Every student would do two of these and they would be different actors and scripts. No scenario required any prior knowledge of medicine or bedside experience. I rotated the cases per interview day so that a student would not know the case in advance through a prior interviewee.

The admissions committee would be given the scores but told that these scores could not yet be heavily weighted, as we did not know yet how they might predict future behavior. We carefully analyzed the results and compared them to the admissions decisions made during the regular interview and to their MCAT score. We found that those with the highest scores on the SP encountered were the most likely to be recommended for acceptance without those offering these assessments, knowing how the applicant had performed in the SP sessions. We also found no correlation of the MCAT with SP performance in general. There was a tendency for those with the highest MCAT scores to do less well in the SP encounters.

Assessment of the data is ongoing. I am not longer overseeing the admissions' process and have happily gone back to the role of a teacher. This SP aspect of the interview is no longer being used. It will be interesting to see if the prior SP scores on interview day will be able to shed any light onto whether we can predict, before accepting a candidate, who might be more likely to go into a primary-care field, who will do well in the SP encounters during medical school and the mandatory clinical skills exam in the fourth year, and who demonstrates empathy and humanism while in medical school. Likewise, those schools using the MMI process are examining and sharing their data. Hopefully as the computers supplant the need for our brains to consume and process all knowledge, we will identify the best way to select for tomorrow's physicians.

I have been on the other side of the bed and want my physician to be more than an MCAT score.

Burnout

Stress is often defined as your body's way of responding to any kind of demand or threat. Stress isn't always bad. In small doses, it is well known that it can help you perform under pressure and motivate you to do your best. But beyond a certain point, stress stops being helpful and starts causing major damage to your health, your mood, your productivity, your relationships, and your quality of life. Recently, this has been referred to as burnout.

The life of a physician is stressful. I am not going to say that our lives are more stressful than others, since I have not walked in their shoes. I find it interesting that I see physicians react quite differently to the same stressors. Some do not seem to be stressed at all, and when asked, they often reply that they see no benefit from it, so they choose not to be stressed. That is unusual and perhaps a bit difficult to believe. I have felt stress throughout my life and only twice did it seem severe. Both times were very reasonable and gave me the opportunity to feel the pressure my colleagues feel on a daily basis. Recently, there has been a focus on stress, wellness, and physician burnout and the impact it has on the practice of medicine and the personal lives of those affected. This is a very good thing and hopefully will lead to useful tools for all of us.

I am not burned out and never have been. I have been very fortunate to be able to say that. I love what I do and look forward to every day as I have over the past forty years of being a doctor. Why? The great thing about getting older is the ability to reflect. One thing I have learned over time is that no physician is perfect, as we are afflicted with the weight of being human. I have had days when I was not as good at my work as other days. I have had things go wrong and rarely was it because I would have done something different in retrospect. Life happens and none of us can predict everything. We do our best and try to move on. I know physicians who cannot move on and carry every negative outcome with them every day until it destroys them.

I tell my students to be more than a physician, and by doing so, they will be a better physician. I was a son. I am a brother, a husband, a father, a grandfather, and an uncle. I was a basketball and baseball coach, and a PTA

218

president. I am a carpenter, a Lionel collector, and a gardener, and I love TV. At various points in my career, I have been a researcher, an administrator, an educator, and a mentor. I am a very good friend and through those friendships I have gained support, laughter, and countless facts. I say all of this because on any given day, when I close my eyes to sleep, I can reflect on what went well that day and end my day on a high note. There is a zero statistical chance that I screwed up in every part of my world mentioned above! Those who choose to be only a doctor will have many days that lead to focusing on the one thing that did not go as planned and record that day as a loss. We are so driven to be right that we fixate on when we are not and push away the countless good things done that day. This is a proven recipe for burnout.

From early on, physicians face the worst in life and are expected to reach out and try our best regardless of the circumstances. Medical students who work with cadavers experience a horrific reality when they are honest about it. That same student seeing a terrible auto accident, a child born lifeless, a person being told they have cancer, a homeless person with pneumonia, or a battered child is told never to react; they must keep that face looking the same. I heard a wonderful physician describe this as learning to lock your feelings in a chest and leave them there. It works. Soon, we start doing the same with events in our own lives. In time we can no longer show emotion and sometimes look down on those that do. Physicians' marriages can fall apart. The resultant isolation can result in substance use, depression, early retirement, and even suicide. Everyone needs someone. People must be able to talk about their feelings and learn to deal with them other than locking them away. Doctors are hesitant to get psychiatric help. They have a hard time accepting they are human.

I do not see the stressors our physician workforce face becoming less in the future. I try to avoid sports analogies but it is fair to say that we are expected to hit a homerun every time we are at the plate. A single is acceptable. A base on balls puts us on base but without applause. When we strike out, and we often do, there is no one saying 'nice try' or looking at our batting average. That patient is often angry, unforgiving, and potentially planning a lawsuit. Medicine is a very demanding game. Newer physicians enter practice with absurd debt. We all live a life that is planned out every fifteen minutes months in advance. Our charts are reviewed and critiqued. We must battle the computer while trying to make a relationship with our patient.

Physicians now, more than ever, need to develop a plan to avoid burnout. We owe this to every patient we see, as many studies have proven beyond any doubt that care provided by a doctor who is experiencing burnout is inferior. We owe it to our families. Physicians frequently express regrets later in life for the many important moments they missed with their children. A dying patient does not lament not making more money.

There are activities that I have found to keep my ship steady and on a good course. One is teaching. I encourage everyone, not just physicians, to teach. It is literally paying it forward. When I am with students and residents (and in my current roles that is most of the time), I light up. I get to pass on what I know and they make it clear that I know much more than I thought. They teach me every day as well. Another is working with those many patients who have not had the good fortune I have had. They make me grateful and humble. The last is telling stories. We all have them to tell and I love telling them. Stories allow us to reflect and learn again. They make dinner conversations come alive. They can immortalize those many little moments that make our lives worth living.

The White Coat

I was working with the medical residents in clinic. It is a clinic that serves our community and takes only Medicaid and Medicare patients. Internists and Internal Medicine Residents see patients there daily and it is very busy. My role this day was to have each patient the resident saw presented to me. I review their charts in advance of the presentation and look at their medications, problem list, and recent lab work. At times, I check other notes in the chart to prepare me to guide and teach the resident who will be presenting the case to me. If it is a first-year resident or a difficult case, I go to see the patient with the resident after they see them first. The pace is fast. The patients are often complex with their medical issues always trumped by their social problems. The residents are wonderful with them and I am impressed by their patience and concern for each patient they see. TJ was presented to me by a first-year resident.

This lady in her twenties came as instructed after being seen in our ER two days before. She had taken a few Tylenol with codeine pills in a suicide attempt. She was assessed as safe to go home with her boyfriend of a few years and see us. It is very difficult to get an appointment with psychiatry quickly. There is a national shortage in this field for many reasons. It does not have the glitz and glamour of some of the specialties. The patients seen day after day have so many issues, and immediate gratification is not part of this field for the provider. The salary is not that of those who do procedures. As a result of all of this, few medical school graduates decide to enter this field. Primary care is usually asked to assume the care of these patients.

The first-year resident was new to me and new to the world of being a medical resident. After so many years of mentoring and teaching in medicine, one gets to know who is going to be good. She was mature, calm, caring, and very bright. She was going to be very good. She presented TJ to me and told me that all the patient did was stare forward and would not answer a single question. She asked the boyfriend to leave (a very wise thing to do) but still got no response. She could not assess the patient as a result. It was now my turn. We walked into the room together and I introduced myself to the patient with a smile and a light touch on her shoulder. I shook the hand of the boyfriend and sat down with them with the resident present. I asked some simple questions and got one-word answers. The door to her had opened a bit. I then asked her if she was able to sleep. She turned her head and looked me in the eyes for the first time and said no. That door had just opened a bit more to let me in. I touched her again and asked what was keeping her from sleeping and she answered, "The voices." I knew now that this was likely an acute schizophrenic episode and knew what to do next. I told her that I know other people who have had the same experience, that it is very real and very frightening, but that we could help her. The door then opened wide and we had a conversation. I spoke with both and all the pieces fell into place. I even got her to laugh at a simple attempt at humor used as a test. This was not depression.

Why did TJ open herself to me and not this wonderful resident? Was it my age (wearing my six decades obviously), my demeanor, my effect, the way I sat and touched her and included her boyfriend, or was it that I was wearing a white coat? I do not know. I am old-fashioned and I feel that a doctor should both look and act professional at all times. I feel we owe that to our patients and I also feel it elicits a different response from our patients. This is not true in the field of pediatrics, as the white coat might scare children at times. I feel this coat tells the patient who I am, and I am very proud of being a doctor. The long white coat says that I am 'a real doctor.'

Things have changed, however, and I likely will have to accept that the days of the white coat are starting to fade away. There are a few studies questioning whether they might actually contribute to the spread of infections. The same thing is being said of long sleeves in general and of ties. Now ties I could do without, although I still wear one at work every day. I realize that the first thing I do when I get in the car after work is to take off the tie and loosen the top button of my shirt. If I am that uncomfortable with a tie, why wear it? Wouldn't people work better and think better if they are comfortable. Perhaps this next generation has it right: be comfortable at work. I had to wear a tie in elementary school and a coat and tie in high school – the joy of a catholic school education. Those wounds are deep and perhaps are why I still dress as I do. If it allowed TJ to open up to me, it was worth it. I do not approve of residents wearing scrubs when seeing patients in the office. Students should look professional at all times; the less you know, the more important it is that you look the part! White coats, if worn, should be clean and ironed. A wrinkled and/or dirty coat, shirt, or blouse tells the patient you do not care how you look. It conveys that you do not care about them. It is not professional.

The White Coat Ceremony has become an important event in medical schools. I never had such an occasion when I went to medical school. We were told we needed to wear a short white lab coat when with patients and to get one at the bookstore. Now it is a major event attended by loved ones with pictures galore! There is a speaker who gives a moving and memorable address focused on humanism and the meaning of the profession. The Arnold Gold Foundation has provided support for these events and has highlighted the importance of humanism in medical education and in medical practice. Now many have the ceremony during orientation – before a student has even seen a patient or taken a class. Personally, I see the white coat as something to be earned and not just given as a part of paying tuition. I feel that every day I spend with patients, I am earning the right to wear this coat – the signal that I am a physician.

Yes, I am old-fashioned! If that means that I value professionalism, how I appear to others, and that I am honored to be a physician, then I welcome being called that. If my appearance played any role in getting TJ to open up and be treated, the white coat served its purpose. I might be wrong but I feel that the mystique of medicine, the way we are with patients, the way we create an atmosphere when with patients, and the way we genuinely care are as therapeutic as anything else we might do in the encounter.

Medical History

One of the great gifts of getting older is that it allows one to see the past while envisioning the future. Medical students and residents, as well as young physicians, do not have the same perspective. In some ways, this is good, as they are more likely to try things that have failed and less likely to be skeptical. I find myself marveling at what has happened in the science of medicine in such a short period of time. I also realize that these changes are exponential and that science-fiction now, as it has been, gives us a look into the future. I also fear that these advances might lead to unethical decisions, further extrapolating costs, a widening gap between the rich and the poor, and the further erosion of the doctor-patient relationship. We must all work to combat this, and we are better equipped when we study the past.

In the 1800s, an Australian physician named Ignaz Philipp Semmelweis made an observation that women who were in the rooms next to a woman with what was then called puerperal fever were getting the illness. He postulated that caregivers were carrying it from one patient to another. He was ridiculed. In 1960, Pasteur discovered that there were bacteria in the air! Rubber gloves were not worn in patient care until 1889. That was not long ago.

Medication discovery and development is only a factor in medical care over the past century. Prior to that, physicians prognosticated, consoled, and occasionally drained an abscess, but had little else to do. Dreser developed aspirin in 1899 and today it remains an incredible medication used to treat pain and fever as well as to prevent heart attacks. Insulin was made available in limited use on 1921. That means that less than one hundred years ago, diabetics died of their illness. The war sparked many medical discoveries and brought us penicillin in 1941. Over the past few decades, there has been an explosion in the pharmaceutical industry and not always for the good. Most new medications are known as 'me-to' drugs – almost identical to an existing med and developed mostly to get a share of the market. There has actually been, in my opinion, a decreased rate in the development of newer agents mostly due to the high cost of research and development as well as the enormous liability.

Death certificates were not even used one hundred years ago. In 1956, we saw the first external defibrillator, and in 1958, the use of cardiopulmonary resuscitation. That means that until a little over fifty years ago, when you died, you died. Technology took off and science-fiction became real. In 1967, we saw the first heart transplant. In 1980, the end of smallpox was announced. In 1973, the CT scan allowed us to see inside the brain and body without surgery. In 1984, the MRI scan made those images amazingly accurate.

We are now seeing the development of medications to treat viral infections and people with HIV can live fairly normal lives and people with Hepatitis C can be cured. A new family of medications known as immunologicals can target specific pathways and offer treatment options for cancer and many other diseases. 'Precision medicine' is the hot topic now.

With the rapid advances in the 1970s, I saw that we began to think we could cure anything. We ended up keeping patients alive and on tubes for long periods of time with the hope that tomorrow there would be an answer. Slowly, patients began to speak up and battle for quality of life. Court cases ensued and such interventions as mechanical ventilation and tube feedings became accepted as extraordinary measures that could be refused or discontinued at the expressed wish of the patient or their surrogate. In 1991, the Patient Self Determination Act was passed that mandated that healthcare institutions ask each patient about their wishes and offered instructions surrounding living wills and durable power of attorney for health affairs documents. It became reasonable to talk openly about wishes at the end of life. Autonomy, the right of a patient with capacity to make their own healthcare decisions, became the rule.

The electronic medical record became the norm. It was touted as a tool that would allow the provider (what used to be called the physician, nurse, etc. in a better time) to access all records at any time and in any place. It would allow for safer medication management and tracking. It would save time. While the EMR has been wonderful in many ways, it is not what it was proposed to be. There are many EMRs and they do not 'speak' with each other. It is no easier to get records when a patient is in an emergency room at another institution that uses a different EMR than it used to be. They might save time but the cost is steep. Younger physicians adapt well, but the EMR has become a major reason for early retirement.

These advances are at a cost that is more than financial. The advances in imaging have resulted in physicians being less skilled at the physical exam. The EMR has built an enormous wall between the patient and the provider – with empathy declining and physicians trying hard to maintain the therapeutic relationship. Drug prices have risen to the point where many cannot afford them. The use of hospitalists has resulted in the patient not having access to their regular doctor when they need them most. If we do not fight the above, we risk losing the very foundation of medicine.

I am encouraged by what I am now seeing. Medical schools, such as the one where I now work, have created entities that focus on humanism, ethics, and professionalism. These topics are being woven into the curriculum. Burnout is now accepted as real and preventable, and schools are dedicating resources to this, as are our residency programs. Compassion has recently been scientifically proven to improve care as well as decrease costs. Medical education knows the value of caring and is making sure that it remains the foundation of medical care.

The Student Clinic

Lucy was a new patient. She was twenty-eight and had a five-year-old son. She lived with her mother and they had all recently moved to America. Lucy did not have health insurance and lived in the city where the free clinic I precept at is located. She made an appointment.

The current estimate of people in this country who do not have health insurance is staggering. There is very real concern that the number will continue to increase. The fact that the current program that assures that all children have access to healthcare is in jeopardy is a black mark on our nation. There may be more people being employed but more employers are now hiring people less than full-time to avoid providing health insurance. If we are the greatest country in the world, it certainly is not on display in how we deal with those in need.

Lucy had felt ill for about four weeks. She felt warm but had not checked her temperature. She had noted a lump in her upper left chest above her clavicle bone. It was not tender. Her left shoulder area felt achy. She had lost some weight and was tired. She was not coughing or sick in any other way. Her past history was unremarkable. She came to this country about six months ago.

Our clinic is financially supported by our hospital and staffed by the medical school. Medical students begin 'working' in the clinic early in their first year. They take on the roles of scheduler, social worker, nurse, provider, and more. They truly run the clinic and organize all tasks under the supervision of physicians assigned to that role. They often serve as interpreters, they follow up with test results, and they provide longitudinal care; they see their patient on subsequent visits. In this clinic, there are also pharmacists at the PhD level who have pharmacy students with them. These students see the patient first and take a medication history. They then accompany the medical students and are part of the overall patient assessment.

If medications are needed, they are dispensed without cost and the students, overseen by the pharmacists, count the pills and label the bottles – in Spanish if needed. The cost of the medications is assumed by the hospital. There are limited medications and all are generic but it is usually sufficient to provide high-quality care. If the patient needs a medication that we do not have, the students find a way to get it for the patient either at a low cost through a local store or by completing charity-care applications with the various companies.

The medical students are set up as teams and these teams work together over the course of the year. It is a medical student in the first, second, and third year. Fourth-year medical students are usually not available, as most do rotations away from the area in that year. The first year takes the patient history after they are taught how to do this during a course in the curriculum. They do the elements of the history and physical only at the level that they know and this provides another opportunity to hone that skill under the supervision of an upper-year student. By the time a student reaches the third year, they take on the role of organizing the data and presenting the case to the attending. The third-year student often has known and cared for the patient for three years and passes the baton to the second-year student when they leave the clinic. Continuity of care is present.

The students then present the case to one of the physicians who is assigned to the clinic on that day. We work the same day each week and it is common for us to get to know the patients, as they are always scheduled to return on that day. We hear the presentations and provide feedback on how to do it better and the students become very proficient at case presentations. We look through the patient's medical record and go to see the patient with the student team. There can sometimes be many people in one small room but I have found that the patients are not threatened by this and welcome it for what it is – many people working to help them. I then focus on what I feel are the critical elements and show the students how to get the best history, how to preform elements of the exam, and how to interact with the patient. It is magical. My clinic days with the students are always the highlight of my week. I get to use all I have learned over the years and pass these skills on to the next generation while helping someone in need. It does not get any better.

What is not appreciated is that the care given in a free clinic designed such as this is superior. Each patient gets a great deal of time dedicated to them. They have many people working together to help them. They have the input of a skilled pharmacist on each visit. They have continuity of care. All care is overseen and directed by an experienced licensed physician who works in an academic setting.

If a patient needs a test or a referral, this is arranged through a mechanism that allows for free testing and consultation. In essence, the hospital system absorbs most of this cost. The hospital where I work is located in one of the most challenging cities in America. They employ most of the physicians and we know that involves serving our community. If a patient is referred to a specialist, that cost is taken on by the hospital. In return, one of the students who cares for that patient in the clinic must accompany their patient to that visit and they provide a bridge to care for their patient while learning from the specialist. If their patient needs surgery, they scrub in. The patient is always at the center of care. The student is learning from these uninsured patients but never at the cost of the patient receiving care that is not equal or better than that given to those with insurance.

The students presented Lucy to me and I was able to provide tips on how to present. We went to see her and I found her to be a wonderful young lady with friendly eyes who smiled as she shook my hand. I did not obtain any information that was different from what I was told. My exam found a mass above the bone in her upper left chest. It was smooth, round, about the size of a grape, did not move and was not tender. There were no other masses or abnormalities. I thanked her for her time and told her we would leave the room for a few minutes and return to talk more.

Over the years of doing exams, one learns what is a bad or a not bad mass. You just know. This was not a good mass. I went over this with the students and told them that only by doing thorough exams over and over again would they come to know normal from abnormal. Over time, they will know what a cancer feels like, what a fatty tumor is, and what a cyst is. This cannot be learned on YouTube or in a book. The hands must be trained to send the signal to the brain and the brain must be programmed to assess the information and process it. The students tend to stare at me and act like sponges soaking up water. Teaching is such a thrill! I asked them to tell me what they thought it was. It is fascinating to watch them think and often shocking to realize what they already know. In this case, I told them I was worried about this either being a lymphoma or tuberculosis. They went quiet. I explained that the age and other symptoms fit both. I told them I would expect other masses – lymph nodes – if this were lymphoma. I also told them that I knew tuberculosis was very common in the country where she came from and can present differently. I had seen a case of scrofula (lymph node TB) only once many years ago, but that is all it took to program my brain and miraculously have that pop into the differential diagnosis.

We then went over what the next steps should be but we needed to focus on the most cost-effective path to making the diagnosis. I know that in another setting, CT scans and a multitude of tests would be ordered for the insured population because they are 'free.' They are costly and we all shoulder those costs. We arrived at a simple chest X-ray, a blood count to look for infection and anemia, and a blood test for tuberculosis (TB). We decided not to do the skin test, as most people from her country get a vaccination that can make the skin test falsely positive. I explained that the chest X-ray would show us if there was active pulmonary TB, or more nodes if it were a cancerous process.

Forms were filled out by the students and we all explained everything to Lucy. She was appropriately concerned but we assured her we would be at her side through this – and it would not cost her anything. Her chest X-ray was normal and her blood counts were fine, but her blood test for TB was positive. We had her come back and see us right after, and the students, with my instructions, told her she had TB and this was curable, was not in a contagious form, and we could do all this at our hospital for free. A biopsy of the mass was done, and one of the students went to the operating room with her for this. It showed TB. She was referred to our TB clinic and treatment was begun – for free. Lucy got what she needed in our free clinic and did so in a climate that educated and practiced cost-effective medicine.

Why does the hospital support our free clinic? Why does the medical school support the salaries of those of us who work there? The latter is easy – we teach the next generation of physicians how to interact with patients, how to do the physical exam, and how to formulate an assessment and a plan. We also mentor; we become a part of the collage of who this student will one day be. The hospital does it partly because it lives its mission to serve the community it is in. There is another side however. Imagine if Lucy went to the emergency room with her initial symptoms. She might have gotten an array of expensive tests and sent home to fend for herself in terms of whom to see – and at what cost. Our emergency rooms are filled with uninsured who get good care. The cost of that care is assumed by the hospital and covered partially by various charity programs funded by the state. These patients do not have what is really needed – a system that connects to the outpatient environment to provide continuity and decrease the need to return to the expensive care given in ERs. Our poor get great care in the hospital. They do not get it outside of the hospital.

The American system of providing for those who cannot afford care is embarrassing. Lucy worked two manual jobs and took care of her family. She couldn't afford health insurance. She was lucky to live in an area that has a clinic such as ours. Most do not. Lucy will be cured and live a long healthy life. My three students now know what scrofula is and will recognize it going forward and pass this on to their students. I get to teach, care for others, and pass on what I know before I retire. I am so very lucky.

Role Model

Throwing things away is sometimes very difficult. My nature is to get rid of things and I have never been tied to objects as necessary for memories. Recently, I decided to go through some things in my desk at home in order to further my effort to save my family this task when I leave this Earth. Age has a way of making you think these crazy thoughts. I found instructions for tools and appliances we no longer had, receipts faded to the point of not knowing what they were from, cards for occasions that I no longer recalled, and many other things that clearly were better off recycled. There also were things that were important to keep and know that I had. Then there were special things I had completely forgotten about. My mother was extremely organized and she gave me a thick brown envelope before she died that I glanced at once but not in detail. Perhaps I thought by doing so, I would speed her departure from this world. Bright people have stupid notions.

She had kept all of my report cards from every year I was in school! I would read them safely now as my mother had a lovely death at the age of ninety-one and I knew she would want me to enjoy this time-travel. The many nuns over the years were apparently rather pleased with me. I was shocked to see I had two comments on deportment – and I thought I was the perfect child! Language in high school was not my strength, but it was Latin and I subsequently found that was a complete waste of my time. I also did not do as well in physical education and this explains my lifetime avoidance of the gym.

One paper I found was a letter from 1976 authored by a physician, EV, who had sent the original to the chair of medicine at the hospital where I would do my residency training supporting my application. I was in the early months of my fourth year of medical school and had decided to pursue a career in internal medicine. The letter was more than kind and brought into focus how strange and wonderful life is.

I was assigned to do my medicine clerkship in my third year at a hospital affiliated with my medical school. This experience is totally with inpatients – patients in the hospital. Students seldom saw office patients at that time. We would see patients with the residents, assume a level of responsibility, and make rounds on the patients daily as a team. We would be joined for part of these rounds by a physician assigned to be the teaching attending for that month. This physician would listen to our case presentations, provide insights, and teach us skills at the bedside. This one doctor would be my view of medicine for this block of time. Medical education is often one of the chance factors of who that person is in terms of what you learn and what you think of that specialty. I struck gold. EV was my attending for this month and I would get to see what a great physician is, how to interact with patients, how much knowledge one person can possess, and how to do so with humility. He sat on the bed and often held the patient's hand. He seemed to know everything, and he treated us all with respect.

I wanted to have more of this man. I was later able to arrange a one-month experience with him in his office. This allowed me to see this part of medicine and showed me how a career in this specialty would be. EV was a doctor's doctor. He saw the most well-known people in the area as well as those without insurance. He treated all the same. He was a specialist in hematology and oncology but also saw patients for general health issues. It was like drinking from a fire hydrant. I loved it. I could see myself doing this for a living. I could dream of doing it as well as EV.

I wanted to have more of this man. I ranked the hospital he was at as my first choice for residency training and matched there. This paper I was now holding in my hand surely played a role in that! Over the next three years, I was able to work with him at times, but not often. In my senior year, he asked me to cover his practice on weekends. I would be paid! This turned out to be the best experience of my residency. I learned phone medicine. I rounded on the patients in the hospital and got to pretend I was an attending physician and see what it would be like to work with residents in my career. This resulted in my choosing to be a primary-care internist and move to a city that had a residency program in that field. Over the next thirty years, I had many occasions where I would ask myself when dealing with a difficult issue: what would EV do? I lost touch with him as we do in life.

Decades later, I was asked to be part of a team to create a new medical school in another state. I went for a tour of the associated hospital and wanted to get a feel for this opportunity. I loved what I was doing and where I was living and had no real intention of moving. On the tour, we walked off the elevator on the fourth floor of the new building and I stopped in my tracks – there was a portrait of EV! I knew he had left the hospital where I trained to be chair of medicine here decades before. When did he retire? Was he alive? I asked the physician showing me around and was told that he was still very active and even seeing patients that day! We walked across the street and went to the office where he saw patients and she knocked on the door – out walked EV. It was an amazing feeling. He said he remembered me and I am not sure he did – he had worked with so many over many years.

I chose to take the job and move. How much of that was due to seeing that painting and then shaking the hand of EV, I will never know. I am not superstitious, but if there is such a thing as omens… I have enjoyed these past eight years and now I am working directly with EV regularly as he creates a center to address humanism, professionalism, ethics, and law at our school. There is no better person to guide this effort in my eyes. Life has an odd way of coming full circle.

We are all a collage of the many people we encounter in our lives. Unconsciously and sometimes consciously, we take on the various traits and mannerisms of those who cross our paths. My path has been full of amazing role models.

The Lecture

I enjoy doing many things and find it valuable to get my mind off work when possible. Medicine as a profession is addicting. It consumes both time and emotions. Like so many other areas in my life that are laudable, my wife is behind it. She vowed to have me home for supper, to have me be a visible and involved husband and father, and to find enjoyment outside of work. I really enjoyed being at my children's events and even coaching their teams. I enjoy going out to eat with friends. I enjoy every moment with my wife. I enjoy a good television series, a movie, and a play. None compares in my mind to hearing a superb lecture. It is a timeless art form. Upon completion, I find myself invigorated, happy to have witnessed it, informed, and compelled to bring what I learned to others. I steal techniques from each lecturer and use them to make my next one better.

I am an introvert and always have been. Those who know me well know this to be true. Those that do not, and feel I am an extrovert, make me proud of the way I hide it. When there is a party, I am always thinking of how to leave. Once again, my wife is the key. She is so very comfortable in any setting and saves me from myself. When we stay at an event, I hate it, she loves it, and others just remember I was there – and that is enough. I am very comfortable talking with a few friends – four total, including my wife and me is ideal. Six is bearable, eight is a test, and more than that is torture.

When I was in about thirteen, my voice became relatively deep. In my freshman year of high school, a nun somehow convinced me to do public-speaking. At the time, boys just did not do that and I suspect she felt my voice would be a factor in success. I have a very good memory and was relatively tall and stood quite straight, thanks to the prodding of my parents. This wonderful nun trained me and I found that I loved it. In public-speaking, you do not have to speak to anyone. You speak to heads, a room, and a space. You hear your own voice and do not have to worry about questions. I then learned that there were contests and prizes. Over time, I became quite good at it and entered such contests as the American Legion's 'Voice of Democracy' contest and went on to win scholarships. I was fortunate enough to get full scholarships in college and was actually able to apply the speaking ones to medical school. My voice was worth something!

After finishing my residency, I found a way to use my enjoyment of speaking again. I taught! Soon, I was asked to take on the position of director of medical education and ran three major education sessions each week. In some, I was the moderator of case conferences and in some, I gave lectures. I always learn the most when I lecture and got into the habit of scheduling myself for at least two grand rounds each year. These are lectures that go into detail on a medical topic. I always picked the ones I knew nothing about. In the months leading up to this, I was forced to become an expert and the incentive was to avoid embarrassment. That works every time. Over the course of a number of years, I had given over one hundred and fifty category-one education conferences. These are such that physicians who attend are given educational credit toward licensure.

Lectures have changed significantly over the past few decades. At first, they were exclusively podium presentations with people in the audience taking notes. Then came the first audiovisuals: acetates and an overhead projector. The skill was to put them on upside down and backward to have the correct view shown on the screen. I practiced for hours! Then came a slide projector. We had a machine that created slides out of a typed paper. I loved that little device. At the same time, we went from nothing to point at to a long wooden stick to a fancy extending wand to a laser pointer the size of a club to penlight laser pointers.

Then came computers! Then came PowerPoint. It is now the standard. It is a source of aggravation for me. People who do not know how to use it drive me nuts. The sources of my frustration include slides that are too busy, print that is too small, the use of bizarre color schemes, people who are not funny putting in humor, the insane infatuation with making things dart around and flip on a slide, movie clips that do not work, slides that make the lecturer rush rather than teach, and oh, so many other things. I recall the early days when not every laptop was compatible with the projector available. I recall relying on bringing a CD and finding there was no disk drive. I always printed out every lecture and often resorted to the good old-fashioned didactic approach – and it was often even more effective.

I prepare extensively for lectures. It shows those who attend that I care. I learn so they can learn. I know to always use a microphone and always test it before the lecture. Too loud and people stop listening, too low and it is useless. I make sure there is a backup microphone or battery. I learn how to adjust the lights and do so even during the presentation to highlight picture slides and keep the audience awake. I never rush. I can be funny, so I use humor but only at the ideal moment. I know exactly how much time I need. There are times when giving a lecture that you know it is going well and you can listen to yourself while talking as if you were in the audience. There are times you know the plan did not work. Every time, the adrenaline rushes.

I give lectures now to medical students and others. Medical school is changing. Most students do not attend lectures anymore. They prefer to watch it on their computer in their apartment, in their PJs, and watch it on a faster speed. I cannot do anything at a faster speed anymore! They reverse and replay. They skip parts they are sure they know. They have all the lecture slides available to them at any time online. Apparently, this works for them. It does not work for those giving the lecture. I have given talks to as many as six hundred people. I had a blast and I performed. It made me want to do the next one, and so on. Now when I give a lecture that is not mandatory, I often see less than ten students present. I prepare the same and feel the quality was the same. The thrill, however, is gone. The inner desire to do a great job is not the same. The payment for a lecturer is in the response. It is the energy in the room. It is the feedback through the eyes, the attention, the questions, and the applause. The lecture in medical school is in jeopardy.

I recently went to the annual American College of Physicians' meeting. It is an enormous collection of internists and the opportunity to learn is overwhelming. There are at least eight different sessions to pick from every ninety minutes. You want to be able to hear them all. Hours are spent planning each day to optimize what you learn. It is an award show for lecturers. I knew my favorite lecturer would be there – Sal. He was speaking on Leonardo Da Vinci as a tribute. There are few true renaissance men around and Sal is one of them. He knows art, literature, and medicine. I had heard him speak many times – he is the best. It began and the audience was packed. He guided us through an in-depth look at what in Leonardo's life made him so creative. Slides of paintings, writings, maps, and more appeared and matched the pace and message perfectly. They never were a distraction and always highlighted what was being said perfectly. Humor was used at all the right moments. His accent further enhanced his message. On top of that, his true humility was shown and this further highlighted the lecture. He ended it at just the right time – leaving us wanting for more but never disappointed. Everyone stood up and applauded for some time. The lecture as a timeless and invaluable tool was in full view.

Teaching

CL was a forty-six-year-old Hispanic female who came to our student-run free clinic for care. This clinic is designed to serve adults in our city who have no insurance at all. I have had the honor of working with the students in this setting and I know the future of medicine is in very good hands from what I have seen in terms of the way these students treat their patients. Every patient is seen and examined by the students and then is presented to me. I then go to see the patient with the students and go over my history and physical while demonstrating techniques and often having the student repeat what I have shown them. The patients do not mind and we make sure each gets care equivalent to those seeing physicians in a private office setting. There is no charge and the medications are given to them free when we have them. If not, we find cheap options for them.

The case was presented to me as a lady with asthma who was not improving since her last visit a few weeks ago. I had not seen her before. She got the inhaler that was ordered and was using it properly. She had a bad dry cough and that was causing her to have bladder leakage. She had a few child births and was already referred to our gynecologists. Now it was my time to play doctor and teacher – no better time in my estimation! I entered the room and washed my hands before shaking hers. My students were with me. She did not speak English and we got the interpreter on the phone. This person can make or break an encounter. I usually test them by asking them to tell the patient something that should elicit a smile or a laugh when told in their native language. It worked and we both laughed. The door was now open to getting to know this lady. She now looked at me quite differently.

I asked her how long she was having coughing and wheezing and was told she had it for three years and it was getting worse. That is what the students told me – but my job is to check if they did a good job. I asked her if she had any pets at home and she said no. Asthma can present as a cough but it is a disease that does not usually start in the mid-forties without a reason. Knowing medicine is central to a good history – it guides us to the best next question. Students do not know these details yet and it gives me a chance to shine. I knew asthma very well. I asked her what changed in her house three years ago and she paused and looked down. When she looked at me, it was with a worried face and she told me she got two parakeets. Interesting that she did not think of birds at pets... I asked her if one of them got sick about three years ago – again, knowing what I was looking for. She told me that they had babies and she now has five – but the mother died soon after the babies came.

My adrenaline was now peaking! This is one of those moments teachers dream of – one that keeps us loving our craft. I knew that there was an infection humans can contract from birds called psittacosis. I had had a patient exactly like her twenty years ago. I hid my excitement and moved on to complete the interview and exam and we left the room. In the hall, I was able to have that special time to go over the case, give tips, and try to draw upon their knowledge while building upon it. I like to ask questions but always tell them I do not care if they do not know the answer as I find they pay attention better and that they usually know much more than they thought they did. I think that learning can and should be fun. Pressure eliminates that enjoyment.

We put all the pieces together and built the picture of this nice lady. No one in her family had asthma and neither did her children. She now lived alone and was the one who took care of her birds. She did not smoke. She has not gone on vacation or left the house for any period of time – a factor that would be interesting if this removal helped her. She was not wheezing on exam. She looked very healthy and the rest of her exam was normal.

The process that begins after the first word of the interview and gets assembled upon completion of the visit is called making a problem list and differential diagnosis. She had two problems today.

1) Possible asthma

2) Urinary incontinence

We then make a list of all the possible causes for each and sort them out by what is the most dangerous (something we should prioritize) and what is most likely (a simple statistical guess). As an internist, I like to make long differential diagnoses. We are noted for doing that. We try not to test for other than the most serious and most likely at the start – saving the others for later if our first approach comes up empty-handed. We came up with psittacosis, asthma, and lung cancer as the things to focus on first in this patient. I told the students that we should not tell her to get rid of her parakeets without proof because if she did and that was not the cause, she would feel terrible. She clearly loved these birds. Even if she did not have the infection, she could still be allergic to them.

We ordered a chest X-ray, a specific lab test for psittacosis and a blood count looking for an elevated eosinophil count. These are white blood cells sometimes elevated in people with allergies. The clinic is supported by our hospital system and they absorb the cost of all tests. It is our obligation to be cost-effective and my obligation to teach my students how to be. Anyone can make a diagnosis by running every test in the book. A good doctor can do so at the least cost. Insurance companies monitor how cost-effective each physician is and give that data back to the physician – and their employer. I think this a good thing, as we should all shoulder some responsibility for how costly medicine has become. I have found that knowledge and a thorough history and physical can pave the way to most diagnoses and I often use tests only for confirmatory purposes. What other job enables a person to teach, diagnose, treat, show off, and have fun while doing it. My life has been a hoot!

The X-ray was normal. The blood test showed a normal cell count and the antibody test for psittacosis was normal. My diagnosis was wrong! She likely had allergies to the birds but no test will show that. We would have to try to find a way to remove her from the environment for a few days and that is not easy. She did not want to get rid of her birds. Her case could have been very unusual. The fact that she did not have psittacosis was not the issue – this case allowed for these students to consider this possibility now and in the future. Many will now include this disease in their differential diagnosis. It was as simple as taking a thorough history in the face of a language barrier while knowing what to look for. The former can be done by a medical student. The latter takes some time...

Chapter 11

Perspective

If you have read this in page order to this point, I want to thank you more than you know for the gift of caring about life. I hope by now you are thinking of stories that you could and should write. I have left two pages at the end of this book for you to jot down some ideas. I have a view of people, events, and history that is unique to me because of what I have experienced, how, and in what context. It is mine and I treasure it. This perspective is not one that I am teaching or promoting, but merely one that I am sharing. Share yours at the table or in a formal setting. Ideas not shared are ideas lost.

Professionalism

I recently gave a presentation to our first-year medical students on professionalism. I enjoy giving presentations, as I tend to use slides more for topic focus than for content and it allows me to just talk as I would if meeting someone for lunch. I often find myself listening to what I say as I say it as if I were in the audience and at the podium at the same time. The human mind is amazing. This particular lecture went very well as I could see in the faces of those present and by the subsequent questions. I enjoyed hearing it too! Defining professional behavior is very difficult. The analogy that I do not enjoy but always seems to work the best is that of pornography – you know it when you see it. This is very true of unprofessional behavior. We have all seen unprofessional behavior unfortunately. There is no place for this in medicine. People come to us at their most vulnerable moments and reach out to us for help. We owe it to them to be our best every moment. That is a lot to ask, but I feel it is central to the profession of medicine.

As my talk progressed, I found myself going down a road I had not prepared for and this road led to a gold mine. I asked the students if they had ever witnessed unprofessional behavior by a physician and there was a unanimous response that they had. I then asked if they had ever acted in a manner that they considered unprofessional or less than ideal. Again, they answered that they had. The next question is what opened an important door: why? The responses came streaming in. Usually questions in a large classroom are met with silence and 'look-aways.' Not on this day! They noted that it was usually because they were tired, stressed, having issues in their personal lives, had not been able to do the things they enjoy such as exercising or going to movies, were ill, or a number of other reasons that all boiled down to wellness.

The recent literature is filled with articles surrounding wellness. All agree that this is a major issue with physicians. If that is true, and I feel it is very true, then unprofessional behavior is becoming common. This is not safe and will result in a major impact on how our profession is viewed by others. What about the profession of medicine that is worthy of the respect that it is given? Those that pursue a career in medicine possess the tools that could be used in another profession with equal financial reward. Thousands of young men and women sacrifice a great deal to get into medical school, and more to become the type of physician they choose.

A professional is simply someone who gets paid for what they do. Hopefully, doctors are more than that. The Association of American Medical Schools created the 'objectives project' a number of years ago that focused on what attributes they wanted to foster in their students. They knew that knowledge alone was not the goal of educating tomorrow's physicians. Among the results of their work included professionalism and encouraging physicians to respond to societal needs. They listed as core humanistic values – honesty and integrity, caring and compassion, altruism and empathy, and respect for self, patients, and peers. They listed a continuing commitment to excellence as well as high ethical and moral standards. These are lofty goals and exactly what should be expected of those who will impact the lives of so many.

The Accreditation Council for Graduate Medical Education (ACGME) core competencies include professionalism. Residency training programs are reviewed to assure that they are focusing on this in those they train. What is it that these organizations are looking for? What is the focus of the teaching involved to develop professionalism? What exactly is professionalism? Among definitions I have read are: medical professionalism is our behavior as physicians. It is how we conduct ourselves as physicians in our interactions with our patients and society. Medical professionalism is a behavior that is predicated on our personal beliefs and our ideas. It encompasses the values, behaviors, and attitudes inculcated into us by our medical school education and postgraduate training along with our daily experiences interacting with patients and fellow physicians.

Medical professionalism is greatly influenced by our contemporaneous social values and norms. Therefore, it remains a flexible concept from age to age, despite maintaining a core set of values. This is critical, as it infers that professionalism can be taught and that it is always in evolution. Medical professionalism is a behavior that defines our relationship as a physician to our individual patients and our relationship to society. It serves as the infrastructure for the trust absolutely necessary to the patient-physician relationship.

One of the fathers of modern surgery, Harvey Cushing, stated, "A physician is obligated to consider more than a diseased organ, more even than the whole man – he must view the man in his world."

We Are Human

My wife recently forwarded me something from the AARP site. Yes, I am at that stage of life and quite proud of it. I get cheaper movie seats, I get discounts on public transportation at certain hours, and I get a powerful lobbying group! I have successfully navigated signing up for Medicare and even the maze that is known as our social security system. Among five-year age groups in the older population, sixty-five to sixty-nine-year-olds grew the fastest. This age group grew by 30.4 percent, rising from 9.5 million to 12.4 million. The sixty-five to sixty-nine-year-old group is expected to grow more rapidly over the next decade as the first baby boomers started turned sixty-five in 2011. Look out. We will be a major voting block and we are accustomed to getting our way! So much for that brief display of pretending I am fine with getting older.

The piece was entitled: *The Doctor Diaries: What Physicians Wish Patients Knew.* It was in AARP – The Magazine, June to July 2018, and written by Joanne Jarrett, M.D. Many very good insights were shared but the ones that struck me were:

Many of us have post-traumatic stress disorder (PTSD).

"I have nightmares about patients down an infinite hall, each with a problem worse than the last. In my short career, I've seen a baby take her last breaths. I've watched a woman, bleeding uncontrollably after giving birth, lose consciousness as I worked, a pool of her blood expanding at my feet. I've heard a woman, after having both legs traumatically severed, saying goodbye to her father, assuming she wouldn't survive. I could go on. We know we signed up for it. But keep in mind when you're tempted to be angry with your doctor that we are under stress, too."

We worry about you.

"We lie awake worried sick about you more often than you'd imagine. We may wonder about you for years after you leave our care. The stakes are so high, and we know it."

We make mistakes.

"Our fear of screwing up is exhausting, weighty, and ever-present. It's the hardest thing about doctoring. We do make mistakes. Be wary of anyone who won't admit that."

There is not a single physician who has not wished at some moment of one day that they were in a different line of work. Many have that thought often. Some go to work every day thinking that and feel they are trapped by loans or the expectations of others. Life is too short to live this way and anyone who made it through the rigorous path to this profession has the grit, intelligence, and ability to do something else – a job that will bring them joy. Those who are depressed can and should seek help. Life is too precious. I also think anyone who does not love what they do is less good at it. Our patients deserve our best.

My 10:30 AM patient was a twenty-five-year-old female named Diane. I had not seen her before but I had other patients with her last name in my practice. I began the process and learned that she had a cough for about three weeks. It was dry, and nothing she took over the counter helped. She never smoked and was not around anyone that did. I also learned that it began on a cruise – on her honeymoon! She had no fever, had not coughed up any blood, had no sinus symptoms, and was a bit tired but had many good reasons why. On exam, she was a strikingly beautiful red-haired female with a personality to match. She lit up the room. Everything was normal, except she had a localized wheeze in her right mid posterior chest on deep breathing. This was likely viral but my rule is that if the exam is abnormal in anyone who has new respiratory issues, I get a chest X-ray. My office is at the hospital, so she went right over to get it. She was alone. Her husband was working. I went to radiology during my lunchtime, as I was curious. This was at a time when we looked at black and white images on a posterior lit view box. Now we pull it up on our computer wherever we are. I got a cold chill as I saw a large mass where I heard the wheeze. She was dead of cancer within months despite sending her to the top people and getting every treatment possible. This was a rare and nasty cancer. I still think of how this young lady's life was cut short. Her husband never remarried.

It was the day after the Super Bowl when AT called with a headache. He was a muscular twenty-six-year-old that I had seen once before for a work exam. I got on the phone and he admitted that he had been drinking quite a bit and inserted proudly that his team had won. I had a light day scheduled and told him to come right down. I am still not sure why. If everyone with a morning headache went to their doctor after the Super Bowl, it would be bedlam. He came in and looked fine. His blood pressure was normal. His neurological exam had a slightly decreased reflex in his left knee and ankle. His great toe strength was decreased on that side. I turned off the lights in the room and looked in his eyes with the ophthalmoscope. I could not believe what I saw. His right eye had changes called papilledema – this indicates pressure on that side of the brain. I arranged for a CT scan and went right over while it was being done. As the slices displaying a large brain tumor were unveiled – one that looked very bad – my heart sank. Despite all the best treatments, he was dead in six months, leaving his wife and a three-year-old son behind.

I could go on and on with similar tales. They are a part of the life of a physician. So many things make no sense – when young people die, cancer, birth defects, pregnancy loss, gunshots, auto accidents, and the list goes on and on. The common threads of all this tragedy are that it is happening to human beings every day and that a physician is usually asked to play a major role in breaking the terrible news and walking those suffering through horrible things – often ending in their death.

People need to know this. We really do care and we are affected by it. Those who say they are not are only pretending and using that as a defense. We always imagine what it would be like if we were on the other side of the bed. We take on these tragedies and must get up and go to work the next day. Usually, a card from a patient, a simple thank you, making a great diagnosis, preventing an illness, or seeing someone recover is enough to keep us doing what we do. Sometimes, sharing a meal with our family, a hug from a wife or one or our children, or a call from a friend is enough to offset the bad times. The good moments far exceed the bad, but the pain of those horrible days can be very difficult. I would still never want to do anything different with my life. I encourage students to be physicians. It is an honor to be able to help others. To help other human beings and to move forward every day, we must accept being humans ourselves.

I Don't Know

Physicians are very skilled in many areas. One thing we are not trained to do is to simply say that we do not know the answer. I have found over the years that patients respond very positively when told that I was not sure what was wrong with them. I made sure I let them know that I would do everything possible to find out what was wrong and that always seemed to be enough. Medicine is a profession of lifelong learning. I also came to know that as I became more experienced over the years, the number of times when I would refer a patient to a consultant to find out an answer resulted in fewer and fewer surprises to me. It was, however, very reassuring for the patient to know that a specialist was also unsure of what was going on.

This inability is ingrained in physicians early on in their training. To get into medical school, a student must have excelled in their education before applying to medical school. Most applicants not only have exceptional grade point averages but also have done amazingly well in a standardized admissions test. I would be willing to wager that none of these tests had as the option to any of the questions: "I don't know." This process is further magnified while in medical school. Students from their very first day of medical school have their eyes on the standardized test known as the USMLE. Their score on this test is a major factor in choosing what path in medicine they may be able to take. This test is taken at the end of the second year and then another version of this test taken at the end of the third year. Once again this test, as well as the multiple practice tests, and all the exams in medical school aimed at preparing the students for this test do not ever include an option of 'I don't know.'

This testing also allows for dangerous behaviors to be embedded in future physicians. Once we put down the answer, we move to the next question and seldom look back. These are timed tests. This leads to a habit of accepting an answer that may not be the best answer. In fact, we are told that answers that are changed are often changed to a wrong answer and this further bolsters the attitude of giving an answer and moving on. We carry this to our career and give an answer to a patient problem and move on. Once again, time is the enemy of exploring other possibilities. In life, however, our answer is something a patient must live with and cope with. It is one that carries tests and treatments. It is a great deal more than filling in the circle next to choice 'C.'

There are multiple studies that explore the personalities of medical students. One such evaluation is that of their tolerance to ambiguity. It is not surprising that medical students compared to other students have a low tolerance to ambiguity. This basically means that they look for very concrete answers to questions. The possibility that there could be more than one answer or no answer is poorly tolerated in this group. What I have found over my years of taking care of patients is that tolerance to ambiguity was a very necessary skill because few patients presented in a textbook fashion.

My career path has recently allowed me to go back to teaching medical students in their first two years. This has opened up the door to learning for me and exploring all of the new explanations there are in terms of molecular biology, genetics, biochemistry, and pharmacology. What I also have found is that the more that I have learned, the more questions I have and that there is still a great many issues for which we do not have an answer. One could argue that every answer can easily be followed by another question as to why it is so. My grandchildren when very young were the ultimate scientists in that they replied to me 'why, Doc' no matter what I told them. That inquisitiveness leads to learning. It all starts by admitting that we might not know.

When to Retire

I am at that stage of life when people retire. My two closest friends just did. They are both busy and happy. They had different career paths but both were extremely successful and admired by all. They made a mark on this world and impacted the lives of many. Is it my turn to hang it up? How can a person be sure? Did I save enough? Can I be busy enough? How long do I have to live? How secure is my independence? No one really ever knows.

Physicians often have a very difficult time retiring. We see medicine not as a job that will end but a lifestyle and mission. We develop a panel of patients who rely upon us, as we need their appreciation. Many of us do not develop hobbies. I do not even golf. In our spare time, we often teach and read medicine and participate in continuing medical education. When we greet others, we hear the word 'doctor' used rather than our first name. We are our profession.

Many hospitals are now instituting mandatory cognitive evaluations for physicians they employ at certain ages. Physicians hate this. Denial is a part of cognitive decline and in the case of a physician, this denial could cost lives. Most seldom see their decline as serious and keep working. There is no one to stop a physician from practicing who is not employed. Other physicians see how one day they might be on the other side of this process. Some rely on the physician for referrals and do not want to have those referrals go away.

I was chair of medicine at a hospital for a number of years. It was the worst job I ever had. People in these positions spend their time at meetings and trying to improve the performance of the physicians they oversee. It is mostly a task dealing with people who are not preforming as expected and are unwilling to change, as they see themselves as always right. We had an older primary-care physician at my hospital that was revered by patients and staff. He was kind and always had time for everyone. He was eighty and wore a smile every day. Two nurses reported a recent change in behavior that led to a chart review where I found multiple incidents of poor judgment. No patient was harmed... yet. I called him in for a meeting and showed him the documentation and asked him to get a full medical evaluation and that we would have someone else co-manage all cases until we have more information.

248

He refused and was shocked by what was said. He insisted that he was as good as he ever was and he had been faithful to our hospital for years and would take his work elsewhere. He was not an employee and we had no say over his right to see patients in his office. One could argue that those patients were at even greater risk of an error as consultants and nurses and others were not observing his decisions as was his care in our hospital. Did we have an obligation to report him to the licensing board or other agencies?

This would be a terrible note on which to end decades of work that was respected and admired. It happens daily. Leaving the game after hitting the winning shot in the championship is everyone's dream. Few have the courage and insight to walk away before our skills deteriorate. Retiring at the right time shows respect for those we care for – it is not leaving them without their doctor. It is making sure they have a doctor who can best care for them. Seasoned clinicians are hard to replace. Medicine is learned best by doing and a new physician does not have the experience to provide the same care as someone who knows the patient well and has seen the varied presentations of many diseases. Wisdom beat knowledge in care.

Every physician should prepare for retirement years in advance. This is much more a matter of garnering interests and hobbies than it is of building the nest egg. A physician without a spouse is usually married to their work and leaving that becomes a nightmare. Building friendships is also important. Upon retiring, one must look forward with enough enthusiasm to erase the loss of what is left behind. The bonds with patients, their appreciation, the excitement of making a diagnosis, the satisfaction of treating, and the pride in having prevented illness, all make our work more rewarding than anyone can realize. Leaving that willingly is an act of putting our patient first for the last time. It is being a professional.

Personally, at the time of this writing, I am not ready yet. I had a serious illness that left me home for some time and realized that I had not done my job preparing for my future. I did, however, drastically change my job and have made it possible to keep working as a result. I now teach and mentor. I still see patients but now with residents and medical students. I get to pass on what I have learned and impact patients now and in the future. Teaching demands that I keep current and I still love learning. My skepticism of new recommendations allows me to question medicine and that is a forum for teaching like no other. My student evaluations will tell me when it is time to move on, so I read them and use them as my guide.

In the meantime, I will try to find things that will enrich my time after this job ends. I will listen to, and thank, colleagues, family, and friends who love and respect me enough to tell me when it is time to leave my work behind. In the meantime, I go to work every day looking to hit the game-winning shot.

Statistics

Millie was a courageous lady who had waged an all-out war on her breast cancer for the past ten years. She was bright and positive and every visit was a mixture of admiration for her and a sense of my own feelings that I could never measure up to her inner strength. More and more people are surviving cancer, thanks to advances in treatment and early detection. We now use the words 'five-year survival' instead of cure, as cancer has a way of recurring many years later. There are many cures and the latest advances in genetic testing are allowing us to target tumors rather than trying to kill the house mouse with a shotgun. The future looks optimistic but I know I will not see the eradication of cancer in my lifetime.

She had seen her oncologist the day before and was offered a new drug that would increase her life expectancy by fifty percent. Anyone hearing this would jump at the chance to live fifty percent longer. Millie was not anyone – she knew this game of statistics well after these past ten years. Millie was in bad shape. She was near the end of her battle and likely had only a month to live. She was in pain from cancer that had spread into many of her bones. She had no appetite – a common problem likely due more to the release of a protein by the cancer cells than a bowel issue. She was weak and more dependent on others now. She did not fear death but loathed the idea of being dependent.

Millie was now sixty-three years old. What had her cancer specialist really told her? If she is likely to die in four weeks and this new drug might increase survival and average of two more weeks in patients like Millie, then it would increase her survival by fifty percent. It is interesting how we phrase things. No one likes to be negative, especially to someone who is dying but we must not sacrifice honestly for optimism. This new drug might not work at all or it might give her more than two more weeks. These statistics are based on average of what happened with many people like Millie. It is an educated guess. If Millie got two more weeks on this Earth, that would really be an increase in life expectancy of 0.4% if her three thousand two hundred and seventy-six weeks on this Earth were used as the comparison factor. Both estimates are correct but convey quite different hopes. The real question for this patient is whether the chance of having another two weeks to live might balance the side effects of the new medication and the weight of all the current issues she is managing. That is her choice alone and she needs facts.

Perhaps her son cannot make it home for another week and she wants to see him before she dies – then two weeks is an extraordinary gift for her. Perhaps she is ready for death and ready to end her fight. She will not be demoralized by the truth. She will be given the facts needed to make critical decisions.

Think of what Millie has already done on her journey with breast cancer. She got mammograms yearly since the age of forty-five. Why did her doctor recommend this? It was based upon statistics. There are studies that show how many mammograms are needed for a population to save one life. This varies widely as per the age of the patient and the study done. Most experts agree that this test is worth the cost. Different guidelines suggest different ages to begin such screening. Mary got her yearly testing and a mass was discovered. Will she be put in the group where mammography worked if she dies of the cancer ten years after discovery? This needs to be known to interpret such studies. Do interpretations of the images by radiologists vary? Yes! How does this factor in? Do the number of false positive readings (no cancer on subsequent testing) and false negative readings (normal test but cancer later found) matter? It should. Does every woman who goes for a mammogram consider all of this? Few do and they rely on us. This is a heavy weight to carry but physicians do so every day.

Once a biopsy of the lesion is done and it is examined microscopically and determined to be a cancer, there are more decisions based upon statistics. Should she have a mastectomy or elect to have the lump removed with sampling of lymph nodes followed by local radiation therapy? Are there specialists locally or should she go to a center in a distant city? Should she have medications to block the response of tumor cells to hormones? Should she have chemotherapy? All of these decisions were made by Millie over these years and based upon the statistics available at the time. She was gambling with her life each step and using math to do so. If there is only a one percent chance something will work, that means only one in one hundred people will benefit. What if you are that one?

Now we have yet another step in this process that is difficult in many ways. Should Millie have genetic testing? The result of such testing now allows physicians to tailor treatment more effectively. If she finds out that she carries what is commonly called the breast cancer gene (BRCA), what does that mean? She will be quoted many statistics including her risk of cancer in the other breast and her chances of passing this gene to her children. Should she tell her children and shift the burden of this real risk to them and their families?

Millie opted against the new treatment. There was a hundred percent chance she was going to die soon and she was ready. She went to Hospice and her family was there every minute. She fought a great fight and I learned a great deal from her. She played the odds very well and that is the best anyone can really do in life.

Extender

A physician extender is a healthcare provider who is not a physician but who performs medical activities typically performed by a physician. It is most commonly a nurse practitioner or physician assistant. The scope of practice for these professionals continues to evolve and many now can function independently. I never worked with an extender when I was in practice. I felt strongly that my patients deserved to see me alone, and a non-physician could not properly meet their needs. I was so very wrong.

MG is a nurse practitioner who works in the clinic where I serve as a preceptor for the internal medicine residents. She sees patients independently – and efficiently. Occasionally, she will ask my advice about a patient and I have yet to add to what she already knew. Her patients love her and ask to be scheduled to see her when they return. My neighbor and new friend is a nurse practitioner who works with cancer patients every day. I see her wear the problems her patients encounter and bring them home with her. She has unique and therapeutic relationships with her patients. She works with a physician and they are a seasoned team that has learned to pull from each other's strengths.

I have always driven a simple car. I never had wealth and when growing up, we often did not have a car – never a new one. One day, a patient had come to see me and told me he had just seen my father driving a new car and stopped to talk to him. Dad told him that his kids had bought it for him. Dad was in his early seventies at the time and retired. He was a policeman and never made much money. I left the room and called my father immediately and told him I heard he just bought a new car and is saying that we bought it for him. He replied that we did because it would be that much less money we would get when he died. He meant it. Dad was great. Every car that I have bought over the years started when I turned the key and got me where I needed to go. A car twice the price would do no better. Does every patient need the Porsche when they can get what they really need from another vehicle?

Cardiothoracic surgeons do not treat arthritis. Neurosurgeons do not treat acne. They have a specialized body of knowledge and skills. Spending their time not using such skills in not efficient or wise. I am an internal medicine specialist. I now have accumulated years of experience – this matters. Time has taught me what my patients need. I formerly thought they needed time with me but have since learned they can benefit from anyone who can give them at least as much time and possesses the knowledge to sort out what they are told and recognize what they know and what they do not know. Knowing what you do not know is the most important skill of any physician. If an extender can give the patient that time and expertise and bounce things off me that they are less comfortable with, that frees me up to spend more time with a patient with whom they are less comfortable. Everyone wins!

Medicine has become absurdly expensive. If a patient can get the same care at a lesser cost, it only makes sense to do so. Primary care is the field that is thought of as the first line in patient care. Even though we spend more time with patients, take on the broadest array of issues, and often prevent illness, we are reimbursed less than those with procedures. Using an extender is economically wise, as it provides for more efficient care while not sacrificing the quality of care. The surgeon can now spend more time in the operating room while the physician's assistant is removing sutures and providing discharge instructions.

The distribution of healthcare providers in this country is very poor. There are many remote areas not served by a physician. Even in crowded cities, there are populations without the same geographic access to physicians. This must change. What we see in the future is a broader and wiser use of extenders. Physicians will have more time to practice at the level of their training that will best serve their patients. We will see patient care often done remotely, utilizing the growing world of tele-health through computers. Medicine is now a team sport tightly linked to technology. I cannot wait to see what is around the corner.

The Underserved

The patients in this country who do not have access to healthcare either because of financial, geographic, or social barriers present a major challenge. The issues surrounding inpatient care are distinct from those in the outpatient setting. Understanding the problems and accepting them is the first step to solving the problem. Physicians have always shouldered a great deal of the burden of this care. We must continue to do so. The duty of providing charity care had been a hallmark of the virtuous physician since the early Middle Ages, and over time had been incorporated into the 'gentlemanly ethic of the noblesse oblige.' However, changes in the healthcare environment transformed healthcare simultaneously into a commodity to be bought and sold on the market as well as a public good – and even a right – expected by citizens from their government.

It was in 1847 when the American Medical Association published its code of medical ethics, that physicians were encouraged as a duty to the public to provide limited, gratuitous services to the poor: "Poverty, professional brotherhood and certain of the public duties... should always be recognized as presenting valid claims for gratuitous services... to indigent circumstances, such professional services should always be freely accorded."

As scientific and business changes took hold and began to shape the demands on the delivery of healthcare, the AMA's code of medical ethics was rewritten in the early 1920s and again in the 1940s to reflect the roles and obligations of physicians practicing within these institutional structures. The duty of charity care was shifted to a section in the code that discusses compensation reflecting the growing insistence that institutions, rather than individual physicians, shoulder some of the burden of caring for the poor.

Inpatient care is currently available to all regardless of their ability to pay. This care comes at a price, however. Charity care consists of services for which hospitals neither received, nor expected to receive, payment because they had determined, with the assistance of the patient, the patient's inability to pay. In practice, however, hospitals often have difficulty in distinguishing bad debt from charity care. Uncompensated care is an overall measure of hospital care provided for which no payment was received from the patient or insurer. It is the sum of a hospital's 'bad debt' and the charity care it provides. One analysis looked at charity care as a percentage of net-operating expenses which ranged from 0.46% to 16.69% in 2016. Nationwide estimates are that there is over $57 billion in uncompensated care provided in this country yearly. The supply and demand for charity care are not geographically aligned. That is, hospitals with the most resources to offer charity care aren't in the places where people most need it.

The care in hospitals and in emergency rooms is for the most part excellent and blind to the ability of the patient to pay. For all patients, the task of setting up discharge begins the day they arrive. Upon discharge, patients are significantly less able to manage than years ago when people stayed longer. It is what happens after discharge that makes all the difference.

For the most part, there is no good system in place for the care of the majority of outpatients who do not have health insurance. Caring for those in need is a fundamental professional commitment. The fact is that people who are socially and economically most disadvantaged are least likely to have satisfactory insurance coverage or regular medical care. They have many illnesses and disabilities that are in need of medical care.

Most physicians leaving their residencies now join large healthcare systems rather than entering private practice. The enormous debt of graduates demands a secure monthly income. These systems are equipped to mitigate overhead and distribute the charity care factor to its physician employees.

Institutions and individual physicians who care for underserved and indigent populations require specific knowledge and resources. I spent the vast majority of my professional life caring for people who were not disadvantaged. They had phones, they could read, they were compliant, and they had friends and loved ones to help them. When I moved to work in a challenged city, I was amazed at how ill-trained I was in what really matters for the population we serve.

Examples of the tools necessary are:

Language: When a physician cares for a patient and is unable to speak their language, they must rely on an interpreter to gain the critical information contained in the interview. It has long been established that the major tool used in the diagnostic process is the patient history. Interpreters help in terms of providing 'what is said' but cannot transmit the critical variable of 'how it is said.' Discussions surrounding mental health are especially difficult in these situations. The use of an interpreter significantly prolongs the time spent with the patient and this decreases the number of patients that can be seen on any given day. Language expertise has become extremely important.

Environment: Studies have shown that living in a disadvantaged neighborhood may be an independent risk factor for diseases such as ASCVD (heart and vascular disease). This risk element was recently shown to be equal to other factors. Many studies have pointed out the numerous risks of this population including violence, substance use, and the challenges of not having access to food and housing.

Prevention: Medical care appropriately focuses on prevention. Identifying risk factors for atherosclerosis becomes a routine part of an outpatient visit. This involves a thorough family history which is often hampered by a lack of knowledge of the health of a parent. It involves getting a lipid analysis and blood sugar. Such tests are difficult or impossible in those who do not have health insurance. Smoking cessation counseling becomes even more of a challenge with a language barrier. As environmental issues become identified as risk factors, the need for the health profession to take on the social problems of the population it serves becomes obvious. Colon cancer will become only something we can detect early in the insured who can afford colonoscopies. The accepted standards for CT scanning of the lungs and abdominal aorta in certain populations become applicable only to the insured or patients who are served by a system that identifies and cares for those without means. New tools to screen for depression and cognitive dysfunction become more a burden than a useful tool when treating those who do not speak English.

Testing: As physicians, we rely on testing to confirm a diagnosis as well as to rule out other possibilities. One can argue that this reliance has become too great. The need to know and the demand to be sure in the face of possible litigation fuel certain aspects of testing. Regardless, in the patient who cannot afford tests, the diagnostic process is severely hampered. One is less able to obtain a CXR for a patient who is coughing or a CT scan in a patient with abdominal pain. This may lead to the need to later admit a patient with pneumonia of diverticulitis and result in even greater expenditures associated with an inpatient stay.

Treatment: Prescribing is another challenge when caring for the uninsured or underinsured patient. Simply being able to read the instructions can be an issue. Affording the medication is the biggest issue and can often result in a patient not getting the medication. Such a patient is less likely to return for care out of embarrassment. In the case of a patient with hypertension, for which there are no symptoms, these patients can go months to years untreated and present as a stroke of myocardial infarction. We now live in a society where the ability to treat is linked to the ability to pay. The many new biologicals being marketed are really only available to those who can afford them. Patients watch TV and hear about drugs for diseases they have but cannot afford. We clearly utilize medications in treating patients for which there are cheaper medications of equal efficacy. Do we have a social obligation to utilize the most cost-effective approach to treatment as stated in The Ethics Manual of the American College of Physicians?

Access: The simple issue of how a patient gets to care is a major barrier, especially in areas where there may not be a provider for many miles. Even in urban communities, the task of getting a bus or a cab for the many without cars is a challenge.

Technology: Open access to one's medical record has become the rule. We can look at our tests online now and make sure the notes are correct. This is another area where the 'have nots' are discriminated against. Studies have shown that such access improves care. Those who do not have computer access of the knowledge to use online resources are denied this care. The gap between the 'have' and 'have-not' continues to widen.

Housing: Many people in this country do not have an address, much less a cellphone. Reminders of appointments or the simple task of telling them about a test result is impossible. These patients cannot access care in a meaningful way. Caring for the homeless is a major challenge and one that is taken on daily by providers in this country. 'Street medicine' has become a means through which medical students volunteer to reach out to the most challenged members of our society.

Diet: The simple matter of dietary changes in a diabetic becomes a major obstacle for the many who do not have access to healthy foods.

Continuity of care: In my practice, I knew instantly when a patient was ill, since I had come to know them via repeated visits over years. The current structure, such as when the care is through resident clinics, does not allow the physician to truly know the patients over time and vice versa. This can lead to unnecessary testing.

If all physicians agreed to care for a very small percentage of the uninsured, our profession can answer the need. One can argue that not all physicians, or their offices, have the ability to manage the many factors that complicate the care of this population as noted above. Systems of care structured such as the National Health Service Corp are better equipped to tackle the societal barriers to care this population faces. The social worker becomes a critical element of care. Such systems need to be supported financially. Physicians could volunteer some of their time to work in such care centers. In doing so, they will learn how to manage this unique population as well as appreciate the privileges of the insured they serve. The challenge of working with these patients is more than balanced by the incredible good that is accomplished. My time caring for this population has given me incredible personal and professional satisfaction. Teaching while doing so is icing on the cake!

I Know How You Feel

Empathy is the ability to understand and share the feelings of others. It is considered a critical skill for a physician and is actually taught in medical school. The problem is that by nature the ability to empathize with another person is often an intrinsic part of that person and when it is taught, it becomes mechanical and loses the element of being therapeutic at times. Just knowing the right thing to say is different than actually having insight into another person's feelings. When we say, "I know how you feel," it is actually a lie in certain circumstances and thus conveys the message that you do not even care enough about that patient to be truthful with them.

I was present at my three children's births. It was an experience like no other. To watch my wife give birth to my first child (who happened to be a good-size baby girl) without any medications at all dumbfounded me. This was in the '70s and the "in" thing was the Leboyer method of childbirth that tries to minimize the trauma for the newborn; delivery occurs in a quiet dimly lit room and immediate bonding between mother and child is encouraged. Katrina was handed to me upon delivery and I was to float her in a large basin of warm water to ease her into this world. I blew it. I was so nervous I was shaking and the water was spilling everywhere. My wife had a good laugh as did everyone. I hold my wife in the highest esteem after seeing her bring our child into this world. I could not tell her that I knew how the pain of childbirth felt, thank god. I could never have done what she did.

Physicians frequently reply to a patient's expression of pain, sorry, anxiety, and loss with the phrase: "I know how you feel." I would like to state that we do not have any idea without having had the exact same experience. I use a phrase like "that must have been difficult, would you like to talk about it more?" My patients have always responded well to that and I am sincere. Part of healing is listening and to listen best is to both hear and understand what is being said.

The physician cannot, and hopefully will not, come to know what all of their patients are feeling through personal experience. That is too costly an education in every way. The message here is that we must try to understand,

and even if we cannot, we must accept that the patient has had a negative experience that is impacting their life. Only by doing so can we truly show empathy and heal them.

Beth came to me after her physician had retired. She was in her early fifties and I knew her but not well. She always seemed to be life of a party, to know everyone and to be the best mother and wife in the world. Her life was enviable from my perspective. Her husband was a terrific guy and they were always together. In the first visit to my office, she relayed her story. It was about five years ago when she began to experience anxiety and it was thought to be due to menopause. It got worse and she was put on medication but it did not seem to work. Gradually, it took over her life. She would no longer go on an airplane because it happened once there. She began to avoid many things and her life changed.

I asked her to give me a description of an episode in detail. She said that without warning she would suddenly not feel right but could not say how. This made her nervous and she began to feel her heart pounding. This made her weak and after a short time it would go away as suddenly as it began. She never passed out. It would happen more when she was tired. Every time she went to the doctor, all tests were normal, including a cardiogram. She began to need more pills and took them regularly to prevent these anxiety attacks. She spoke of these episodes in such a way that it made me wonder if this was anxiety/panic – it just did not seem like what I knew this to be like. It did not feel like when I would become anxious. I asked her to come to my office on a bad day and not take her anxiety medication the morning she came. I made her sit in the waiting room and promised to examine her the moment it happened. It didn't. I had her come back the next day. At around ten o'clock, she got anxious and came right back. Her heart rate was 160! I got an immediate cardiogram and she had an abnormal rhythm – not the fast heart rate someone with anxiety can get.

Tests were done and she was referred to a cardiologist. An abnormal conduction pathway in the heart was found and ablated. She never had another "anxiety attack" and was able to stop her medication. Her life returned to normal. I cannot really say why I did what I did with Beth but I think it was that I actually knew what anxiety was and did not feel her problem was that. I knew how she should have felt through my experiences in life. Experiencing life makes us better doctors.

A Business

There are quite a few things I would have done differently in my journey. The vast majority of my life I am very pleased with – even in retrospect. I would not have taken Latin in high school. It was clearly a scam being sold by the nuns as the basis for all other languages and I was told I would use it often if I became a doctor. I never used it. I would have read more. I never liked to read and I am not sure why. I have always been very active and sitting proves a challenge – unless I am writing or using the computer to look things up. I keep trying to read but realize that perhaps I have a touch of ADHD. I would have learned to play an instrument. My children all did, thanks to my wife and the many friends who do all have a wonderful way to relax and unwind. The one big thing I would have done was to take a course in business in my residency. I was prepared well for medicine but very poorly to run the business needed to practice medicine.

Medicine is a business. I made many mistakes that ended up costing me time and money. The one thing I try to do is to not look stupid. I always looked stupid in the business side of my practice. Learning by mistakes is costly. When I left my residency, it was not unusual to start up a practice on your own. I had no idea what I was doing. Today, it is unheard of to start your own practice. The costs of educational loans, the usual costs of living, and the layers of bureaucracy make going it alone now nearly impossible. I did not have help with all the paperwork, licensing, salary, hiring, and so many things. I did not have a guaranteed income and had many weeks with no income. The majority of a physician's income is through insurance company payments and these can take twelve weeks or more to arrive. What I did have was freedom. I could make my own schedule, take any days off I needed, and decide on who to hire and who to work with. It was wonderful. Today's new physicians are basically employees like in any business.

Primary care medicine is the group of specialties that are the frontline. We consider family medicine, internal medicine, pediatrics, and most would include gynecology in this group. We are usually the first to be called for a patient complaint and focus on prevention and wellness. We sort out problems, most of which we treat well ourselves and refer to specialists as needed. The primary task is cognitive and relies heavily on communication with the patient. In general, we do not have a great deal of procedures or ways to generate income outside of patient visits. Insurance companies reward doctors who do procedures but do not seem to value cognitive skills and time with each patient as much. Our income is lower but I know for a fact that we shoulder no fewer burdens. Granted, one slip in a surgical procedure could cost a life but few consider that we make more than one decision on each patient we see every day – any of which might negatively affect a patient. We carry that weight daily. I know that I am paid well now, but for the first ten years of my practice, my income was very low – despite twenty-three years of education.

I say this because I have learned that in this business called medicine the operating margin is critical. The fixed costs of running a practice are considerable and they do not change. Income only occurs when one generates more than is going out for expenses. Whether two patients are seen or twenty-two, it costs the same to run the office. These costs go up every year while insurance payments per level of care go down. Therefore, income goes down unless more patients are seen. To see more patients means to either work longer hours or see more patients in the same time period. The latter encroaches on time for the patient; the former encroaches on time for the family. The doctor loses out both ways. I have seen in my own practice the effect of the need to control costs in many ways. I once had a nurse who saw every patient – now it is a medical assistant. I once wrote my chart records – I now have an enormously expensive electronic medical record. I once was able to return most of my patient calls – now there are layers of people between the patient and the physician.

Hiring employees, deciding on a benefits package, saving for retirement, getting malpractice insurance, doing estimated tax payments, negotiating for everything, learning how to read and argue the many contracts along the way, having a billing system, and an answering service are just a few of the realities of medicine as a business. I learned how to do all of this and I eventually did it all very well but at a cost. The cost was time I could have been home with family or doing carpentry. The cost was time with patients. There are only twenty-four hours in a day and sleep is mandatory. I do not think we can ever go back to when I started my little business. Medicine has changed and I am honestly not sure it is for the better in the way we now approach our patients. People do not see what goes on behind the curtain when they go to the doctor and I do not expect them to. They have their own problems and we will be there to help them.

A Miracle

He was lying peacefully in bed when I first saw him – a man in his twenties appearing healthy and fit. The room was silent except for the rhythmic noise of the ventilator. His hospital gown was neat and there was a large crucifix in the front gown pocket. A woman, whom I was told by the nurses was his mother, was sitting next to him, holding his hand and quietly reading from a small leather-bound book. He had rosary beads arranged on his gown. Off in the corner was a man, his father, staring out the window. Their lives would never be the same. This tragic scene is all too common.

I chair the ethics committee at an urban teaching hospital in New Jersey and often do medical ethics consultations. These are never uplifting and seldom lead to closure. I was asked to see this patient, as he was declared brain-dead and his parents were invoking the religious exemption which is unique to New Jersey's law. This young man was found unresponsive and underwent the process of resuscitation as per protocol and his heart rhythm and blood pressure were restored. The prolonged oxygen deprivation resulted in brain swelling and herniation. He met all the criteria for brain death after the narcotics that caused his demise were proven to be no longer in his system. These criteria, now over fifty years old, have been well proven in adults and there has not been an adult who met all criteria who has recovered.

The opioid epidemic is real and is not abating. We seem to have become numb to it despite the press coverage, the movies, and the shared personal experiences. The fact that I work for a hospital that serves an extremely challenged population was not the reason for this consult – this horror strokes families of all socioeconomic groups.

I had prepared well before entering the room by reviewing the chart in detail, talking to the physician, and talking to his nurse at length. The nurses are the key. They know the patient best, they understand the family, they share in the hourly grief, they get the difficult questions, and they grasp what cannot be written down. I also knew that this young man was tested and proven free of infections had normal kidneys and a strong heart. The Organ Sharing

Network was on the floor and asked to meet with me. I told them I prefer to go in alone and would talk to them when I return.

Upon entering the room, I introduced myself and told them that I represented the hospital's ethics committee. Their quiet nod made it clear they were expecting my visit and the fact they did not react and ask me to leave offered a glimmer of hope. I next said that I was told they were refusing to accept their son's brain death based on a religious exemption. I saw no reason to ease into this and also saw no benefit in asking how they knew of this law. We are a nation that lives on the web and use Google for everything. I asked what religion they practiced. The first response opened the door – the mother said they were Roman Catholic. Knowing that religion well, I quickly responded that this religion does not object to the brain-death criteria. As if rehearsed, the father lifted a book that was on his lap. She turned and pointed and said they were also practicing in a branch of the Episcopal Church. The door now closed. The state law, as written, does not demand that a certain religion have documented positions in place on this subject and does not require proof of participation by parents or children. They told me their son went to church regularly.

Knowing they had insisted on a full code status for their son, I next asked what they would consider as proof of their son's death. She replied that when his heart stopped, that would be God's way of saying he was taking their son. The door opened again. I then asked why they were insisting that we try to restart his heart if it stopped and whether that would be an act against the will of God. The door opened wider. She immediately replied that if it were God's will, what we did would not work. The door closed. I then mentioned that when I entered the room, I noticed that they were both praying and how clear it was how much they loved their son. I asked softly what they were praying for. The immediate reply was 'a miracle.'

What is a miracle? Is it just a significant statistical aberrancy? Is it merely the fact that an occurrence cannot yet be explained scientifically? Is it the will of God? It is different things for different people. In medicine, we must always recognize religion as part of someone's being. It is not to be explained and never to be argued with, especially in such a devastating situation. I quietly left the room.

Upon entering the nursing station, I relayed what had happened and the representative of the Organ Sharing Network had a look on her face that made me know that a door might still be open. She walked into the room, put her hand on the mother's shoulder, and introduced herself followed by telling her that she 'represented the miracle they have been praying for.' I was struck by the words and immediately wondered what might happen. The mother softened and soon thereafter, they had consented to organ donation. Many people will now live longer because of their son's last gift. Some will see again and some will be able to heal. Perhaps the parents' grief and the likely unfounded guilt that all parents feel when a child's path veers from our dream will be less in the coming years.

Perhaps their prayers were answered. Whether that is by God or by science matters less to those who are organ-donor recipients.

Chapter 12

COVID-19

I was 'finished' with this book and was ready to start searching for the best way to get it to anyone who might enjoy reading it. Then life changed in a way that has been beyond imagination. I could not close a collection of stories surrounding ethics, humanism, and professionalism without some mention of this pandemic. I could not discuss parts of my life and ignore this painful episode. The writings by so many talented people in so many respected publications to date have captured these past weeks and their effects on all of our lives more profoundly than I ever could. I thank them for amazing insights that coming generations can read. The end to this nightmare is not in sight. I embrace science and am as hurt by the recent unwillingness to embrace science as anything else. We must learn from this. It will happen again. That is why we all must study history.

The Health Professional in a Pandemic

Before you read this, I feel it is necessary for me to be open and honest regarding who I am so that you can best understand what follows. Much of this is elsewhere in the book, but when I decided to write this book, I wanted the reader to be able to open it up at any chapter and read knowing some background to better understand where the thoughts came from. It is certainly not a novel in which one chapter leads to the next.

I am an internist and have practiced for four decades in both the outpatient and inpatient environment. I was in the ICU as a medical student at the time ambulances brought people with severe pneumonia to our ER in Philadelphia that turned out to be Legionnaire's Disease. We had no idea what it was at the time. I practiced before and during what was and is AIDS and saw how our healthcare system reacted. It was often less than admirable. These were all terrible and tests of how our healthcare system responds to infections. They were nothing compared to COVID-19!

I am also a medical ethicist and chair the bioethics committee at Cooper University Hospital in Camden, New Jersey, as I write this. I am honored to work with an amazing group of informed and dedicated people every day. My view is through the eyes of a physician but I have made sure that what follows is applicable to all who care for people everywhere. We share a purpose, a mission, and a resolve.

"The practice of medicine is an art, not a trade; a calling, not a business; a calling in which your heart will be exercised equally with your head," said William Osler.

"Medicine is not," as Francis Peabody said, "a trade to be learned, but a profession to be entered."

"A profession is characterized by a specialized body of knowledge that its members must teach and expand by a code of ethics and a duty of service that, in medicine, puts patient care above self-interest and by the privilege of self-regulation granted by society. Physicians must individually and collectively fulfill the duties of the profession." From: The American College of Physicians Ethics Manual.

We take an oath to serve the sick. Traditionally, the ethical imperative for us to provide care has overridden the risk to the treating physician and all those who provide direct care even during epidemics. Healthcare providers' ethical obligation to the welfare of patients is a fundamental tenet of the medical profession. The social contract between medicine and society also requires physicians to treat all in need of care. All should evaluate their risk for becoming infected with pathogens, both in their personal lives and in the workplace, and implement appropriate precautions, including following guidelines for hygiene, protective garb, immunization, and constraints for exposure designed to decrease spread of infection.

Because Covid-19 may be transmitted from patient to provider and pose risks to a provider's health, some providers may be tempted to avoid the care of infected patients. It is at this time that we all must realize what we have chosen to do in our professional life and to do that with resolve and pride while making sure we utilize all the resources available that are known to keep us safe. We and our hospitals are obligated to provide competent and humane care to all patients regardless of their illness. We are one in our dedication to limit occupational exposure through rigorous infection-control methods.

The guiding principles for healthcare delivery during catastrophes may shift from autonomy and beneficence to utility, fairness, and stewardship. Physicians, nurses, and all who battle this disease together should participate in the development of guidelines for the just delivery of healthcare in times of catastrophe, being mindful of existing health disparities that may affect populations or regions.

We are not our best when anxious or fearful. There are resources for all and we must take advantage of these. We share a scientific profession that mixes the art and science of medicine daily. We must do all we can daily to be our best. We owe this to our patients, our family, our neighbors, and future generations. Medicine is best when done as a team. A team relies on everyone and it is our ethical obligation to endeavor to be our best. Reaching out to others has never been more important. In helping one another, we help our patients.

We are not obliged to be heroes. We are obliged to serve those in need and to do so utilizing what we know will keep us safe. In being safe, we can serve more people in the weeks ahead. Ethical behavior guides all of us daily and will allow us to be better for our patients and our community. Each day that we embrace the care and comfort of our patient while working to balance doing good for that patient with the good for all is one we will be proud of. Ethics is a unique part of being human.

Society is seeing healthcare providers as courageous, selfless, kind, and truly dedicated to those we serve. We are. We are paving the way for future generations to see healthcare as a special calling and want to follow us. In doing what we do now, we are also serving future generations.

Benched

I grew up loving to play sports. That does not mean I was any good at any of them, but I loved to play. In those times, you got up in the summer and on Saturdays, went out, came home for meals, and then home to sleep. My parents seldom asked where I was. I was 'out' and that was fine. There was no concern for safety and everyone in my life was within a walking distance. We did not need a car or a bus. I do not recall using a phone either. We just went 'out' and magically our friends would gather, ideas developed, and a plan took off. Those were wonderful times when we learned to be social and creative, and we were physically active.

Success is a matter of being lucky enough to happen to find out what you are good at, and perhaps even turn that into profit. My youth taught me not to consider being a professional athlete! I was tall but not tall enough. I was in good shape but never had stamina. I was competitive but never at the risk of injury. I was neither fast nor tough. I had good skills in observation and never had the need to be the star (thank God!). Basketball became my sport, since I liked to run short distances, I liked to pass, and I could defend. Since you could have a good game with six people and a great one with ten, there was always a chance to have enough people to play. We had a playground two blocks from my home and that should have been my mailing address. Pine Street Playground. I loved it there.

We would pick a captain who would pick his team. I would usually be the last picked and sometimes sat on the bench. It built resilience, I suppose, but it mostly was depressing. Back then, not everyone got a trophy or made the team. We were prepared better for the reality of life.

Fortunately, I found what I was meant to be – a physician. It had everything I loved: science, mystery, memorization, human interaction, constant stimulation, and positive feedback. I also loved to teach, and being in academia allowed me to do it all – for decades. An illness that kept me home for a time taught me that I would not be good at retirement. My plan was to do all that I loved for as long as I can. Put me in the room with a patient and I was happy.

Add a student or resident in that setting and I was in heaven. My days have been full, challenging, and filled with human interaction.

Then came COVID-19... All my classes became online interactions where people became tiles on my computer. Because of my age and other conditions, I was told not to be at clinic but to supervise tele-health visits. I was benched from the game I love. Because of my expertise in medical ethics, I was asked to be on many committees online, dealing with the pandemic at our hospital. This turned out to be a great deal of work and it allowed me to see what wonderful people worked at the hospital. It was, however, an enormous burden, as it was looking directly at what this virus was doing to patients and their families as well as those caring for them.

People were going to work every day, knowing the risk of catching this infection and usually working longer and harder than ever before. They faced the added weight of worry surrounding coming home to those they loved, fearing giving it to them. Hopefully, people will now see the courage and dedication of those in healthcare. I honestly felt horrible every day that I was working from home while they were out there doing what I honestly would have wanted to do. I understood that my risks should I get this infection are greater than most, and that I also would have the risk of bringing it home to someone also in the same category. I volunteered to do more from home mostly out of a sense of guilt.

There is also an enormous sense of loss. I love being with students and residents. I love to teach and read faces. I love to joke and tell stories. That was all taken away. When one teaches in a small group, each person in the room has a personality but the group itself takes on a life and a feel. Online teaching does work and without it we would be lost, but it can never replace that feel for the room. I did not realize it until the school shut down but there was always a student who would drop by and ask my advice or just talk. I get to watch them grow and sadly watch them go. An email or a call can never come close to the feeling of those random interactions. This all came to a sudden halt. I am sure the learners have been even more impacted that me.

Extra time is a commodity that I often did not have. This is not a complaint, since I liked being busy and always found things to do. Now I had time to think and I have found that is not good, especially at this time in the world and this time in my life. Time to think means time to explore issues best not explored. Should I retire? Can I retire with what this pandemic is doing to my resources? I knew that things would never be the same. I knew that this was not going to be 'over' and that we still have no idea what lies ahead. When could I pick up my new granddaughter? When can we have the treasured sleepovers with the grandsons? When can we safely get on a plane to visit our son? When can I be at the bedside? When can I be in the classroom? I wish I did not have the time to think about these things – but I do!

As humans, we adapt. I will adapt and create my new norm amidst the new norm. That is what we do. Perhaps we can all rise up and make something better out of this. Can we accept what we did wrong and prevent that for the future? Will the value of human life be seen as greater than the value of money? I only hope that I can be around to see what the answers are and hope that we become better for all of this. I am thankful that I am safe and that I am doing all I can to make others safe. I am on the bench but still part of the team. When the time comes to put me in the game, I will be grateful and give all that I have.

Visitor

I spent many weeks as a patient in the hospital a few years ago and was encephalopathic during the entire stay. This means that I could speak and interact and at times especially to those who did not know me and appeared normal. I was told that I would give coherent lectures to the medical students who came to see me on rounds, only to not remember doing so an hour later. I am sure that I was assumed to have capacity and could consent to tests and treatments. The fact was that I still do not remember anything of that time even years since. My wife was at my bedside daily and made every decision during that horrible time and she guided me to wellness. She was more than a visitor.

COVID-19 has taken away visitors from the hospital. Throughout the country, people lie in bed alone for what is often the singular, most challenging time of their life. Families are forced to stay home – wondering how their parent, spouse, child, or friend is doing. The nursing staff and others at the hospital are given the added task of being family to each patient. At a time when they are already burdened by what this terrible virus is doing, they now must take on this new role. They are doing it daily and doing it with compassion. Finally, people are seeing how amazing healthcare workers are. In the absence of family at the bedside, all are reaching to technology as we are through social distancing every day. They are bringing family into the room through FaceTime, using phones and computer tablets – even showing patients how to Zoom, Google Meet, and so many other forums that have risen up to help us fill the social needs we all seek.

What is obvious to those who treat people in the hospital now is that everyone is very ill. COVID has stopped elective surgeries. People do not even come to the emergency room now unless they are seriously ill for fear of exposure. The non-COVID patient is getting little attention in this pandemic by the media. They lie in beds in every hospital, fighting to recover without visitors while fearing they will get the virus and bring it to loved ones once discharged.

We no longer 'visit' anyone. A small tile on our phone or computer of those we love must suffice. Everything has changed. Anything that can be put off until another time is put off. How many procedures now done electively will become needed as emergent ones due to the delay in diagnosis is frightening. We all spend every day in fear of even going for a walk and coming within six feet of someone well. Going to the grocery store has become living a game of Pacman where we push a cart up an isle until we see someone coming toward us and turn to avoid them. Going to a place where the likelihood of coming into contact with an ill person is unheard of – a doctor's office, a pharmacy, or an emergency room. The entire topic of the Tsunami that will hit our healthcare system of those putting off care until this pandemic is controlled (a time we all must have faith in despite current facts) is beyond the scope of this writing.

The COVID patient in the hospital presents yet another challenge. Not only can they not have visitors, but all those they see are also stripped of humanity. It is a nightmare. Caregivers are now making badges with their faces on them to wear on their protective clothing so a patient might get some idea of what they look like. Each encounter is a vivid reminder of how serious what they have is. The many tales of how those who treat these patients going above and beyond are both heartbreaking and enlightening.

So why not open the doors and let those who want to visit come? Isn't it their right? Shouldn't it be up to each patient to have a willing visitor come to see them? Autonomy means that the patient has the right to choose as long as they are informed and have the capacity to understand. Autonomy has been the ruling principle in medical ethics for decades. Autonomy now has yielded to justice – the principle that must guide us in a pandemic. Our decisions must be focused beyond self and to society. We must look to the good of many as well as the one. Every visitor to a hospital right now must be treated as a possible vector that can carry this horrible virus to and from the hospital. We have no idea yet who is infected, how exactly it is carried, and who it will kill next. These are simple facts. Allowing visitors is likely to continue the spread of COVID-19 and, in doing so, continue to fill our hospitals with patients who are alone.

These are horrible times. Science-fiction is now reality. What about the patient who is dying in the hospital? What about the child? Rules are created in every hospital and exceptions are part of all rules. People working within hospitals who know the relative risks are making these decisions every day. The reality of the patient who is in the dying stage of COVID-19 is that they are sedated, unable to talk because they are on a ventilator, and they are unaware. The visitor may want to say goodbye and know they were there. The patient will not know either. The fact that someone wants to visit despite the risk shows the incredible love that they have for this dying person. No doubt that the patient would have felt the same. Part of love is protecting. The last thing I would want if dying of COVID would be to have those I love risk getting this disease or bringing it to others. The last vision I would want for them is to see me in an ICU on a ventilator.

My parents are no longer alive. When I close my eyes, I see my father standing tall in his police uniform and I smile. I see my mother baking chocolate-chip cookies and I salivate. My wife is resourceful and brilliant and would have found a way to direct my care from home if not allowed at my bedside. She would have gotten me well. We owe it to those we love, as well as to those we do not know, to do our part to control the spread of this heartless virus. Not visiting a hospital right now is an act of love for all.

Adapting

Change is a constant. Slow change often goes unnoticed. When I look at old photographs, as this social distancing has resulted in many doing now since we are forced to be home and kill time, I see a different person in those old slides than the one now in my mirror. Expected change gives us a little time to adjust and often brings out the best in us. We prioritize, find ways to let go, and embrace the inevitable. Unexpected rapid change is the very definition of stress and this is what COVID-19 has done to the world. We must try to accept, as there is little else to do, adapt quickly, and find someone to guide us. This latter issue is now so difficult for me. I am a scientist. I am an ethicist. I want the truth and I need to know I can trust what is being told to me. I am very good at accepting when someone tells me they do not know. Being told mistruths is insulting. It also is dangerous because when someone believes they know something, they stop looking for other answers.

My patients expected me to tell them the truth and I did. If I did not know, I told them. It has worked for decades. Not knowing made me work harder. Complacency kills. I hope by the time anyone reads this, we will be well, have gotten an effective vaccine, have a medication to prevent death from this virus, and we will be back to life as we knew it. I need to hold on to these hopes as we all do. I also need to be honest with myself and prepare for a new normal.

Everything has changed. Anything that can be put off in terms of healthcare until another time is put off. How many procedures now done electively will soon become emergent ones due to the delay in diagnosis is frightening. We all spend every day in fear of even going for a walk and coming within six feet of someone. Our dogs have never been healthier. Going to the grocery store has become a reenactment of a game of Pacman where we push a cart up an isle until we see someone coming toward us and turn and go the other way to avoid them. Going to a place where the likelihood of coming into contact with an ill person is unheard of: a doctor's office, a pharmacy, or an emergency room. The entire topic of the Tsunami that will hit our healthcare system when all those putting off care until this pandemic is controlled (a time we all must have faith in despite current facts) is beyond the scope of this writing.

Tele-health is here to stay – part of the 'new normal.' It should be. To make someone take time off work, get a babysitter, drive, or take a bus only to get to a physician's office and wait to be told all is well and to come back in one year is absurd. We now know that blood-pressure readings done by a patient at home are more accurate than in our office, as coming to our office can put your pressure up! So many things can be effectively treated on a telephone visit. Add a video component and we get to truly converse and read some non-verbal clues. Save the office visits for those who really need it.

I teach and it energizes me. I now see my students as a small tile on my phone or computer. I teach first-year medical students now three days per week – same group of nine for the year. They know one another well and the dance has been well rehearsed and actually is working online as a result. How this will translate into a new group of nine next year is unknown. The problem right now is that this block is musculoskeletal and it was to be the beginning of their cadaver experience. This is so much more difficult to teach without the benefit that a dissection offers. It is not the same and that is sad in so many ways. Medical students seldom go to lectures anymore. They watch it when they feel like, usually at a faster speed. The move to online education was easy in that venue.

I teach clinical skills. I love the physical exam. We use the simulation lab a great deal and standardize patients. Medicine relies on these skills and I do not see how we can duplicate teaching the physical exam in an online fashion. Perhaps I am nostalgic and there will be a way. To me, being good with people requires being with people. I can 'feel' when in a room with patient. It is what makes the patient's visit magical.

Whatever happens, I plan to keep working. This new norm needs me and many like me – old-fashioned docs who love what they do and know that it is all built on humanism, professionalism, and ethics. We will fight to keep these as the essence of the practice of medicine. The new norm must be built on this foundation.

Table 1 – Content by Category

Chapter Title	Page	Category	Message	Other
Preface	15	Intro	Explanation	
Gross Anatomy	46	Learning	Cadavers	Tests
Surgical Block	52	Learning	Medical School	Idols
The Odor	18	Medicine	Competence	Choices
They Stayed Together	22	Medicine	Dementia	Competence
The Call	55	Medicine	Med School Admin	Big Moments
Being Sued	68	Medicine	Lawsuits	Medical-Legal
Bad People	71	Medicine	Sociopath	Trust
Make the Last First	73	Medicine	Diagnosing	Career Path
Dark	75	Medicine	Disability	House Call
Suicide	81	Medicine	Competency	Suicide
Old Photos	87	Medicine	Diagnosing	Acromegaly
What Finger?	89	Medicine	Self-mutilation	Family
Ask Your Doctor	91	Medicine	Advertising	The Profession
Confidentiality	94	Medicine	Breaking	Medical-Legal
I'm Not Nuts	97	Medicine	Open Access	Paternalism
Billy Smokes	106	Medicine	Human Value	Birth Selection
Delivering Bad News?	108	Medicine	Dying	Happiness
He Wrote	110	Medicine	Surrogates	Ethics
Capacity	112	Medicine	Capacity	Ethics
He Loved to Sing	114	Medicine	Dying	Competence
Our Path Do Cross	117	Medicine	Advance Directives	Ethics
Bad Idea	119	Medicine	Confidentiality	Abuse
Stroke	123	Medicine	Caring for	Luck
Pastoral Care	125	Medicine	Humanism	Dying
Intent	147	Medicine	Double Effect	Ethics
A Brick Wall	149	Medicine	Firing a patient	Compliance

Alone	151	Medicine	DNR	Advance Directives
The Guardian	154	Medicine	Guardianship	Quality of Life
Brain Death	157	Medicine	Brain Death	Religion
STD	160	Medicine	Honesty	Human Nature
No Big Deal	163	Medicine	Honesty	Business
Personalized Medicine	166	Medicine	Genetics	Ethics
A Different Time	173	Medicine	Doctors	History
Alcohol	175	Medicine	Substance abuse	Labeling
What Is a Disease	178	Medicine	Labeling	Humility
CME	180	Medicine	Education	Bias
Teens	183	Medicine	Adolescent Health	Behavior
Fear	186	Medicine	HIV	Professionalism
Calories	189	Medicine	Obesity	Labeling
911	192	Medicine	Access to Care	Phones
Alternative	194	Medicine	Vitamins	Wisdom
What Would You Do?	198	Medicine	Guidelines	Evidence-based
Journals	209	Medicine	Conflict	Learning
Why Learn	212	Medicine	Knowledge	CME
Burnout	218	Medicine	Stress	Wellness
The White Coat	221	Medicine	Professionalism	Mental Illness
Medical History	224	Medicine	History	Empathy
Professionalism	241	Medicine	Defining it	Wellness
We Are Human	243	Medicine	Stress	Tragedy
Statistics	251	Medicine	Decision Making	Cancer
Extender	254	Medicine	Cost	Time with patients
The Underserved	256	Medicine	Disadvantaged	Distribution
I Know How You Feel	261	Medicine	Empathy	Anxiety
A Business	263	Medicine	Time with Patients	Costs
Miracle	265	Medicine	Death	Religion
Our Dogs	20	Personal	End of life	Ethics
Yes, Sister	32	Personal	The Journey	Influences
Coming Home Late	34	Personal	Parenting	Respect
Coaching	37	Personal	Life style	Parenting
The Flood	39	Personal	Books	Tragedy
Love	41	Personal	Relationships	Marriage

Research	42	Personal	Careers	Ethics
Medical School	49	Personal	Debt	Education
Fork in the Road	58	Personal	Influences	Career Decisions
Moving	64	Personal	Career	Costs
Bad People	71	Personal	Career	Costs
On Call	78	Personal	Life style	Risk
Midnight Mass	84	Personal	PAS	Death
Hernia	99	Personal	Experience	Humility
Post-Op	128	Personal	Pain	Labeling
Mom	131	Personal	Dying	Caring for Relatives
Religion	133	Personal	Priests	Humor
People Watching	136	Personal	Refection	Observing
Reentry	138	Personal	Medical history	Skills
Payback	141	Personal	Diagnosing	Role Models
Footsteps	143	Personal	Parenting	Choices
Meetings	196	Personal	Business	Time
When to Retire	248	Personal	Professionalism	Whistle Blowing
Burning Up	24	Teaching	Mental Illness	Experience
The Northern Lights	26	Teaching	Learning	Experience
Medical Education	61	Teaching	History	Costs
The Attending	101	Teaching	Diagnosing	Diabetes
The Number	201	Teaching	Test Scores	Student stress
Communication	205	Teaching	Language Barrier	Cultural
The Interview	207	Teaching	Parental expectation	Failure
Tomorrow's Physician	214	Teaching	Humanism	Computers
The Student Clinic	227	Teaching	Uninsured	Mentoring
Role Models	231	Teaching	Memories	Teachers
The Lecture	234	Teaching	Changes	Medical School
Teaching	237	Teaching	Language	Experience
I Don't Know	246	Teaching	Humility	Testing effects

Table 2 – Content by Message

Chapter Title	Page	Category	Message	Other
Preface	15	Intro	Explanation	
Gross Anatomy	46	Learning	Cadavers	Tests
Surgical Block	52	Learning	Medical School	Idols
911	192	Medicine	Access to Care	Phones
Teens	183	Medicine	Adolescent Health	Behavior
Our Paths Do Cross	117	Medicine	Advance Directives	Ethics
Ask Your Doctor	91	Medicine	Advertising	The Profession
The Flood	39	Personal	Books	Tragedy
Brain Death	157	Medicine	Brain death	Religion
Confidentially	94	Medicine	Breaking confidentially	Medical-Legal
Meetings	196	Personal	Business	Time
Capacity	112	Medicine	Capacity	Ethics
Moving	64	Personal	Career	Cost
Research	43	Personal	Careers	Ethics
Stroke	123	Medicine	Caring for Family	Luck
The Lecture	234	Teaching	Changes	Medical School
The Odor	19	Medicine	Competence	Choices
Suicide	81	Medicine	Competency	Suicide
Bad Idea	119	Medicine	Confidentiality	Abuse
Journals	209	Medicine	Conflict	Learning
Extender	254	Medicine	Cost	Time with patients
Miracle	265	Medicine	Death	Religion
Medical School	49	Personal	Debt	Education
Statistics	251	Medicine	Decision Making	Cancer
Professionalism	241	Medicine	Defining it	Wellness
They Stayed Together	22	Medicine	Dementia	Competence

Make the List First	73	Medicine	Diagnosing	Career Path
Old Photos	87	Medicine	Diagnosing	Acromegaly
Payback	141	Personal	Diagnosing	Role Models
The Attending	101	Teaching	Diagnosing	Diabetes
Dark	75	Medicine	Disability	House Call
The Underserved	256	Medicine	Disadvantaged	Distribution
Alone	151	Medicine	DNR	Advance Directives
A Different Time	173	Medicine	Doctors	History
Intent	147	Medicine	Double Effects	Ethics
Delivering Bad News?	108	Medicine	Dying	Happiness
He Loved to Sing	114	Medicine	Dying	Competence
Mom	131	Personal	Dying	Caring for Relatives
CME	180	Medicine	Education	Bias
I Know How You Feel	261	Medicine	Empathy	Anxiety
Our Dogs	20	Personal	End of Life	Ethics
Hernia	99	Personal	Experience	Humility
A Brick Wall	149	Medicine	Firing a patient	Compliance
Personalized Medicine	166	Medicine	Genetics	Ethics
The Guardian	154	Medicine	Guardianship	Quality of Life
What Would You Do	198	Medicine	Guidelines	Evidence-Based Care
Medical History	224	Medicine	History	Empathy
Medical Education	61	Teaching	History	Costs
Fear	186	Medicine	HIV	Professionalism
Std	160	Medicine	Honesty	Human Nature
No Big Deal	163	Medicine	Honesty	Business
Billy Smokes	106	Medicine	Human Value	Birth Selection
Pastoral Care	125	Medicine	Humanism	Dying
Tomorrow's Physician	214	Teaching	Humanism	Computers
I Don't Know	246	Teaching	Humility	Testing Effects

Fork in the Road	58	Personal	Influences	Career Decisions
Why Learn	212	Medicine	Knowledge	CME
What Is a Disease	178	Medicine	Labeling	Humility
Teaching	237	Teaching	Language	Experience
Communication	205	Teaching	Language Barrier	Cultural
Being Sued	68	Medicine	Lawsuits	Medical-Legal
The Northern Lights	26	Teaching	Learning	Experience
Coaching	37	Personal	Lifestyle	Parenting
On Call	78	Personal	Lifestyle	Risk
The Call	55	Medicine	Med School Admin	Big Moments
Reentry	138	Personal	Medical History	Skills
Role Models	231	Teaching	Memories	Teachers
Burning Up	24	Teaching	Mental Illness	Experience
Calories	189	Medicine	Obesity	Labelling
I'm Not Nuts	97	Medicine	Open Access	Paternalism
Post-Op	128	Personal	Pain	Labeling
The Interview	207	Teaching	Parental Expectation	Failure
Coming Home Late	34	Personal	Parenting	Respect
Footsteps	143	Personal	Parenting	Choices
Midnight Mass	84	Personal	PAS	Death
Religion	133	Personal	Priests	Humor
The White Coat	221	Medicine	Professionalism	Mental Illness
When to Retire	248	Personal	Professionalism	Whistle Blowing
People Watching	136	Personal	Refection	Observing
Love	41	Personal	Relationships	Marriage
What Finger?	89	Medicine	Self-Mutilation	Family
Bad People	71	Medicine	Sociopath	Trust
Burnout	218	Medicine	Stress	Wellness
We Are Human	243	Medicine	Stress	Tragedy
Alcohol	175	Medicine	Substance Abuse	Labeling
He Wrote	110	Medicine	Surrogates	Ethics
The Number	201	Teaching	Test Scores	Student Stress
Yes, Sister	32	Personal	The Journey	Influences
A Business	263	Medicine	Time with Patients	Costs
The Student Clinic	227	Teaching	Uninsured	Mentoring
Alternative	194	Medicine	Vitamins	Wisdom

The Reader's Ideas

The Reader's Ideas

CPSIA information can be obtained
at www.ICGtesting.com
Printed in the USA
BVHW060125240221
600896BV00010B/1481